BRITISH BATTLES OF THE NAPOLEONIC WARS 1793–1806

DESPATCHES FROM THE FRONT
The Commanding Officers' Reports From the Field and At Sea.

BRITISH BATTLES OF THE NAPOLEONIC WARS 1793–1806

Compiled by John Grehan and Martin Mace
With Additional Research by
Sara Mitchell and Robert Cager

Pen & Sword
MILITARY

First published in Great Britain in 2013 by
Pen & Sword Military
an imprint of
Pen & Sword Books Ltd
47 Church Street
Barnsley
South Yorkshire
S70 2AS

Copyright © John Grehan and Martin Mace, 2013

ISBN 978 1 78159 3 325

The right of John Grehan and Martin Mace be identified as Authors of this Work has been asserted by them in accordance with the Copyright, Designs and Patents Act 1988.

A CIP catalogue record for this book is available from the British Library. All rights reserved. No part of this book may be reproduced or transmitted in any form or by any means, electronic or mechanical including photocopying, recording or by any information storage and retrieval system, without permission from the Publisher in writing.

Printed and bound in India by Replika Press Pvt. Ltd.

Pen & Sword Books Ltd incorporates the Imprints of Pen & Sword Aviation, Pen & Sword Maritime, Pen & Sword Military, Wharncliffe Local History, Pen and Sword Select, Pen and Sword Military Classics and Leo Cooper.

For a complete list of Pen & Sword titles please contact:
PEN & SWORD BOOKS LIMITED
47 Church Street, Barnsley, South Yorkshire, S70 2AS, England
E-mail: enquiries@pen-and-sword.co.uk
Website: www.pen-and-sword.co.uk

Contents

Introduction	vii
List of images	x
List of maps	xi
British Battles of the Napoleonic Wars, 1793 to 1806	1
The Despatches	
1. Famars – 23 May 1793	23
2. Hondschoote and the Siege of Dunkirk – 6 to 8 September 1793	26
3. Toulon – 18 September to 18 December 1793	30
4. Saint Florent – 7 February to 18 February 1794	39
5. Martinique – 23 March 1794	43
6. St Lucia – 1 April 1794	46
7. Bastia – 4 April to 19 May 1794	48
8. Guadeloupe – 11 April to 12 April 1794	51
9. Beaumont-en-Cambrésis – 26 April 1794	55
10. Tourcoing – 18 May 1794	58
11. Tournay – 22 May 1794	62
12. The Glorious First of June – 1 June 1794	64
13. Calvi – 19 June to 10 August 1794	67
14. Fleurus – 26 June 1794	70
15. Boxtel – 15 September 1794	72
16. Genoa – 14 March 1795	74
17. Île de Groix – 23 June 1795	77
18. Hiéres Islands – 13 July 1795	79
19. Saint Lucia – 24th May 1796	81
20. & 21. The Capture of St Vincent and Grenada	84
22. Cape St Vincent	89
23. Trinidad – 21 February 1797	92
24. Fishguard – 23 February 1797	96
25. San Juan – 17 April to 2 May 1797	98
26. Santa Cruz de Tenerife – 22 July to 25 July 1797	100
27. Camperdown – 11 October 1797	102
28. Ostend – 19 May 1798	104

29.	The Nile – 1 August to 3 August 1798	109
30.	St George's Caye – 3 September to 10 September 1798	111
31.	Ballinamuck – 8 September 1798	118
32.	Tory Island – 12 October 1798	121
33.	Seringapatam – 5 April to 4 May 1799	123
34.	Callanstoog – 27 August 1799	126
35.	Krabbendam – 10 September 1799	131
36.	Bergen – 19 September 1799	133
37.	Alkmaar – 2 October 1799	137
38.	Castricum – 6 October 1799	146
39.	Brión (Ferrol) – 25 and 26 August 1800	149
40.	Alexandria – 21 March 1801	151
41.	Copenhagen – 2 April 1801	155
42.	Algeciras Bay – 6 July to 12 July 1801	159
43.	Boulogne – 15 August to 16 August 1801	164
44.	St Lucia – 22 June 1803	169
45.	Ally Ghur – 1 September to 4 September 1803	172
46.	Assaye – 23 September 1803	173
47.	Pulo Aura – 14 February 1804	176
48.	Cape Finistere – 22 July 1805	179
49.	Trafalgar – 21 October 1805	181
50.	Cape Ortegal – 4 November 1805	185
51.	Blaauwberg – 8 January to 18 January 1806	188
52.	San Domingo – 6 February 1806	196
53.	Maida – 4 July 1806	199

Index of Persons	203
Index of Military and Naval Units	206

INTRODUCTION

It is the job of the historian not only to assemble facts and present them to their public but also to interpret those facts. Much is lost and gained in such interpretations, everything being dependent upon the inclination of the author. That each new book on any subject can claim to be different from those that preceded it is ample proof of this.

Where then lies the truth? Which interpretation shall be judged the correct one? All will have their merits either in accuracy, detail or brevity. But only one account will be authentic – that delivered by the man who witnessed the events in person.

Battles, however, are notoriously difficult to describe, the individual solder being able to see little beyond his immediate vicinity. Only the most senior officers can have a holistic view of the unfolding events and their possible short-term consequences. It is to those persons that we must turn.

Until the Great War of 1914–1918, the Napoleonic Wars were the most described conflict in history. Since then the outpouring of books has scarcely diminished. These works have been histories, memoirs and biographies, all written after the event. All have been written in the knowledge of what happened next. All coloured by hindsight. All subject to interpretation.

So what are presented in this volume are the reports from the commanding officers in the field or at sea, taken directly from the original despatches. In the main they were written on the day, or the days immediately following the battle in question. Often they represented the first knowledge the British people had of the battle or its outcome.

Some of these are comparatively brief accounts of the battle just won or lost. Others, particularly those conducted many hundreds, or even thousands, of miles away, are comprehensive reports detailing the entire campaign, from its commencement to the final, decisive battle. They are reproduced here as they were 200 years ago.

Some place names were spelt differently in the eighteenth and nineteenth centuries and we have retained the original spellings. We have not corrected the original text for spelling errors or grammatical blunders. What is written here is what was reproduced either in the despatch itself or the copy published in the relevant issue of *The London Gazette*.

Readers will therefore note considerable differences between the grammar and spelling of Georgian times and the present day. For instance, that which today we consider to be the American way of spelling honour, i.e. without the 'u', was in fact how it was spelt in Britain in the late eighteenth and early nineteenth centuries, though this changed towards the end of the period in question to the modern spelling. It was also the case with favour/favor, though there was no consistency in the use of either of these words. Readers will also see that increase was encrease and many other unfamiliar spellings can be spotted throughout the various despatches; chase, for instance, is often chace.

The seemingly arbitrary use of capital letters has been retained as has the very individualistic style of writing displayed by some officers. It would seem that all nouns, not just proper nouns, began with a capital, as did numbers when they were written in words. It must be stressed, however, that there is little consistency and these observations should not be regarded as standard rules, and towards the end of this period this use of such capital letters fell out of practice. This caveat includes the use of hyphens in military ranks. Even in the same despatch, Major Generals, Brigadier-Generals, etc. can be both hyphenated and non-hyphenated. Some names also, it will be noticed, are occasionally spelt differently in the same despatch.

Anyone that chances to read the original printed documents of this era will note the apparent use of the letter 'f' in place of the letter 's'. This letter is in fact not an 'f' but an elongated 's' which has its origin in the days before the printing press when hand-written script was highly elaborate. When the printing press came into being the printers of the day adopted the most popular scripts of the day, which included the elongated 's'.

Finally, we must acknowledge that transcribing such a large amount of text from documents that are 200 years or more old can sometimes be challenging. Whilst every effort has been directed towards complete accuracy, it is not impossible that, in the reading of faded print, errors have been made.

Most of these reports included a list of the casualties incurred in the battle. These, and most references to them, have not been included in the despatches in this book. This is because they would make for very uninspiring reading and would make the book unacceptably bulky. For the same reason, where articles of capitulation and details of stores seized during successful assaults are listed, these also have been omitted, as well as some enclosures relating to other aspects of particular engagements.

This book makes no attempt at providing a comprehensive history of the British military involvement in the French Revolutionary wars or the early First Empire period. Its sole object is to present the despatches of the commanding officers. We have not attempted to include every action involving Britain's armed forces during this era. The remit of the book is to provide the reports of large-scale engagements from senior officers exercising independent commands. In some instances, where the engagements were combined operations involving both the Army and the Navy, separate reports were submitted by both the naval and military commanders. Where these are available or appropriate they have been included.

What are presented here, therefore, are the only genuinely authentic and comprehensive accounts of these, often momentous, military and naval actions, unsullied by retrospection or by subsequent personal bias.

This then is our assembly of facts, raw and untainted. Their interpretation is yours alone.

John Grehan and Martin Mace
Storrington, 2013

Images

1. Captain John Jervis.
2. Lord Howe's action.
3. Vice Admiral Horatio Lord Nelson.
4. The Battle of Camperdown.
5. Sir Ralph Abercomby.
6. Admiral Sir Robert Calder's action.
7. The Battle of Assaye
8. Admiral Sir Sidney Smith.
9. Battle of the Nile.
10. Frederick, Duke of York.
11. 1st Earl Howe.
12. Action off San Domingo.
13. 1st Viscount Duncan.
14. Charles Cornwallis.
15. The 'Last Effort and Fall of Tippoo Sultaun'.
16. The Battle of Cape St. Vincent.
17. The Battle of Copenhagen.
18. The Battle of Trafalgar.

Maps

1. Battle locations in Europe — xii
2. Battle locations, rest of the world — xiii

British Battles of the Napoleonic Wars 1793-1806

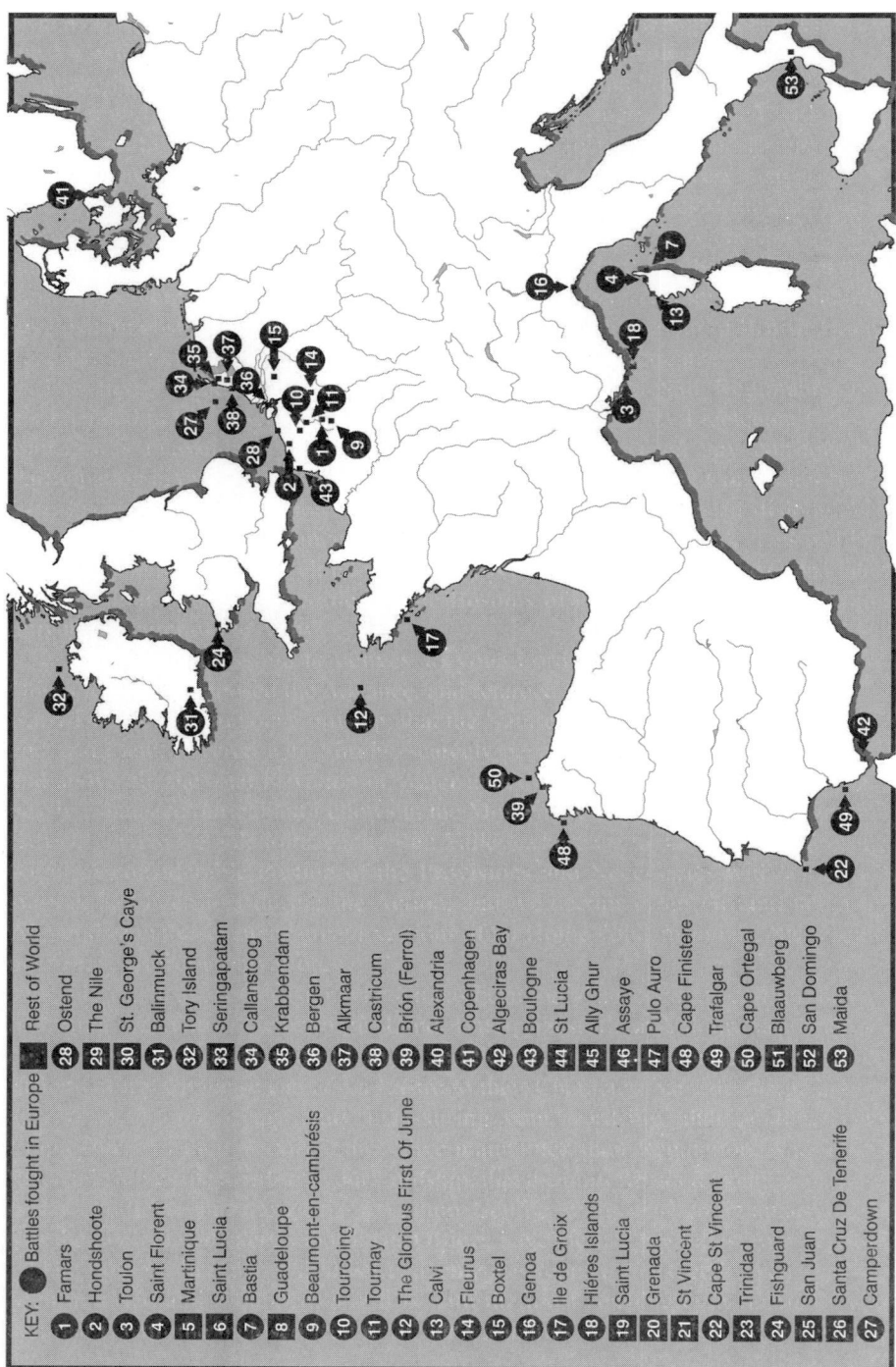

British Battles of the Napoleonic Wars 1793–1806   xiii

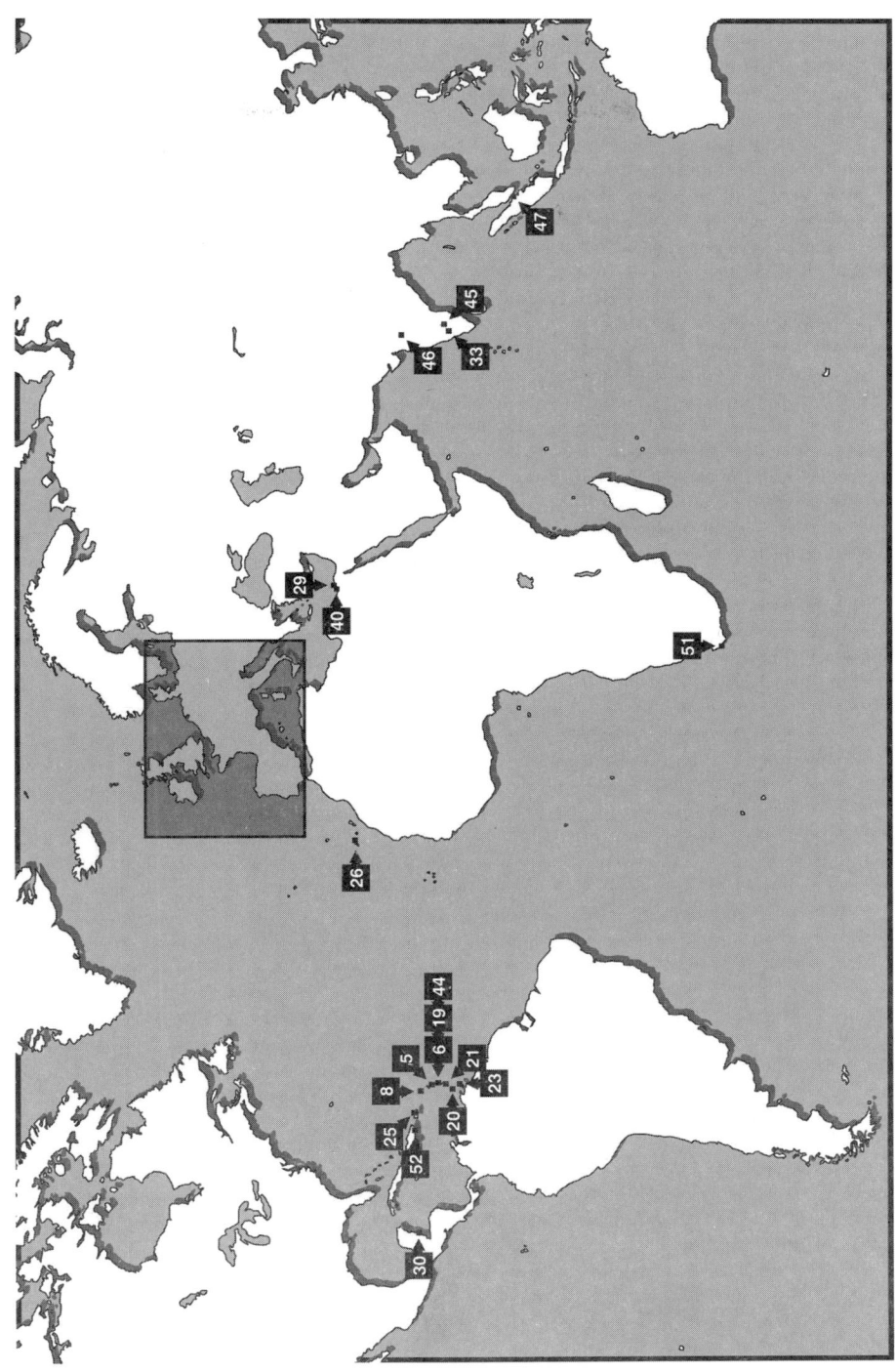

British Battles Of The Napoleonic Wars 1793 To 1806

France was in a state of turmoil. The Revolution, which started in 1789, had brought liberty, equality and fraternity to the masses but it had led to social chaos and economic collapse. France needed a war, an enemy for her people to fight to distract them from the failures of the Revolutionary government. So, on 20 April 1792, the French Assembly declared war on Austria. It marked the start of a conflict which ravaged Europe and spread across much of the world for the next twenty-three years.

At last able to raise the cry *'La patrie en danger!'* France called for volunteers to defend the country and the principles of the Revolution. An invasion of France by a combined Austro-Prussian army under the command of Ferdinand of Brunswick was turned back at Valmy in north-eastern France, and French troops occupied Savoy and Nice. French armies continued to experience success. Following victory at the Battle of Jenappes, Austrian forces were driven out of Belgium (at that time the Austrian Netherlands), the Rhine was crossed and Frankfurt and Mainz were occupied.

Britain remained aloof from the events across the Channel but she had promised to support the neutrality of the Dutch Republic, which was at that time the richest country in Europe and a vital trading partner. Holland's wealth made her a natural target for the impoverished French Government and, on 1 February 1793, eight days after the execution of Louis XVI signalled France's final breach with its monarchy, war was declared on both Britain and Holland. Britain consequently joined with Austria, Prussia, Spain, Portugal, Holland, the Ottoman Empire and many Italian states in the First Coalition against France.

Henry Dundas, the Secretary of State for the Home Department, sought to take advantage of the state of war to strip France of her colonies. The wealth won in the East and West Indies would help fund the war on the Continent. But events across the Channel moved far too quickly for Dundas.

Within a matter of days of the declaration of war French troops invaded Holland and the *Stadholder*, William V of Orange, appealed to Britain for immediate help. The objective of the French was the occupation of the Schedlt and the vital port of Antwerp. This was a direct threat to Britain, which saw the retention of the Dutch coastline and the great anchorages of the Scheldt in friendly hands as key to its financial and defensive policy.

Britain responded by sending the Duke of York across the Channel with the Brigade of Guards, which landed at Helvoetsluys on 25 February. A plan of operations was established in which the Allies were to drive the French out of the Low Countries and then march on Paris, end the Revolution, and restore the monarchy. An Austrian army led by Prince Frederick Josias of Saxe-Coburg-Saalfeld, along with forces from Hanover, joined the Duke of York and reinforcements were sent from Britain. Saxe-Coburg took overall command, the entire force amounting to around 90,000 men.

At the beginning of April the Allied leaders set out their campaign strategy. Austria was scarcely able to fund its war effort so Britain agreed to provide financial support but only providing the Coalition forces helped Britain achieve its war aims on the Continent, the principal one at this stage being the capture of Dunkirk. Not only would the capture of this important port shorten the British Expeditionary Force's communications with Britain, its possession would also prove a valuable bargaining counter at any future peace negotiations.

The Austrians agreed and the Allied army marched into France, with its first tactical objective being the capture of the fortress of Valenciennes, but before Saxe-Coburg could lay siege to the fortress he had to make sure that no French forces could intervene. He therefore moved against the army of General François Drouet Lamarche which was camped at **FAMARS** some three miles south of Valenciennes. Saxe-Coburg decided to attack, with the main assault being spearheaded by the Duke of York with his Anglo-Hanoverian force supported by a number of Austrians.

The Allies successfully stormed Famars, the French losing more than 3,000 men and seventeen pieces of artillery. This victory enabled the Allied forces to carry out their attack upon Valenciennes, which fell to Saxe-Coburg on 28 July. Though Saxe-Coburg now wanted to move against Cambrai, the Duke of York was under strict instructions to seize Dunkirk.

The defences of Dunkirk, which included 8,000 men under the command of General Joseph Souham, were thought to be in a poor state of repair and vulnerable to capture. York concentrated at Menin and split his command into two forces; the right column of 22,000 British troops he led directly to invest the town of Dunkirk, while to protect his left flank was the 14,500-man covering army of the Hanoverian Field-Marshal Freytag consisting of his Hanoverian troops and ten squadrons of British cavalry. The Duke drove Souham's men back into Dunkirk, taking the Rosendahl suburb on 24 August, then digging in to besiege Dunkirk from the east side. However, the siege looked as though it might be a protracted affair, as York had neither siege artillery nor the manpower to properly surround the town.

Meanwhile, large numbers of reinforcements were received by the French *Armée du Nord* bringing it up to a strength of around 45,000 men, now under the command of General Jean Nicholas Houchard. With this force he attacked, and overwhelmed, the troops under Freytag forming the protective cordon around the Allied forces besieging Dunkirk at **HONDSHOOTE**.

French successes, however, proved to be short-lived. Saxe-Coburg won two significant victories, and Prussian forces under the Duke of Brunswick captured Mainz before sweeping through the Rhineland, mopping up small and disorganized elements of the French army. Brunswick also gained a significant victory over the French at the Battle of Pirmasens.

Faced with defeat on every front, the French Government enacted a *levée en masse*, calling for the compulsory enlistment of 300,000 men. Many in France were unhappy with the Revolution, the south and west of the country in particular remaining staunchly monarchist, and when troops tried to enforce the decreed conscription many regions rose up in rebellion. Amongst those places determined to oppose the Government was **TOULON**.

Royalist forces seized control of Toulon and, directed by the Baron d'Imbert, called for aid from the Coalition powers. Britain and her allies were quick to respond and, on 28 August, Admiral Lord Hood and Admiral Juan de Lángara of the Spanish Navy committed a force of 13,000 British, Spanish, Neapolitan and Piedmontese troops to the French Royalists' cause.

This was a serious blow to the Republic. Toulon was the most important naval arsenal of the country and in its sheltered waters were thirty warships. If the place was lost France would have no hope of challenging Britain at sea, therefore risking the loss of her overseas territories. Its loss would also set a dangerous precedent for other areas that menaced the Republic with revolt. The very survival of the Revolution and all it stood for was at stake.

On 1 October, Baron d'Imbert proclaimed the young Louis XVII to be king of France. The French royalist flag of the *Fleur-de-Lys* was raised above the battlements of Toulon and the great French naval base was delivered into the hands of the British navy.

French Revolutionary forces were sent to the area and soon some 12,000 men under Carteaux had besieged the port and begun to mount counter-attacks. In charge of the French artillery was a young Corsican officer called Napoleon Bonaparte.

It was the energetic and brilliant Captain Bonaparte who devised the plan that would eventually lead to the evacuation of Toulon by the Allied forces. His scheme was to capture the forts of l'Eguillette and Balaguier, on the hill of Cairo, the guns of which would be able to cut communications between the inner and outer harbours – La Petite Rade and La Grand Rade.

The first assault upon the heights failed, and the Allies, now alerted to the danger, stengthened their defences. Nevertheless, the French mounted a more determined operation to seize the position which was finally taken on 17 December. The following day Admiral Hood ordered Captain Sidney Smith to destroy the French ships and the arsenal prior to the evacuation of Toulon. Sidney Smith was only able to destroy thirteen of the French warships in Toulon, the rest survived to be used against the British in the years to come.

Having lost Toulon, it was then considered essential that the port should be blockaded by the Royal Navy. To be able to do this Lord Hood needed a base in the Mediterranean and just such a place was found in the form of the French-held island of Corsica. In the spring of 1793 the islanders had revolted against the Republicans and had driven them into the island's coastal fortresses of **SAINT FLORENT**, Bastia and Calvi. The Corsican leader Pascal Paoli appealed to Britain for help and Hood decided to take advantage of the situation.

British ships under Captain Nelson blockaded the port, and troops and sailors were landed under the command of Major General David Dundas. The town was dominated by two strong forts, one being the Mortella Tower to the north and the other the Convention Redoubt. When these had been captured the French surrendered, though a large number of the defenders were able to escape to **BASTIA**, which was Hood's next objective. The tower of Martella had proven to be so resilient that its construction was used as the basis for the Mortello Towers that were later erected around the south and east coasts of Britain when the fear of invasion from across the Channel was at its height.

Bastia was the largest place in Corsica and was held by around 5,000 troops. Hood had at his disposal just 1,200 plus the loyal Corsicans. Despite the odds, Hood was determined to attack the port. Dundas disagreed and he eventually returned to the UK. Nevertheless, Hood pressed on, and Captain Nelson landed to the north of Bastia and established siege batteries.

With the port blockaded by the Royal Navy, and under persistent bombardment, the situation in Bastia became increasingly desperate. On 19 May, General Gentili surrendered. Hood was now able to turn his attention to the last French stronghold, **CALVI**.

Nelson, with the new Army commander, General Charles Stuart, again landed to help lead the attack upon the port. On 12 July the Anglo-Corsican forces assaulted the town. Nelson was severely wounded in the head and lost an eye. The struggle continued until 10 August when, with the town in ruins, the garrison surrendered. The French had held out for forty days.

Further success followed as Britain began operations in the Caribbean with attacks against the French-held islands. The West Indies at this time were of immense importance to the French. They accounted for a third of France's trade, mainly in sugar, cotton and coffee, and one fifth of the French population derived their income from this trade. In January 1794 a British force under Admiral Sir John Jervis, with some 7,000 men under the command of Lieutenant General Sir Charles Grey, reached Barbados after a six-week voyage. From Barbados, Grey's force, divided into five brigades, sailed across to the French-held island of **MARTINIQUE**. Grey's men seized Fort Royal and Fort Saint Louis on March 22, and the last French stronghold, Fort Bourbon, was taken two days later. From there Jervis landed Grey's troops on **ST LUCIA**. The principle French garrison at Morne Fortune surrendered on 1 April.

Grey's and Jervis's next moved against **GUADELOUPE.** On 20 April, after two or three batteries, including the principle one of Palmiste, had been carried, with some resistance, and no great loss, General Collot, commanding at Fort Saint-Charles, capitulated on honourable terms. In doing so he surrendered to Great Britain Guadeloupe and all its dependencies, which included the islands of Marie-Galante, Désirade, and the Saintes.

Back in the main theatre of operations, the opposing forces in Flanders rested and regrouped over the course of the winter of 1793/4. Though some of the troops sent to the West Indies under Grey had been withdrawn from the army in Flanders, reinforcements were sent out to join the Duke of York from Britain as the country moved onto a war-footing and efforts to enlist more men started to bear fruit. Saxe-Coburg's army was now more than 100,000 strong but the *levée en masse* had yielded a vast number of recruits and the French *Armée du Nord*, under General Pichegru, numbered around twice that of the Allies it opposed. Nevertheless, it was the Allies who moved first. They advanced through Belgium at the beginning of April in three columns, their first objective being the capture of the fortress of Landrecies. The French counter-plan was to attack the besieging forces whilst sending a relief column into Landrecies.

The Prince of Orange commenced siege operations covered by the rest of the Allied army, which formed a semi-circle around the fortress. On 26 April 1794, the French attacked. The Duke of York's contingent was at **BEAUMONT-EN-CAMBRESIS** at the western end of the Allied line and was the target of General de Brigade René-Bernard Chapuy's 30,000-strong corps.

Chapuy (or Chapuis) found York's force strung out across a low ridge and drove in the British outposts. The British were taken by surprise, as the French approach had been concealed by a heavy fog, but Chapuy failed to take advantage of the situation. Instead of attacking immediately he manoeuvred his troops in front of the British line for two hours, giving York the chance to gather his men for a counter-stroke.

In the ensuing battle the French were roundly beaten, losing some 7,000 men. Chapuy himself was taken prisoner, along with Pichegru's orders for the campaign which were still in his pocket.

Saxe-Coburg's Chief-of-Staff, General Mack, urged the Allies to follow up the victory at Beaumont-en-Cambresis by attacking the French. He identified the 50,000-strong gathering formed by the divisions of Souham and Moreau situated on the River Lys between Courtrai and Aalbeke as being isolated and he planned to surround them. The Duke of York's corps' part in the operation was to attack from the north-west from Tournay to **TOURCOING** and pin Souham and Moreau against the Lys whilst the Austrians completed the encirclement of the French.

The Duke of York carried out his task well – but the Austrians failed. The British found themselves unsupported in the midst of the French army. Though they managed to cut their way back through the French, the British were badly mauled. The Allies then withdrew into an armed camp at **TOURNAY** (Tournai), the defeat at Tourcoing having cost them around 5,500 men as well as sixty guns.

This failure marked a turning point in the campaign. The Austrians were becoming increasingly disillusioned with the war in Flanders, seeing no end in sight. The Prussians, with their own problems, likewise were on the point of pulling out of the war. Nevertheless, plans for a renewal of the offensive were being considered when Pichegru, who had been absent at Tourcoing, attacked the Allied positions with around 60,000 men on 22 May.

This time the French were driven back with heavy losses, but after the battle

General Mack resigned, making it clear that he did not believe that the French could ever be driven out of Belgium. Following this, on 24 May, the Austrian Emperor Francis II, called for a vote amongst the commanding officers in Flanders. York voted to continue the fight, the others for a withdrawal.

Gradually, the Coalition forces retreated. The French followed and York withdrew behind the Scheldt. He was joined there by a fresh force from England which had been hastily landed at Ostend under Lord Moira to try and save the port. With French forces encircling Ostend, Moira abandoned the place and marched north to meet up with the rest of the army on the Scheldt.

After the Battle of Tourcoing, command of a part of the *Armée du Nord* was combined with General Jourdan's Army of the Ardennes to form the Army of Sambre-et-Meuse. With this force Jourdan laid siege to the fortress of Charleroi.

On 16 June 1794 Saxe-Coburg attacked Jourdan and managed to break the French stranglehold around the fortress. Two days later Jourdan counter-attacked and re-established his investment of Charleroi. Saxe-Coburg gathered his forces together once more and on 26 June the Allies attacked the French at **FLEURUS**. Saxe-Coburg's efforts failed to relieve the fortress, which surrendered that same day.

June 1794 also saw the first major fleet action at sea between Britain and France. Surrounded by enemies, France had been experiencing considerable problems obtaining food from the rest of Europe. A solution to this was sought by turning to France's colonies in the Americas, and the growing agricultural strength of the United States.

To transport the food, a huge convoy (figures vary from between 117 to 350 ships) was formed in Chesapeake Bay where it was to be met by the French Atlantic Fleet under the command of Admiral Villaret de Joyeuse.

Aware of the developing situation, Lord Howe with the British Grand Fleet was watching the French warships in Brest. De Joyeuse, however, managed to slip out of port and sail to the States, setting off back to France with the vital convoy under his protection.

When Howe realized that he had let Villaret de Joyeuse escape he set off after the French but with the vast expanse of the Atlantic before him, he had little hope of finding the enemy fleet. For eight days Howe searched the Atlantic in vain then, on 25 May, a straggler from the French fleet was spotted and was followed. It led Howe straight to the French battle fleet of twenty-six warships.

On what became known as **THE GLORIOUS FIRST OF JUNE**, Howe attacked, destroying a quarter of the French fleet. After the battle Howe had to be helped from his quarterdeck by his officers and was too exhausted to pursue Villaret.

It was nearly a fortnight before Howe returned to Portsmouth with his prizes. Though a great victory for the Royal Navy, Villaret had achieved his objective, as the convoy of food reached France and famine was averted.

Back in Flanders, the Austrians continued their withdrawal, effectively giving up their century-long control of Belgium. As the Austrians withdrew, so York was compelled to pull back. On 24 July the Allies crossed the Dutch frontier.

There followed a brief period of respite for the Allies whilst the French focused their efforts on capturing the border forts. When Pichegru, with the *Armée du Nord*, renewed the French offensive at the end of August, York was obliged to pull back to the line of the River Aa where he was attacked at **BOXTEL** on 15 September. It was at Boxtel that Arthur Wellesley, the future Duke of Wellington, came under fire for the first time as Lieutenant Colonel of the 33rd Regiment of Foot.

Following the battle York was compelled to withdraw even further north, taking up a position behind the Meuse. On 18 September the Austrians were beaten again. York, seeing nothing but the prospect of further loss of territory, proposed a counter-attack to halt the French. This had to be abandoned when the Hanoverian contingent of his army refused to take part and the Duke was recalled to London. The Hanoverian General Wallmoden took over command of the Anglo-Hanoverian forces.

As winter approached the situation of the British army was looking increasingly perilous and a retreat behind the flooded River Waal was considered its only hope of finding a suitable defensive position. Yet, against all the principles of eighteenth-century warfare, instead of settling down for the winter, the French attacked across the frozen river.

The Allies retreated in complete disarray, falling back upon the Yesl. The retreat brought with it the final collapse of the Dutch Republic, and the Prince of Holland fled to England in a fishing boat. The British army fell back into North Germany but received no help from the Prussians, who were already engaged in secret meetings with the French to end their participation in the war.

In early March the British Government sent transports to the Wesser to evacuate what remained of the army. On 13 April 1795 the infantry embarked at Bremen, with the cavalry and a small force of artillery remaining behind to protect Hanover.

Though its forces had been driven from the Continent, the excesses of the Jacobins and their offerings to *Madame Guillotine* in France had roused great animosity and dread in Britain, and rather than accept that the Coalition was dead she tried to revive it. Large subsidies were offered to Russia and Austria to continue fighting and, whilst they happily took the gold, no more armies were put into the field.

Effectively alone, Britain had to decide which course of action could offer the greatest prospect of damaging the Revolution and encouraging Royalist opposition in France. The latter – promoting internal disorder – appeared to be the most effective and an operation to help the Royalists in the south-west of France was approved.

An expedition was mounted from Portsmouth on 13 June 1795, consisting of a convoy of fifty transport ships accompanied by a Royal Navy squadron of three ships of the line and six frigates under the command of Commodore John Warren, part of Admiral Lord Bridport's fleet. The ships carried 2,500 French émigrés and volunteer prisoners of war, along with sixty pieces of artillery and a vast amount of arms and provisions. The convoy was destined for Quiberon Bay in southern Brittany, where the *Fleur-de-Lys* would be raised against the *Tricolour*. A fleet under Villaret de Joyeuse attacked Warren's squadron on 23 June 1795, but was forced to retire quickly towards the **ÎLE DE GROIX** chased by Bridport's fleet. The French were overtaken and brought to battle with three of their ships being captured and the remainder scattered along the coast. The expedition, however, was a disaster. Most of the equipment was captured by the Republicans at Quiberon Bay as well as six of the transport ships.

There was also a reversal in the Caribbean. In April a French squadron had slipped through the blockade of Rochefort and reached Guadeloupe in June. After fierce fighting, the British withdrew to the eastern half of the island. In December they were forced to evacuate the island altogether and fighting also broke out in the Windward Islands. In March 1795 the black populations of Grenada, St Vincent and St Lucia rebelled against the British occupying forces, which retreated into their garrisons. Though reinforcements from Britain helped regain some measure of control in Grenada and St Vincent, the British lost some 2,000 men in the fighting and from disease.

In the Mediterranean, Vice-Admiral Hotham moved the Mediterranean Fleet from its base at Saint Florent to Leghorn (now Livorno) on the north-western coast of Italy. News of the move soon reached the French at Toulon, who saw this as a chance to re-capture Corsica. A strong naval force under Rear-Admiral Pierre Martin, including a squadron of thirteen ships of the line with 5,000 troops, sailed for Corsica on 3 March 1795.

News that the Toulon fleet was at sea reached Hotham on 8 March and he put to sea the following day. The two fleets came within sight of each other on 12 March but it was not until the morning of the 13th that the British were able to close with the French and on the 14th the main engagement took place off **GENOA**. The result was a significant victory for Hotham.

Martin escaped to the safety of the **HYÈRES ISLANDS** off the French coast, sending the more heavily damaged of his ships to Toulon for repairs. Martin's fleet was reinforced by a squadron from Brest under *Contre-Admiral* Renaudin and on 7 June the combined force put to sea.

That afternoon the French force was spotted by Captain Nelson in *Agamemnon*, who alerted the rest of the Mediterranean Fleet. Martin tried to out-run the British but on 13 June the rearmost French ships were overtaken. In the resulting battle one French ship was lost; the rest were able to retreat to Toulon.

With the French gaining the upper hand in the West Indies, Pitt decided to mount a huge amphibious operation to secure the islands of the Caribbean once and for all. Sir Ralph Abercromby was given command of 15,000 men and a naval squadron and ordered to take all the French and Dutch islands in the Caribbean. The Caribbean had become the main theatre of operations for British forces. Abercromby arrived in April of 1796 and re-took **ST LUCIA**. He followed up this by seizing **ST VINCENT** and **GRENADA** in June.

Closer to home Britain faced further problems when Spain, having made peace with France, declared war on Britain in October 1796. The French and Spanish navies could now count a combined force of thirty-eight ships of the line compared with the British Mediterranean Fleet of just fifteen ships of the line, and the Royal Navy was forced to abandon positions on Corsica and Elba. These two forces clashed in February 1797.

The Spanish fleet of twenty-seven ships of the line left Cartagena on 1 February with the intention of joining up with the French fleet at Brest. The combined force would then sail to Cadiz where it would provide the escort for a large merchant convoy.

The Spanish ships, under the command of Admiral Don José de Cordóba, encountered heavy winds which blew them far out into the Atlantic. In the meantime, the British Mediterranean Fleet, under Admiral Sir John Jervis, had sailed from the Tagus with ten ships of the line to try to intercept the Spanish fleet. On 6 February, Jervis was joined off **CAPE ST VINCENT** by a reinforcement of five ships of the line from the Channel Fleet under Rear-Admiral William Parker. Though still considerably weaker than the Spanish fleet, Jervis attacked, capturing four Spanish ships and killing some 3,000 men. Whilst the Spaniards had been dealt a devastating blow, most of their ships were able to retreat to Cadiz.

At the Admiralty it was thought that the Spaniards had been so severely beaten that Jervis would be able to closely blockade Cadiz harbour and therefore prevent convoys from the Americas reaching the port. Accordingly Jervis blockaded the entrance to Cadiz but the Spanish, under Vice-Admiral Mazarredo, attacked the British ships with a flotilla of gun-boats. In the confined waters of the Outer Harbour the gun-boats had a distinct advantage and were able to inflict considerable damage upon the big warships. Jervis was forced to withdraw further out to sea, which allowed several convoys to slip in and out of the port.

Jervis looked for another way to stop the treasure ships reaching Cadiz and he learnt that the convoys frequently stopped en route at Tenerife in the Canary Isles. On 14 July 1797, Jervis sent the recently promoted Rear-Admiral Nelson with a squadron of nine ships and some 4,000 men to capture the main port, **SANTA CRUZ DE TENERIFE**. Under Captain Troubridge of HMS *Culloden*, 1,000 men were landed on the 22nd but, amidst much confusion, they failed to penetrate the Spanish defences. Nelson himself led the next attack but was wounded in his right arm. The soldiers and sailors tried to storm the Spanish position but were driven off. Under the cover of a truce, the British forces were allowed to withdraw peacefully.

Operations also continued in the Caribbean and, with Spain now an ally of France, Abercromby attacked the Spanish island of **TRINIDAD** in February 1797. With some eighteen ships commanded by Rear-Admiral Henry Harvey and 10,000 soldiers and marines, Abercromby reached Trinidad on 15 February. In addition to a strong garrison and a powerfully armed battery on Gaspar Grande island, a Spanish squadron including four ships-of-the line was found anchored in Chaguaramus Bay. Consequently the troops were landed further up the coast, some five miles from the capital, Port-d'Espagne (Port of Spain). Rear-Admiral Harvey then placed his ships to prevent the Spanish squadron from sailing out to sea. When it was clear to the Spaniards that there was no possibility of escape and with the British troops advancing towards Port-d'Espagne they set fire to their ships. On 21 February the govenor, José Maria Chaon, surrendered.

Abercromby followed this up with an assault upon Puerto Rico. He reached the waters off the capital, **SAN JUAN**, on 17 April with a force estimated at possibly as many as 13,000 soldiers and marines and a total of sixty or sixty-four warships and transports. The Spaniards, supported by a number of warships, were determined to resist and the following day the British ships began bombarding points where the Spanish had taken defensive positions to prevent a landing. Eventually Abercromby was able to land a few troops but they could make little impression upon the Spanish positions. On Sunday, 30 April, Abercromby accepted that he was not going to be able to take San Juan and he called off* the attack and withdrew to the ships.

The largest collection of Spanish ships was still the squadron at Cadiz and, as well as maintaining the blockade of that port, the Royal Navy also had to keep a careful eye on the French fleet and, since the occupation of Holland (which had then become the French-controlled Batavian Republic), the powerful Dutch fleet. The latter was blockaded within its harbour in the Textel by the British North Sea fleet under Admiral Duncan. At the start of October, Duncan was forced to return to Yarmouth for supplies. Seeing this as an opportunity to conduct a brief raid into the North Sea, Admiral De Winter took his ships to sea, returning to Holland a few days later – only to find that Duncan was waiting for them. At the Battle of **CAMPERDOWN**, eleven Dutch ships were taken by Duncan's men, the rest being forced to disperse.

The year of 1797 saw the collapse of the First Coalition. Repeated success by the recently promoted General Bonaparte saw his army advance through Italy and into Austria, and, at the same time, other French forces under Hoche and Moreau penetrated through Germany and bore down on Austria from the west. The Austrians sought peace, effectively ending the War of the First Coalition. Only Britain remained at war with France.

With peace in Europe, France could concentrate its efforts against Britain and the result was a direct assault upon the British mainland. Four French warships under the command of Commodore Jean-Joseph Castagnier, landed approximately 1,400 men near **FISHGUARD** in Pembrokeshire on 22 February. Discipline amongst the French troops, a large proportion of whom were irregulars, soon broke down and many deserted. On the 23rd, a hastily assembled force of around 500 British reservists and militia, including the Pembroke Yeomanry, attacked the French. Realizing the hopelessness of their situation, the French surrendered the following morning. This was the last ever invasion of the British mainland. The Pembroke Yeomanry was granted the battle honour 'Fishguard', becoming the first volunteer unit to receive a battle honour. It remains the only unit still serving in the British Army to bear the name of an engagement on British soil.

An easier option to sailing all the way around Britain was to simply cross the Channel, and at Dunkirk a vast camp was formed and a great flotilla was assembled. Fishing boats were collected from along the Dutch and French ports, barges were taken from the rivers and canals, and the shipyards buzzed with activity. Encamped within a day's march of Dunkirk was the invasion army, estimated at 200,000 strong, and it was to be commanded by the Republic's most successful general, Napoleon Bonaparte.

Britain took the threat of invasion very seriously and around its southern and eastern coast the ring of Martello Towers began to rise. But it was not Britain's way to simply wait to be invaded and a scheme was laid to attack **OSTEND** where many of the invasion barges were being gathered. The raiding force, under the command of Sir Charles Grey, destroyed the Bruges Canal Gates and rendered inland navigation from Flushing to Ostend impossible.

The events of the previous months had demonstrated just how difficult an invasion of Britain would be, and the attack upon Ostend indicated just to what degree the Royal Navy commanded the waters of the Channel. The vagaries of the weather also meant that even the best laid plans could, quite literally, be blown off course. Yet, if a direct assault upon Britain was at best problematical, she might be seriously damaged by other, and easier, means.

With European markets denied to her, Britain's economy had become reliant upon the developing markets in India and the New World. Any attempt at attacking the territories in the Americas would be faced with exactly the same perils, or even greater ones, as trying to transport an army across the Channel. But India could be approached overland. Whilst a march through Europe and Asia would be impracticable, if an army could be shipped across the Mediterranean to Egypt it would cut the march in half.

Though the Royal Navy was dominant in the Channel and across the Atlantic, it was less able to control the Mediterranean against the combined strength of the French and Spanish navies. An expedition to Egypt therefore seemed quite likely to succeed. Bonaparte, who first proposed such a venture, was placed in command of the expedition and he assembled a force of 35,000 men and a powerful fleet at Toulon. On 19 May 1798, the armada sailed for the Orient, reaching Malta on 9 June, which was seized from the Knights of St John. The armada continued on to Egypt but a British squadron under Rear-Admiral Nelson had set off in pursuit. Nelson had no idea where the French convoy was heading and he scoured the eastern Mediterranean in search of the French ships.

Bonaparte reached Egypt without interference from Nelson. After landing the troops, the French ships, commanded by Admiral François-Paul Brueys D'Aigalliers, anchored in Aboukir Bay twenty miles north-east of Alexandria. It was here, on 1 August 1798, that Nelson found the French fleet and immediately attacked. Brueys was killed at what became known as **THE BATTLE OF THE NILE**, and all but four of the seventeen French warships were captured or sunk.

The battle completely changed the naval balance of power in the Mediterranean. Britain now possessed an unrivalled superiority in the Mediterranean, which she retained for the rest of the war.

Such a position of dominance was not experienced by Britain in the New World. After its defeat in Puerto Rico, a strong Spanish force was despatched from Mexico to try and capture the British settlement of Belize. The Spanish force, consisting of thirty-five vessels with more than 2,000 soldiers and sailors tried to force its way through the Montego Caye shoal only to find it defended not only by the 700-strong British garrison but also by the natives who had agreed to support them and who had been armed by the Superintendent of the settlement, Lieutenant Colonel Thomas Barrow. The culmination came on 10 September when the Spanish and the small contingent of British ships lined up against each other off **ST GEORGE'S CAYE**.

The Spaniards were driven off in confusion. The battle is still celebrated every 10 September in Belize as St. George's Caye Day or National Day.

France continued to look at invading British soil and an opportunity of doing just that presented itself in early 1798. The Society of United Irishmen, led by Wolfe Tone, launched an uprising against British rule in Ireland in May, and the rebels appealed to France for help. A small French force under General Humbert was landed at Killala, County Mayo. The British responded by amassing a force of 26,000 men under Lord Cornwallis, the recently appointed viceroy. Cornwallis divided his force into two columns, giving command of the second column to General Lake. The two columns combined to overcome the Franco-Irish forces at the Battle of **BALLINAMUCK** on 8 September. Humbert was compelled to surrender.

None of this was known in France and a force of 3,000 reinforcements sailed from Brest in nine warships. Aware that the French might make such an attempt, a squadron under Commodore John Warren was keeping watch on the approaches to Ireland. One of Warren's frigates spotted the French convoy and the British squadron set off in pursuit. For three weeks the French managed to elude Warren's ships but on 12 October they were brought to battle near **TORY ISLAND** off the coast of Donegal. Only two frigates and a schooner escaped destruction out of the ten ships in the original French squadron. Wolfe Tone was captured and hanged.

Napoleon's planned expedition through the Middle East to India involved joining forces with Tippu Sultan, the ruler of the Kingdom of Mysore in the south-west of the country. Tippu was a supporter of the French and a bitter opponent of the British. In order to deny Napoleon a foothold in India an operation to remove Tippu from power began in March 1799.

A large British and compliant Indian force provided by the Nizam of Hyderabad under the command of General George Harris marched into Mysore and laid siege to Tippu's capital **SERINGAPATAM** on 5 April.

It was not until 1 May that the attackers were able to erect breaching batteries but by 4 May a large breach had been blown in the walls and the fortress was stormed. Tippu was killed defending the walls.

The peace in mainland Europe that followed the collapse of the First Coalition in October 1797 lasted only until the following year and in December 1798, Britain, Russia, Turkey and Austria joined together to form the Second Coalition. The Coalition powers planned to attack France from all sides, including a combined Anglo-Russian force which would invade the Batavian Republic and drive into northern France.

On 23 August 1799, Sir Ralph Abercromby landed the first of his 12,000 men on the Helder coast near **CALLANSTOOG**, even though the Russian army had not yet arrived. The Dutch resisted but were driven off and the British were able to establish themselves on the land. They were then able to occupy the roadstead of Nieuwe Diep which would provide the rest of Abercromby's men, and the Russians when they arrived, with a safe disembarkation point.

Having disembarked his force, Abercromby took control of the Zijpe polder, which was an area of reclaimed land that had a protective bank with a deep drainage canal that acted like a moat. Abercromby strengthened this barrier by erecting batteries and building additional protective earthworks at points along the embankment. The Dutch forces were reinforced by French troops and, by 9 September, General Brune commanded approximately 25,000 men. The following day he attacked. The Batavian divisions delivered a frontal assault upon the villages of Eenigenburg and **KRABBENDAM**, whilst the French division would turn Abercromby's flank. Krabbendam was taken twice by the attackers but both times they were driven out and, with the other attacks also failing, Brune called off his troops.

After the battle, the Russians arrived, as well as more British troops, making the combined force between 30,000 and 40,000 strong, which then came under the command of the Duke of York. With this powerful force he attempted to break out from the Zijpe polder on 19 September.

The operation actually began on 18 September with Sir Ralph Abercromby leading his 18,000-strong left-hand column through the night. The state of the roads caused considerable delay and Abercromby did not reach his objective until much later than expected. Meanwhile the fighting began on the morning of the 19th with the Russian column attacking **BERGEN** but they were unsupported by the British, who had not even lined up, the respective commanders having failed to synchronize watches. The Russians were driven back with heavy losses. The third column, under General Pulteney, also experienced considerable difficulty crossing the terrain, which was broken with watercourses and dykes. The result of all this was the Anglo-Russian attack was uncoordinated and was beaten back. Abercromby's column was not even engaged.

After the battle Russian reinforcements arrived, making up for many of the losses sustained in the Battle of Bergen. The Duke of York was still determined to break out of his beach-head but bad weather stopped him from re-commencing operations for two weeks, by which time the Franco-Dutch forces had further strengthened their positions. Soon only a narrow strip of land, all but surrounded by water, offered an avenue of attack for the Duke.

The breakout began on 2 October with, once again, Abercromby attempting a flank march whilst the other three columns attacked towards Bergen. As before, the coordination between the Coalition forces was poor. Abercromby marched seven miles before he encountered any serious opposition at Egmont. This place was taken after heavy fighting by the British but they were too exhausted by their march to be able to move to assist the other columns. However, the weight of the Anglo-Russian forces proved too great for the French and Batavians, and Brune withdrew leaving Egmont and **ALKMAAR** in Coalition hands.

With the retreat of the Franco-Batavian army the greater part of the North Holland peninsula was now in Anglo-Russian hands and the Duke of York quickly pressed his advantage by advancing upon Brune's new line about six miles from Alkmaar that stretched from the North Sea through Castricum to Akersloot. Sickness and casualties had reduced York's command to around 27,000 men.

On 6 October York probed the Franco-Batavian positions. Though believed to be only a reconnaissance to test the strength of the enemy, early gains prompted the

Russians to persist with their advance. York was obliged to support the Russians, bringing on a general engagement. The Coalition forces captured **CASTRICUM**, which changed hands several times throughout the battle. Darkness put an end to the fighting, with both sides in the same positions in which they had started the day. That night York held a council of war in which it was agreed that the Coalition forces would withdraw back to their original beach-head of the Zijpe polder. All the gains achieved in the previous fighting were given up.

Hemmed in with his back to the sea, and with the weather deteriorating as winter approached, York was now faced with the prospect of a long siege and a growing sick list. With no possibility of achieving any success, York decided to abandon the expedition and save what troops he could, and he approached Brune with an offer of an honourable capitulation. After some bartering the Convention of Alkmaar was signed, some 8,000 prisoners were exchanged, and on 19 November the Anglo-Russian forces completed their departure from the Continent.

The following year, 1800, saw the Royal Navy mount an assault upon the Spanish port of **FERROL**. It was hoped that if this major port with its arsenal was captured the Spaniards might be induced to break off relations with France and make peace with Britain.

A considerable force of 15,000 men and between 80 and 100 ships took part in the expedition. On 25 August 1800, the troops commanded by Sir James Pulteney landed on the beach of Doniños to take the Castle of San Felipe covered by the guns of the British warships under Admiral Pellew. Instead of an easy victory, the defences of Ferrol proved to be formidable and the Spaniards intent upon resistance. Discouraged, the troops re-embarked and the expedition was abandoned amid much acrimony between the Royal Navy and the Army.

The next significant move by Britain was against the French forces in Egypt. In August 1799 Napoleon had left his troops to return to France and they were now under the command of General Menou.

On 8 March 1800, a 14,000-strong British army led by Sir Ralph Abercromby landed in Aboukir Bay. After securing his beach-head Abercromby advanced towards **ALEXANDRIA** before the main French army marched up from Cairo. Abercromby positioned his troops with his right resting on the Mediterranean and his left on the inland lake of Aboukir. Menou attacked on the 21st. The two forces were evenly matched but it was the British who held their ground and beat off the attack. During the fighting Abercromby was caught alone by a detachment of French cavalry, and was mortally wounded.

The French withdrew into Alexandria, which was then besieged by the British force. On 2 September, with no hope of receiving any help from France, the French surrendered.

The success in Egypt had been the result of Britain's dominance of the sea, and it was the Royal Navy which was the country's principle weapon in the war against France. As well as preventing French ships and those of her allies from sailing, the Navy also insisted on stopping and searching neutral ships and, if they were seen to be carrying goods to France, their cargoes were seized. Understandably, this angered many of the neutral countries and, in 1800, Russia, Norway-Denmark, Sweden and Prussia formed the League of Armed Neutrality to ensure free trade with France. Britain viewed this as being beneficial to France and in early 1801 the British Government assembled a large fleet at Great Yarmouth with the objective of breaking up the League. Britain wanted to strike at the Danish contingent of the Norwegian-Danish fleet before the ice-bound Russian fleet could join them when the Baltic thawed. Admiral Hyde Parker was sent to Denmark to try and separate the Danes from the rest of the League, by force if necessary. After diplomatic efforts had failed, Parker allowed Vice-Admiral Nelson to attack the Danish fleet moored along the quayside at **COPENHAGEN**. Three Danish ships were destroyed and twelve captured, though only one was retained to take the wounded back to England; the rest were burnt. Despite promises of assistance, the Swedes did not intervene on the side of the Danes. The loss of the Danish fleet precipitated the disintegration of the League, which officially ceased on 23 October 1801.

As well as fighting against the northern League, the Royal Navy still had to guard the Channel, as a large invasion force was being assembled by the French at **BOULOGNE**. On 4 August 1801, Vice-Admiral Nelson attempted to bombard the vessels collected in Boulogne harbour, but with little effect, being unable to sail close to the port because of the coastal gun batteries. Nelson renewed his operations on 15 August with a surprise night attack, but this ended in confusion and was called off the following morning.

The Royal Navy was still endeavouring to keep the French and Spanish navies blockaded within their own ports and in the summer of 1801 this led to a protracted engagement off the Spanish coast. An attempt was made by the French Toulon fleet to join the Spanish and French ships at Cadiz. The Toulon ships, under the command of Admiral Charles Linois, sailed down to **ALGECIRAS** and anchored in the bay. A British squadron led by Admiral James Saumarez attacked the anchored ships in the First Battle of Algeciras on 6 July 1801. A number of French ships were damaged, but none were captured.

The battle (the Second Battle of Algeciras) was renewed on 12 July. Five Spanish and one French ship of the line sailed from Cadiz to help escort Linois' ships into Cadiz. As they sailed that night, Saumarez pounced. In the confusion of a night engagement two huge Spanish ships, each of 112 guns, collided and exploded, and a French ship was captured.

The French and Spanish ships had combined, but the British blockade of Cadiz was resumed.

Whilst the opposing navies were fighting to the death, the diplomats were talking and, on 30 September, a preliminary peace treaty between Britain and France was signed. After further talks agreement was reached and on 25 March 1802 the Treaty of Amiens was formalized.

Under the terms of the agreement, many of the territories gained by British forces over the preceding years were handed back to their previous occupiers: France, Spain and Holland. Britain also agreed to evacuate Egypt.

*

Peace lasted for little more than a year. Neither Britain nor France fulfilled all of their treaty obligations and both sides were suspicious of the others' motives. On 18 May 1803, Britain declared war on France and shortly afterwards formed the Third Coalition with Austria, Russia, Portugal and others including the Kingdom of Naples. Amongst the first moves undertaken by Britain was the recapture of **ST LUCIA,** which was one of the countries that had been returned to France the previous year. Led by Commodore Samuel Hood and Lieutenant General Grinfield, a strong force set out from Barbados on 19 June. The squadron reached Choc Bay two days later, and the troops, disembarking without opposition, immediately set themselves up at La Vigie and Castries. The French retired to the main stronghold of the Morne Fortune, which was stormed at 0400 hours on June 22 and in less than an hour the works were carried at the point of the bayonet.

In India the Governor-General, Richard Wellesley, sought to further erode French influence and extend British control across the sub-continent. Internal disputes amongst the leaders of the Maratha Confederacy presented him with the opportunity he sought.

On 4 September the British East India forces under General Lake stormed the fort of **ALLY GHUR** (Aligarth), which was fortified and commanded by the French officer Pierre Cuillier-Perron. During the battle the British lost possibly as many as 900 men.

Lake then moved against Delhi. He was met by the Maratha of Scindia's army led by the French General Louis Bourquin at the Jumna river. During the battle fought on 11 September, the Maratha's forces were soundly beaten with many of them being driven into the river. Delhi surrendered three days later.

A second column of a little less than 10,000 men under the command of Major General Arthur Wellesley attacked a much larger Maratha army at **ASSAYE** on 23 September. Though the British were victorious, they had suffered heavy casualties and were unable to pursue. Further victories at Argan and Gawilghur, coupled with Lake's success in the north, led to Britain taking control of most of India.

Britain's prosperity owed much to her trade with her overseas territories, India being the most important of these. Though there was no longer any prospect of Napoleon invading India, as First Consul and soon to crown himself Emperor of France, he still sought to disrupt British shipping in the Indian Ocean.

Anticipating the ending of the Treaty of Amiens, in March 1803 Napoleon dispatched a small squadron to the Île de France from where it would operate against the East Indiamen crossing the Indian Ocean. As soon as war was declared, *Contre-Amiral* Charles-Alexandre Durand Linos began attacking British merchant ships.

Durand wintered at Batavia where news reached him of the sailing of the annual 'China Fleet'. The cargoes carried by these ships were immensely valuable but no warships were available to act as escorts. The East Indiamen, however, were well armed with up to thirty-six guns mounted for their defence and it was decided that collectively ships of the convoy were strong enough to see off any French warships.

On 14 February 1804, Durand sighted the convoy and the following day, off the coast of **PULO AURO**, he attacked. The convoy was under the command of Commodore Nathaniel Dance and he ordered four of his lead ships to fly the blue ensign, indicating that they were warships. These ships had also been painted to resemble ships of the line. Unnerved, Durand broke off the action and the convoy continued on safely to England.

With the renewal of hostilities between Britain and France, the Royal Navy once again re-established its blockade of the French ports. As it was evident that the French, even combined with their allies, could not defeat Britain at sea, Napoleon sought, yet again, to end the war by invading Britain. As in 1801, a large force was assembled at Boulogne. The so-called *Armée d'Angleterre* was brought to a total of 150,000 men, more than sufficient to defeat the few regular troops and militia stationed in Britain. All Napoleon needed was control of the Channel long enough to ship his army to the open beaches of southern England.

To accomplish this it was arranged that the French navy would escape from the British blockades of Toulon and Brest and threaten to attack the West Indies. This, it was hoped, would compel the British fleet to chase after the French ships, leaving the Channel unguarded. The French squadrons would rendezvous at Martinique and then double-back to Europe. They would land troops in Ireland to raise yet another rebellion and tie down the British forces before continuing to Boulogne to escort the *Armée d'Angleterre* across to England.

On 29 March 1805, Vice-Admiral Villeneuve's Toulon fleet managed to evade Nelson's blockade, reaching Martinique on 12 May accompanied by six Spanish men-of-war from Cadiz. There they waited for the Brest fleet but Admiral Ganteaume was unable to break through the British blockade.

Whilst waiting for the Brest ships, Villeneuve attacked the British-held island of Diamond Rock. However, Villeneuve soon learnt that Nelson had reached the Caribbean, and he set off back across the Atlantic, capturing a British convoy on the way. The Franco-Spanish fleet was intercepted off **CAPE FINISTERE** on the evening of 22 July 1805, by Robert Calder's squadron which had been blockading Ferrol and Rochefort. For three hours the opposing forces battled, with neither side being able to achieve a decisive result. Calder did not renew the battle the following day, which later resulted in a court-martial. Villeneuve took his ships into Cadiz, where he was blockaded once again.

Villenueve's failure led to Napoleon abandoning his plans to invade Britain and he turned instead to counter the other main Coalition countries, Austria and Russia, which had mobilized their respective armies. As Napoleon advanced eastwards, on 16 September 1805, he ordered Villeneuve to sail at the first opportunity. He was to join up with a further seven Spanish ships of the line at Cartagena and sail to Naples where he was to land the soldiers his ships carried to reinforce his troops there opposing the Austrians.

On 20 October Villeneuve sailed. That evening Nelson's fleet was spotted. The following day off **CAPE TRAFALGAR** the opposing fleets engaged. The resultant

British victory was one of the most decisive in the history of naval warfare. Twenty-one French and Spanish ships were captured and one destroyed.

Four French ships of the line escaped along with four frigates. These were spotted by Captain Baker of HMS *Phoenix*, who was able to inform the squadron under Sir Richard Strachan of the enemy's position. Strachan caught up with the French ships off **CAPE ORTEGAL** on the morning of 4 November. All four battleships were captured, leaving the Royal Navy as undisputed masters of the seas.

Believing that the French navy would not risk putting to sea again for a long time, the blockade of the French ports was relaxed during the winter of 1805/6. The Brest fleet, however, which had not been involved in the Trafalgar campaign, remained intact and was able to put to sea on 13 December 1805. splitting into two divisions, the French fleet's objective was to attack British shipping in the Atlantic.

The ships under *Contre-Amiral* Urbain de Leissegues' command were badly damaged by storms and put into **SANTO DOMINGO** for repairs. They were spotted there by a British squadron under Vice-Admiral John Duckworth on 6 February 1806. The French could not escape and so formed up to fight, but in the ensuing battle all their ships of the line were either captured or burnt. The battle of Santo Domingo was the last fleet engagement of the war between French and British capital ships in open water.

Britain could now look at recovering the territories relinquished under the terms of the Treaty of Amiens and at capturing those of its enemies. The first move in this the direction took place at the beginning of 1806 when two British brigades, under command of Lieutenant General Sir David Baird, attacked the Batavian Republic's South African Cape Colony. Throughout the 6th and 7th of January the troops were landed to the north of Cape Town. Despite being inferior in numbers the Dutch, under Lieutenant General Jan Willem Janssens, attacked the invaders who had formed up on the slopes of **BLAAUWBERG** mountain. The Dutch forces were driven inland whilst the British advanced upon Cape Town, which surrendered on 10 January.

The decision of Naples to join the Third Coalition led to France invading that country in the spring of 1806. Though King Ferdinand fled the country, and Joseph Bonaparte was installed on the Neapolitan throne, the Neapolitans refused to accept French rule. A large body of Neapolitan troops occupied the key fortress-port of Gaeta and rebellion broke out in Calabria. The French responded by sending an army under Marshal Andre Masséna to capture Gaeta. Britain wanted to support the uprising, not by joining the defenders in Gaeta but by initiating further insurrections in the rear of the besiegers.

A force of more than 5,000 men under Major General John Stuart landed in the Gulf of Sant'Eufemia on 30 July 1806. At the same time a French force of at least the same size, led by General Reynier, moved to confront the British. On 4 July the opposing forces met on the plain of **MAIDA**. The battle lasted just fifteen minutes, the French being routed. Stuart, however, felt that he lacked the numbers to be able to attack Masséna's forces besieging Gaeta and he marched to Reggio where he embarked on the ships of Admiral Sidney Smith.

Despite Britain's supremacy at sea, there appeared no possibility of defeating

France on the Continent. In 1806 no one could possibly have envisaged the great victories of the Duke of Wellington in the Iberian Peninsula and at Waterloo. Until then, Britain continued to send its ships and its soldiers across the seas, learning failure as well as success.

The Despatches

1

The Battle Of Famars

Whitehall, May 27.

The following report was received in Whitehall on the evening of 26 May from the Duke of York's Adjutant-General Sir James Murray. It was delivered by Captain Craufurd, the Duke's Aide de Camp:

Famars, May 25, 1793.

SIR,

I AM happy to have the Honor of informing you, that the Combined Forces, under the Command of the Prince of Saxe Cobourg and of His Royal Highness, have defeated the Enemy, and driven them from the strong Camp of Famars.

    A Body of Sixteen Battalions, viz. the Brigade of British, Two Battalions of Hanoverian Guards, Two Battalions of Hanoverian Grenadiers, and Eight Battalions of Austrian Infantry, with Six Squadrons of British Light Dragoons, Four of Hanoverian and Eight of Austrian Cavalry, with a great Proportion of heavy Artillery, assembled very early in the Morning of the 23d, under the Command of His Royal Highness. They were to arrive at Day-Break upon the Bank of the Ronelle, near the Village of Ortie, to establish Bridges to pass the River, and turn the Right of the Enemy. Another Column, of nearly equal Force, under General Ferraris, was destined to attack the Works which had been thrown up upon the right Bank of the Ronelle, and, after carrying them, to second the Operations of His Royal Highness as Circumstances might direct: A Column, under the Command of General Colloredo, was employed to observe Valenciennes; another, under General Otto, to cover Quesnoy. The Enemy attempted an attack upon the latter, in which they were repulsed, with the Loss of Three Pieces of Cannon: Two were taken by a Detachment of Hussars. A thick Fog occasioned some Delay in the Advance of the Troops. Upon their Approach to the Ronelle several Batteries were opened from the opposite Side, but from such a Distance as to produce little Effect.

    They were answered and kept in Awe by the Austrian and Hanoverian heavy Artillery. After some Time spent in cannonading, Two Divisions of Hussars passed the River without Opposition at a Ford in the Village of Mershe. His Royal Highness ordered the Brigade of Guards, Two Battalions of Austrian Infantry, Six Squadrons of British and Two of Hanoverian Light Cavalry, to pursue the same Route, in order to take the Batteries in Flank, and secure a Passage for the Rest of his Troops. This Movement had the desired Success; the Enemy retreated from all their Posts, falling back upon a Redoubt which they had thrown up upon the commanding Heights behind the Village of Famars.

General Ferraris, after cannonading some Time, attacked, upon his Side, and carried the Entrenchments by Assault. The Troops of the different Nations displayed the utmost Firmness and Intrepidity in this arduous Undertaking. The British Troops, who had this Opportunity of distinguishing themselves, were the Brigade of the Line, viz. the 14th and 53d Regiments, with the Battalion formed from their Light Infantry and Grenadier Companies, commanded by Major-General Abercromby. Seven Pieces of Cannon and near 200 Prisoners were taken in the Redoubts. Some Squadrons of French Cavalry appearing at this Time, and threatening the Flank of the Infantry, though superior in Number, they were attacked with the greatest Valour by the Regiment of Hanoverian Garde de Corps. The Contest was of the severest Kind; the Squadrons mixed with one another, and the French were defeated, though not without considerable Loss to the Garde de Corps; the Regiment had, upon that and other Occasions, Three Officers killed, One taken, and Four wounded, and 67 killed and wounded, Non-commissioned Officers and Privates. The Rest of the Hanoverian Troops lost about 35 Men killed and wounded.

His Royal Highness advanced, with a Part of the Troops, to a hollow Way, within a small Distance of the Works; but observing, from the Disposition of the Enemy, that they could not be carried at that Time without considerable Loss, from which no proportionable Benefit would arise, he thought it better to defer the Attack till next Morning at Day-break, approaching and turning them in the Night.

The Enemy, apprehensive of the Consequences of such a Movement, abandoned the Works as soon as it was dark, and withdrew into Valenciennes. This important Position is now occupied by His Royal Highness, who has been joined by the Rest of his Column.

It appears that the French Generals, foreseeing they could not defend the Passage of the Ronelle, and unwilling to risk the Event of a decisive Engagement in so confined a Situation as that between the Ronelle and the Scheldt, made early Preparation for Retreat. They passed the Scheldt, and were seen marching towards Denain. Captain Craufurd, Aide de Camp to His Royal Highness, observing a Column of Baggage, which was proceeding towards the River, took Two Squadrons of the 11th Regiment of Light Dragoons, though the Convoy was at that Time rather in the Rear of their own Works, and attacked and dispersed the Troops who escorted it, killed and wounded between 50 and 60, took 56 Prisoners, and 8 Waggons and 30 Horses. The Enemy advanced in Force from the Camp, and attempted to cut off this Detachment; they however effected their Retreat with the Loss of only 3 Men killed and 3 Horses. The Enterprize and good Conduct of Captain Craufurd upon this Occasion, as well as the Behaviour of the Men and Officers of the 11th Regiment of

Light Dragoons, has been highly approved of by His Royal Highness.

General Clairfait, upon his Side, attacked and carried the Heights of Anzain, a Post of the utmost Consequence, which, to a certain Degree, overlooks the Citadel of Valenciennes, and which compleats the Investment of the Place.

In this Manner, with a Loss of Men, which must be deemed very inconsiderable when compared with the Importance of the Object which has been attained, have the Enemy been obliged to abandon a Position upon which they had placed great Reliance, which they had occupied long, and fortified with Care, and to leave Valenciennes and Coudé to their Fate.

In the Variety of Attacks which took Place, I cannot at this Moment state with Precision the Loss upon either Side: That of the Combined Armies is very small upon this Side of the Scheldt, not above 250 Men killed and wounded: That of General Clerfayt's Corps by Anzain was more considerable than any other, and equal perhaps to the Whole. That of the Enemy was unquestionably much greater.

Captain Craufurd, who carries this Letter, will explain any further Particulars of which you may be desirous to be informed.

I have the Honor to be, &c.
(Signed) J.A. MURRAY.

2

The Siege Of Dunkirk And The Battle Of Hondschoote

Whitehall, August 28.

THE following Dispatch was this Morning received from Colonel Sir James Murray, Adjutant-General to the Forces under the Command of His Royal Highness the Duke of York, at the Office of the Right Honourable Henry Dundas, His Majesty's Principal Secretary of State for the Home Department.

Lefferinck's Hocke, August 16, 1793.

SIR,

I Have the Honor to inform you, that His Royal Highness intended upon the 24th to attack the Enemy, who were still posted at some Distance from Dunkirk, in order to get Possession of the Ground which it was necessary to occupy previous to the Siege. They hastened the Execution of his Design by attacking the Out-Posts between the Canal of Furnes and the Sea. Lieutenant-General Dalton advanced with the Reserve, which was encamped upon that Side, to their Support. The Enemy were repulsed, and driven, with Loss into the Town. One Piece of Cannon and a few Prisoners were taken. The Ardour of the Troops carried them further in the Pursuit than was intended, so that they came under the Cannon of the Place, by which Means a considerable Loss has been sustained. This was likelier to happen, and more difficult to be prevented, from the Nature of the Country, which is covered with Trees and strong Enclosures.

Lieutenant-General Dalton was killed with a Cannon Shot towards the Conclusion of the Attack. The Loss of this excellent Officer must be severely felt. The Courage and Ability, which he has displayed in the Course of many Campaigns, raised him to the highest Rank of Estimation in the Army in which he served.

His Royal Highness has likewise to lament that of Colonel Eld, of the Coldstream Regiment, and of other valuable Men. The Troops behaved with their usual Courage. The Two British Battalions which were engaged were commanded by Colonel Leigh and Major Mathews, and the Grenadier Battalion of the Hessians by Lieutenant-Colonel Wurmb. His Royal Highness is particularly sensible of the Exertions of Major-General Abercromby and Major-General Verneck, who were with the Advanced Guard, as likewise of those of Lieutenant-General Wurmb.

The Army have taken up the Ground which His Royal Highness intended they should occupy: The advanced Posts within a short Distance of the Town.

I have the Honor to be, &c.
J.A. MURRAY.

Whitehall, September 10.

THE following Dispatch was this Morning received from Colonel Sir James Murray, Adjutant-General to the Forces under the Command of His Royal Highness the Duke of York, at the Office of the Right Honourable Henry Dundas, His Majesty's Principal Secretary of State for the Home Department.

Lefferinck's Hocke, September 7, 1793.

SIR

I Have only Time, before the Departure of the Messenger, to have the Honor of informing you, that Field-Marsahl Freytag attacked a Post of the Enemy, at the Village of Arnecke, upon the Morning of the 5th. A considerable Number of Men were killed, and Five Officers and upwards of 60 Men taken.

Upon the following Day the Enemy made an Attack upon the Whole of the Field-Marshal's Posts, as well from the Town of Bergues as from the Camp of Caffel. The Troops behaved with the utmost Bravery, and the Enemy were repulsed at Warmouthe, Esckelbeck and several other Places; but, by Means of great Superiority of Numbers, they got Possession of Bambecke, Rousbrugghe and Poperinghe.

From the Lose of these Posts, the Field-Marshal found himself under the Necessity of falling back, in the Night, upon Hondschoot, where he means to encamp this Day. I shall have the Honor of transmitting to you further Particulars as soon as I become acquainted with them.

Upon the Evening of the 6th, the Enemy made a Sally from Dunkirk. Their Attack was chiefly directed against the Right, where they kept up a heavy Fire for some Time; but the 14th Regiment of Infantry, commanded by Major Ross, (Lieutenant-Colonel Doyle being ill) and the Austrian Regiments of Starray and Jordis, being ordered up to support that Part of the Position, they were driven back into the Town. The Behaviour of the Troops is worthy of every Commendation.

I am sorry to add that the Loss has been considerable, though that of the Enemy was much greater. I inclose a Return of that which the British Troops have sustained; that of the Austrians is about 150 Men; the Hessians were very little engaged.

It is with infinite Regret I must add, that Colonel Moncrieff has received a Wound of the most dangerous Kind. The Loss of an Officer of Spirit, Activity and Genius like his must ever be severely felt; and it is particularly to be lamented at the present Moment.

I have the Honor to be,
with the greatest Respect,
SIR, &c.
J.A. MURRAY.

Whitehall, September 11.

R. Richard Lawrys Acting Lieutenant of His Majesty's Fireship the Comet, dispatched by Rear-Admiral Macbride fromt Gravelines Pitts, arrived this Afternoon at the Office of the Right Honourable Henry Dundas, His Majesty's Principal Secretary of State for the Home Department, with a Dispatch from Colonel Sir James Murray, Adjutant-General to the Forces under the Command of His Royal Highness the Duke of York, of which the following is a Copy.

Furnes, September 9, 1793.

SIR,

IT is with extreme Sorrow that I have to acquaint you with the unfortunate Event of an Attack which the French Army made upon that of Field-Marshal Freytag upon the 8th Instant. The latter was posted, as I have had the Honor of informing you, at Hondschoote, the Right upon the Canal, the Left extending towards Leyrel.

The Enemy had made an Attack the preceding Evening in which they had been repulsed; but upon that Day attacking upon every Point, notwithstanding the greatest Exertions of Bravery of the Troops and of Ability in General Wallmoden, who then commanded them, they succeeded in forcing the Center of his Line. He retired behind the small Canal which runs from Bulsam to Steenkirk.

The Loss has been very severe. His Royal Highness has not as yet received any Return, nor have any further Particulars been transmitted. Many gallant Officers have fallen. The whole Loss in the different Actions is supposed to be near 1500 in Killed, Wounded and Missing; that of the Enemy has been unquestionably greater. Three Pieces of Cannon, and between Two and Three Hundred Prisoners have been taken. I understand that the Hanoverians have lost the same Number of Cannon.

Upon the 7th His Royal Highness sent Two Battalions of Hessians to General Walmoden's Support, but finding that Aid to be ineffectual, he was reduced to the Necessity of collecting his whole Force, by abandoning the Position he had taken near Dunkirk. Thirty-two of the heavy Guns, and Part of the Stores provided for the Siege, were left behind, there being no Means of carrying them off.

The Army marched last Night, and encamped this Morning near Adinkerque.

It appears that the Enemy had collected a Force for this Enterprize from every Quarter of the Country, from the Armies of the Rhine and the Moselle, and particularly that which had occupied the *Camp de Cæsar*. They were commanded by General Houchard, who is said by the Prisoners (though with what Degree of Truth cannot be ascertained) to have been mortally wounded at Rexpoede.

In the Retreat upon the Night of the 6th, His Royal Highness Prince Adolphus and the Field Marshal were, for a short Time, in the Possession of the Enemy. A Patrole of Cavalry, which ought to have been in their Front, having taken another Road, they went into the Village of Rexpoede, through which one of the Columns was to pass, but which was then occupied by the Enemy. His Royal Highness was slightly wounded with a Sword upon the Head and Arm but I have the Satisfaction to say, that no bad Consequences are to be apprehended. The Field-Marshal was wounded in the Head, and, I am happy to add only in the same Degree. He has, however, been unable, since that Time, to take the Command of the Army. Captain Oustar, one of His Royal Highness's Aides de Camp, was killed, and another, Captain Wangenheim, very severely wounded.

From this Situation His Royal Highness and the Field-Marshal were relieved by the Intrepidity and Presence of Mind of General Walmoden, who, upon discovering the Enemy were in Possession of Rexpoede, had immediately collected a Body of Troops, attacked it without Hesitation, and defeated them with great Slaughter.

I must repeat that nothing could exceed the Steadiness and good Behaviour of the Troops in these repeated Engagements. Lieutenant-General Sir William Erskine commanded the Rear Guard, and much is due to his Conduct and Military Skill.

The Enemy made a Sortie on that Night, and another on the Evening of the 8th; in both of which they were repelled without much Loss on our Side.

I have the Honor to be, &c.
(Signed) J.A. MURRAY.

P.S. The Cavalry, from the Nature of the Country, have been very little engaged.

3

Siege Of Toulon

Whitehall, January 15, 1794.

This Morning Sir Sydney Smith and Major Moncrief arrived at the Office of the Right Hon. Henry Dundas, His Majesty's Principal Secretary of State for the Home Department, with Dispatches from Vice-Admiral Lord Hood and Major-General David Dundas, of which the following are Copies and Extracts.

Victory, Hières Bay, December 20, 1793.

It is my Duty to acquaint you, that I have been obliged to evacuate Toulon, and to retire from the Harbour to this Anchorage.

It became unavoidably necessary that the Retreat should not be deferred, as the Enemy commanded the Town and Ships by their Shot and Shells; I therefore, agreeable to the Governor's Plan, directed the Boats of the Fleet to assemble by Eleven o'Clock, near Fort la Malgue, and am happy to say the Whole of the Troops were brought off to the Number of near 8,000, without the Loss of a Man; and in the Execution of this Service I have infinite Pleasure in acknowledging my very great Obligations to Captain Elphinstone for his unremitting Zeal and Exertion, who saw the last Man off; and it is a very comfortable Satisfaction to me that several Thousands of the meritorious Inhabitants of Toulon were sheltered in His Majesty's Ships.

I propose sending the Vice-Admirals Hotham and Colby, with some other Ships, to Leghorn or Porto Ferrara, to complete their Wine and Provisions, which run very short, having many Mouths to feed, and to remain with the Rest to block up the Ports of Toulon and Marseilles. Circumstances which had taken Place made the Retreat absolutely necessary to be effected as soon as possible, and prevented the Execution of a settled Arrangement for destroying the French Ships and Arsenal. I ordered the Vulcan Fireship to be primed, and Sir Sydney Smith, who joined me from Smyrna about a fortnight ago, having offered his Services to burn the Ships, I put Captain Hare under his Orders, with the Lieutenants Tupper and Gore, of the Victory, Lieutenant Pater, of the Britannia, and Lieutenant R.W. Miller, of the Windsor Castle. Ten of the Enemy's Ships of the Line in the Arsenal, with the Mast-House, Great Store House, Hemp-House, and other Buildings, were totally destroyed, and before

Day-Light all His Majesty's Ships, with those of Spain and the Two Sicilies, were out of the Reach of the Enemy's Shot and Shells, except the Robust, which was to receive Captain Elphinstone, and she followed very soon after, without a Shot striking her. I have under my Orders Rear-Admiral Trogoff, in the Commerce de Marseilles, Puissant and Pompée, of the Line, the Pearl, Arethusa and Topaze Frigates, and several large Corvettes, which I have manned, and employed in collecting Wine and Provisions from the different Ports in Spain and Italy, having been constantly in Want of one Species or another, and am now at short Allowance.

Don Langara undertook to destroy the Ships in the Bason, but, I am informed, found it not practicable; and as the Spanish Troops had the guarding Vessels, which contained the Powder of the Ships, I ordered into the Bason and arsenal on my coming here, as well as that from the distant Magazines, within the Enemy's reach, I requested the Spanish Admiral would be pleased to give Orders for their being scuttled and sunk; but, instead of doing that, the Officer to whom that Duty was entrusted, blew them up, by which Two fine Gun Boats, which I had ordered to attend Sir Sydney Smith, were shook to Pieces. The Lieutenant commanding One of them was killed, and several Seamen badly wounded. I am sorry to add, that Lieutenant Goddard, of the Victory, who commanded the Seamen upon the Heights of Grasse, was wounded, but I hope and trust not dangerously.

I beg to refer you for further Particulars to General Dundas respecting the Evacuation of Toulon, and to Sir Sydney Smith as to the burning the Enemy's Ships, &c. on which Service he very much distinguished himself; and he gives great Praise to Captain Hare, of the Fireship, as well as to all the Lieutenants employed under him.

It is with very peculiar Satisfaction I have the Honor to acquaint you, that the utmost Harmony, and most cordial Understanding, has happily subsisted in His Majesty's Army and Fleet, not only between the Officers of all Ranks, but between the Seaman and Soldiers also.

I herewith transmit a Copy of Sir Sydney Smith's Letter to me, with a List of the Officers employed under him. I have the Honor, &c.

HOOD.

P.S. The List of the Ships at Toulon that were burnt, and those remaining, has been received since writing my Letter.

Toulon, December 18, 1793.

MY LORD,

Agreeably to your Lordship's Order, I proceeded with the Swallow Tender, Three English and Three Spanish Gun-Boats, to the Arsenal, and immediately began making the necessary Preparations for burning the French Ships and Stores therein. We found the Dock-Gates well secured by the judicious Arrangements of the Governor, although the Dock-Yard People had already substituted the Three-Coloured Cockade for the White one. I did not think it safe to attempt the Securing any of them, considering the small Force I had with me, and considering that Contest of any kind would occupy our whole Attention, and prevent us from accomplishing our Purpose.

The Galley Slaves, to the Number of at least 600, shewed themselves jealous Spectators of our Operations. Their Disposition to oppose us was evident; and being unchained, which was unusual, rendered it necessary to keep a watchful Eye on them on Board the Galleys, by pointing the Guns of the Swallow Tender and One of the Gun-Boats on them, in such a Manner as to enfilade the Quay on which they must have landed to come to us, assuring them, at the same Time, that no harm should happen to them if they remained quiet. The Enemy kept up a cross Fire of Shot and Shells on the Spot from Malbousquet, and the neighbouring Hills, which contributed to keep the Galley Slaves in Subjection, and operated, in every Respect, favourably for us, by keeping the Republican Party in the Town within their Houses, while it occasioned little Interruption to our work of preparing and placing combustible Matter in the different Store-Houses, and on Board the Ships; such was the Steadiness of the few brave Seamen I had under my Command. A great Multitude of the Enemy continued to draw down the Hill towards the Dock-Yard Wall, and as the Night closed in they came near enough to pour in an irregular though quick Fire of Musquetry on us from the Boulangerie, and of Cannon from the Heights which overlook it. We kept them at bay by Discharges of Grape Shot from Time to Time, which prevented their coming so near as to discover the Insufficiency of our Force to repel a closer Attack. A Gun-Boat was stationed to flank the Wall on the Outside, and Two Field Pieces were placed within against the Wicket usually frequented by the Workmen, of whom we were particularly apprehensive. About Eight o'Clock I had the Satisfaction of seeing Lieutenant Gore towing in the Vulcan Fireship. Captain Hare, the Commander, placed her, agreeably to my Directions, in a most masterly Manner, across the Tier of Men of War, and the additional Force of her Guns and Men diminished my Apprehensions of the galley Slaves rising on us, as their Manner and occasional tumultuous Debates ceased entirely on her Appearance. The only Noise heard among them was the Hammer knocking off their Fetters, which Humanity forbade my opposing, as they might thereby be more at Liberty to save themselves on the Conflagration taking Place around them. In this Situation we continued to wait most anxiously for the Hour concerted with the Governor for the Inflammation of the Trains. The Moment the Signal was made, we had the Satisfaction to see the Flames rise in every Quarter. Lieutenant Tupper was charged with the Burning of the General Magazine, the Pitch, Tar, Tallow and Oil Store-Houses, and succeeded most perfectly; the Hemp Magazine was included in this Blaze. Its being nearly calm was unfortunate to the Spreading of the Flames, but 250 Barrels of Tar divided among the Deals and other Timber, insured the rapid Ignition of that whole Quarter which Lieutenant Tupper had undertaken.

The Mast-House was equally well set on Fire by Lieutenant Middleton, of the Britannia. Lieutenant Pater, of the Britannia, continued in a most daring Manner to brave the Flames, in order to complete the Work where the Fire seemed to have caught imperfectly. I was obliged to call him off, Lest his Retreat should become impracticable: His Situation was the more perilous, as the Enemy's Fire redoubled as soon as the amazing Blaze of Light rendered us distinct Objects of their Aim. Lieutenant Ironmonger, of the Royals, remained with the Guard at the Gate till the last, long after the Spanish Guard was withdrawn, and was brought safely off by Captain Edge of the Alert, to whom I had confided the important Service of closing our Retreat, and bringing off our detached Parties, which were saved to a Man. I was sorry to find myself deprived of the further Services of Captain Hare: He had performed that of placing his Fireship to Admiration, but was blown into the Water, and much scorched, by the Explosion of her Priming, when in the Act of putting the Match to it Lieutenant Gore was also much burnt, and I was consequently deprived of him also, which I regretted the more, from the Recollection of his Bravery and Activity in the warm Service of Fort Mulgrave. Mr Eales, Midshipman, who was also with him on this Occasion, deserves my Praise for his Conduct throughout this Service. The Guns of the Fireship going off on both Sides as they heated, in the Direction that was given them, towards those Quarters from whence we were most apprehensive of the Enemy forcing their Way in upon us, checked their Career. Their Shouts and republican Songs which we could hear distinctly, continued till they as well as ourselves were in a Manner thunderstruck by the Explosion of some Thousand Barrels of Powder on board the Iris Frigate, lying in the Inner Road, without us, and which had been injudiciously set on Fire by the Spanish Boats, in going off, instead of being sunk, as ordered. The Concussion of Air, and the Shower of falling Timber on Fire, was such as nearly to destroy the Whole of us. Lieutenant Patey, of the Terrible, with his whole Boat's Crew, nearly perished; the Boat was blown to Pieces, but the Men were picked up alive. The Union Gun-Boat, which was nearest to the Iris, suffered considerably. Mr. Young being killed, with Three Men, and the Vessel shaken to Pieces. I had given it in Charge to the Spanish Officers to fire the Ships in the Bason before the Town, but they returned, and reported that various Obstacles had prevented their entering it. We attempted it together, as soon as we had compleated the Business in the Arsenal, but were repulsed in our Attempt to cut the Boom, by repeated Vollies of Musquetry from the Flag Ship and the Wall of the Battery Royale. The Cannon of this Battery had been spiked by the judicious Precaution taken by the governor, previously to the Evacuation of the Town.

The Failure of our Attempt on the Ships in the Bason before the Town, owing to the Insufficiency of our Force, made me regret that the Spanish Gun-Boats had been withdrawn from me to perform other Service. The Adjutant Don Pedro Cotiella, Don Francisco Riguelme, and Don Francisco Trusello remained with me to the last; and I feel bound to bear Testimony of the Zeal and Activity with which they performed the most essential Services during the Whole of this Business, as far as the Insufficiency of their Force allowed it, being reduced, by the Retreat of the Gun-Boats, to a single Fellucca, and a Mortar-Boat which had expended its Ammunition, but contained 30 Men with Cutlasses.

We now proceeded to burn the Hero and Themistocles, Two seventy-four Gun Ships, laying in the Inner Road. Our Approach to them had hitherto been impracticable in Boats, as the French Prisoners who had been left in the latter Ship were still in Possession of her, and had shewn a Determination to resist our Attempt to come on Board. The Scene of Conflagration around them, heightened by the late tremendous Explosion, had however awakened their Fears for their Lives. Thinking this to be the Case, I addressed them, expressing my Readiness to land them in a Place of Safety, if they would submit; and they thankfully accepted the Offer, shewing themselves to be completely intimidated, and very grateful for our humane Intentions towards them, in not attempting to burn them with the Ship. It was necessary to proceed with Precaution, as they were more numerous than ourselves. We at length completed their Disembarkation, and then set her on Fire. On this Occasion I had nearly lost my valuable Friend and Assistant, Lieutenant Miller, of the Windsor Castle, who had staid so long on Board to insure the Fire taking, that it gained on him suddenly, and it was not without being very much scorched, and the Risk of being suffocated, that we could approach the Ship to take him in. The Loss to the Service would have been very great, had we not succeeded in our Endeavours to save him. Mr. Knight, Midshipman of the Windsor Castle, who was in the Boat with me, shewed much Activity and Address on this Occasion, as well as Firmness throughout the Day.

The Explosion of a Second Powder Vessel, equally unexpected, and with a Shock even greater than the first, again put us in the most imminent Danger of perishing; and when it is considered that we were within the Sphere of the falling Timber, it is next to miraculous that no one Piece, of the many which made the Water foam around us, happened to touch either the Swallow or the Three Boats with me.

Having now set Fire to every Thing within our Reach, exhausted our combustible Preparations and our Strength to such a Degree that the Men absolutely dropped on the Oars, we directed our Course to join the Fleet, running the Gauntlet under a few ill-directed Shots from the Forts of Balaguier and Aiguillecte, now occupied by the Enemy; but fortunately, without Loss of any Kind, we proceeded to the Place appointed for the Embarkation of the Troops, and took off as many as we could carry. It would be Injustice to those Officers whom I have omitted to name, for their not having been so immediately under my Eye, if I did not acknowledge myself indebted to them all for their extraordinary Exertions in the Execution of this great National Object. The Quickness with which the Inflammation took Effect, on my Signal, its Extent and Duration, are the best Evidences that every Officer and Man was ready at his Post, and firm under most perilous Circumstances.

We can ascertain that the Fire extended to at least Ten Sail of the Line, how much further we cannot say. The Loss of the Great Magazine, and of the Quantity of Pitch, Tar, Rosin, Hemp, Timber, Cordage and Gunpowder, must considerably impede the Equipment of the few Ships that remain. I am sorry to have been obliged to leave any, but I hope your Lordship will be satisfied that we did as much as our circumscribed Means enabled us to do, in a limited Time, pressed as we were by a Force so much superior to us.

I have the Honor to be, &c.
W. SYDNEY SMITH

On Board the Victory, Hieres Bay, Dec. 21, 1793.

SIR,

IN my letter of the 12th Instant I had the Honor to acquaint you, that from the 30th of November to that Time no particular Event had taken Place, and that the Fire of the Enemy was less frequent. During this Period they were daily receiving Reinforcements from every Quarter, and both Sides were busily employed, we in strengthening our Posts, and the Enemy in establishing new Batteries against Cape Brun and Malbousquet, but principally against Fort Mulgrave, on the Heights of Balaguier.

From all concurring Accounts of Deserters, and others, the Enemy's Army was now between 30,000 and 40,000 Men, and an Attack upon our Posts was to be daily expected. These, from their essential though detached Situations, had been severally strengthened, in the Proportion their Circumstances required, having such central Force in the Town as was deemed necessary for it's immediate Guard, and for affording a Degree of Succour to any Point that might be more particularly attacked.

For the complete Defence of the Town and it's extensive Harbour, we had long been obliged to occupy a Circumference of at least Fifteen Miles, by Eight principal Posts, with their several intermediate dependent ones; the greatest part of these were merely of a temporary Nature, such as our Means allowed us to contract; and, of our Force, which never exceeded 12,000 Men bearing Firelocks, and composed of Five different Nations and Languages, of which 9000 were placed in or supporting those Posts, and about 3000 remained in the Town.

On the 16th, at Half past Two o'Clock in the Morning, the Enemy, who had before fired from Three Batteries on Fort Mulgrave, now opened Two new ones, and continued a very heavy Cannonade and Bombardment on that Post till next Morning. The Works suffered much. The Number of Men killed and disabled was considerable. The Weather was rainy, and the consequent Fatigue great.

At Two o'Clock on the Morning of the 17th the Enemy, who had every Advantage in assembling and suddenly advancing, attacked the Fort in great Force. Although no Part of this temporary Post was such as could well resist determined Troops, yet, for a considerable Time, it was defended; but, on the Enemy entering on the Spanish Side, the British Quarter, commanded by Captain Conolly of the 18th Regiment, could not be much longer maintained, notwithstanding several Efforts were made for that purpose. It was therefore, at last, carried, and the remains of the Garrison of 700 Men retired towards the Shore of Balaguier, under the Protection of the other Posts established on those Heights, and which continued to be faintly attacked by the Enemy. As this Position of Balaguier was a most essential one for the Preservation of the Harbour, and as we had no communication with it but by Water, 2200 Men had been placed there for some Time past. On the Night preceding the Attack 300 more Men had been sent over, and on the Morning of the 17th 400 were embarked still farther to support it.

When the firing at Balaguier ceased, we remained in anxious Suspence as to the Event till a little before Day-Light, when a new Scene opened, by an Attack on all our Posts, on the Mountain of Pharon. The Enemy were repulsed on the East Side, where was our principal Force of about 700 Men, commanded by a most distinguished Officer, the Piedmontese Colonel de Jermagnan, whose Loss we deeply lament; but on the Back of the Mountain, near 1800 Feet high, steep, rocky, deemed almost inaccessible, and which we had laboured much to make so, they found Means, once more, to penetrate between our Posts, which occupied an Extent of above Two Miles, guarded by about 450 Men, and, in a very short Space of Time, we saw, that with great Numbers of Men, they crowded all that side of the Mountain which overlooks Toulon. The Particulars of this Event I am not yet enabled to ascertain, but I have every Reason to think that they did not enter at a British Post.

Our Line of Defence, which, as I have mentioned, occupied a Circumference of at least 15 Miles, and with Points of which we had only a Water Communication, being thus broken in upon, in its Two most essential Posts, it became necessary to adopt decisive Measures, arising from the Knowledge of the Whole of our actual Situation. A Council of the Flag and General Officers assembled. They determined on the Impracticability of restoring the Posts we had lost, and on the consequent Propriety of the speediest Evacuation of the Town, evidently, and by the Report of the Engineers and Artillery Officers, declared untenable. Measures of Execution were taken from that Moment. The Troops were withdrawn from the Heights of Balaguier without much Interruption from the Enemy, and in the Evening such Posts as necessarily depended on the Possession of Pharon were successively evacuated, and the Troops drawn in towards Toulon. The Forts D'Artigues and St. Catherine still remained, together with the Posts of Sablettes, Cape Brun, and Malbousquet, from which last the Spaniards withdrew in the Night, in consequence of the supporting Post of Neapolitans, at Micissey, having left the Battery there established, and abandoned it without Orders. Every Attention was also given to enforce the Tranquillity of the Town. In the Night the Combined Fleets took a new Station in the Outer Road.

Early in the Morning of the 18th the Sick and Wounded, and the British field artillery, were sent off. In the Course of the Day the Post of Cape Brun was withdrawn into La Malgue, the Post of Sablettes was also retired, and the Men were put on Board. Measures were arranged for the final Embarkation, during the Night, of the British, Piedmontese and Spaniards, who occupied the Town, and of the Troops of the same Nations, who were now at La Malgue, amounting in all to about 7,000 Men, for the Neapolitans had, by Mid-Day, embarked.

Having determined with Lieutenant-General Gravina, commanding the Spanish troops, that, instead of embarking at the Quays and in the Arsenal of the Town, our whole Force should assemble near Fort La Malgue, and form on the Peninsula which from thence extends into the Harbour, every previous Disposition was made, and every Care taken to conceal our Intention. The Arsenal and Dock-Yard were strictly guarded. The Troops were ranged accordingly on the Ramparts, and the Tranquillity of the town was much ensured from the Time the Enemy began to throw Shells and Shot into it; which they did from our late Batteries at Micissey and Malbousquet.

About Ten o'Clock at Night Fire was set to the Ships and arsenal. We immediately began our March, and the Evacuation of the town, which it was necessary should be made with Secrecy and Expedition. The Fort of St. Catherine having, without Orders, been quitted in the Course of the Day, and possessed by the Enemy. The consequent early Knowledge of our March, had we taken the common Route, through the Gate of Italy, and within Musquet Shot of that Fort, might have produced great Inconvenience; we therefore, by a Sally Post, gained an advanced Part of the Road, and without Accident were enabled to quit the Town, arrive at Fort La Malgue, and form on the rising Ground immediately above the Shore. The Boats were ready, the Weather and the sea in the highest Degree favourable: The Embarkation began about Eleven o'Clock, and by Day-Break on the 19th the Whole, without Interruption, or the Loss of a Man, were on Board Ship.

The great Fire in the arsenal, the blowing up of the Powder Ships, and other similar Events which took Place in the Night, certainly tended to keep the Enemy in a State of Suspense and Uncertainty.

As the Security of this Operation depended much on the Protection afforded from the happy Situation of Fort La Malgue, which so effectually commands the Neck of the Peninsula, and the judicious Use that should be made of it's Artillery, this important Service was allotted to Major Koenier, with 200 Men, who, after seeing the last Man off the Shore, and spiking all the Guns, effected, from his Activity and Intelligence, his own Retreat without Loss.

Captains Elphinstone, Hollwell and Mathews superintend the Embarkation and to their indefatigable Attention and good Dispositions we are indebted for the happy Success at so important an Operation. Captain Elphinstone, as Governor of Fort La Malgue, has ably afforded me the most essential Assistance in his Command and Arrangement of the several important Posts included in that District.

It is important for me to express, but in general Terms, the Approbation that is due to the Conduct and Merits of the several Commanding Officers, and indeed of every Officer, in every Rank and Situation. Troops have seldom experienced, for so long a Time, a Service more harassing, distressing and severe; and the Officers and Men of the Regiments and Marines have gone through it with that Exertion, Spirit and Good-Will, which peculiarly distinguish the British Soldier. At Fort Mulgrave, Lieutenant Duncan, sen. of the Royal artillery, was so essentially useful, that to his Exertions and Abilities that Post was much indebted for its Preservation for so Long a Time.

The general Service has been carried on with the most perfect Harmony and Zeal of the Navy and Army. From our Deficiency in Artillery-Men, many of our Batteries were worked by Seamen: They, in Part, guarded some of our Posts, and their Aid was peculiarly useful in Duties of Fatigue and Labour. In all these we found the Influence of the superior Activity and exertions of the British Sailors.

It was the constant Attention of Lord Hood to relieve our Wants and alleviate our Difficulties.

The Sardinian Troops we have always considered as a Part of ourselves. We have experienced their Attachment and good Behaviour, and I have found much Assistance from the Ability and Conduct of the Chevalier de Revel, and from Brigadier-General Richler, who commands them.

Notwithstanding the undefined Situation of Command, I found every Disposition and Acquiescence in Lieutenant-General Gravina, commanding the Spanish Troops, to execute every proposed Measure which the common Cause required.

The Loss of the British on the 17th at Fort Mulgrave, and on the Heights of Pharon, amounts to about 300 Men, of which, during the last Four Days, no exact Account could be procured: And, as the Troops, in embarking, were put on Board the nearest and most convenient Ships, till they are again united in Corps, I cannot have the Honor of transmitting particular Returns, nor even knowing the Detail of Circumstances that attended the Attack of those Posts.

It is now about Three Weeks that, from the unfortunate Accident of General O'Hara being made Prisoner, the Government of Toulon devolved on me; my best Exertions have not been wanting in that Situation, and I humbly hope that His Majesty may be pleased to look upon them in a favorable Light.

I beg Leave to add, that the Battalion of Royal Louis, and Two Independent Companies of French Chasseurs, raised at Toulon, have behaved, on every Occasion, with Fidelity and Spirit. They embarked at La Malgue, to the Number of about 600 Men, and are now with us.

I have the Honor to be,
With the most profound Respect,
SIR,
Your most faithful and
Obedient humble Servant,
DAVID DUNDAS,
Lieut. Gen.

4

Siege Of Saint Florent

Whitehall, March 11.

DISPATCHES, of which the following are Copies, were Yesterday received at the Office of the Right Honourable Henry Dundas, His Majesty's Principal Secretary of State for the Home Department, from Vice-Admiral Lord Hood and Lieutenant-General David Dundas.

Victory, St. Fiorenzo, Feb.22, 1794.

SIR,

HAVING received repeated Information how much the French were straightened for Provisions in Corsica, I had, for a considerable Time past, kept Ships constantly cruising between Cape Corse and Calvi, and, after my leaving the Road of Toulon, I judged it more necessary to prevent Succours being thrown in as much as possible, my Mind being impressed with the Importance the Island must be of to the French, in the State the Ships and Arsenal of Toulon were, and that it was very much so to Great Britain, as it contained several Ports, and that of St. Fiorenzo a very good one, for the Reception of His Majesty's Fleet in this Part of the Mediterranean. I therefore determined to make an Attempt to drive the French out of it, so soon as I could get a sufficient Supply of Provisions and Wine, being in Expectation of the former from Gibraltar and from Port Mahon and Alicant; and in the Mean Time I signified to General Dundas my Intention of sending Lieutenant-Colonel Moore and Major Koehler to Corsica, and requested he would give them proper Instructions for informing themselves of General Paoli's real Situation and that of the French; and after they had been there a Week I received, in the Afternoon of the 23d of last Month, a very encouraging Report, and at the same Time certain Information that the French had actually embarked at Nice 8000 Troops which were, at all Risque, to push for the Island, under Convoy of Two Frigates, a Covette, Zebeck, and other Armed Vessels. That same Evening I detached Three more Frigates to the Senior Officer, the more effectually to line the Coast, and to guard Bastia also; at the same Time I ordered the Ardent and a Sloop off Villa Franca, and, in case he found the French Frigates there, Captain Sutton was directed to call to him the Diadem and other Cruizers from before Genoa, and Cruize from Villa Franca to Antibes; but if he found the French Frigates sailed, he was to proceed, and join me off St. Fiorenzo, as I intended to put to Sea the next Morning. I could not, however, get away until the Afternoon, for Want of Wind. At Four o'Clock I weighed Anchor, accompanied by Sixty Sail of Ships and Vessels, including Army Victuallers, Horse Transports, and others, having 1800 unfortunate Toulonese on board, and the Victory and Princess Royal had 400 more. I gave the Convoy in Charge of the Gorgon, with Three Gun Boats to bring up the Rear. Just at Sun-set next Evening I was within Three Miles of Isle Roussa, where Lieutenant-Colonel Moore was waiting, but having no Frigate or Cutter with me, I was unable to send for him; but observing the Juno at some little Distance, I made her Captain's Signal, and directed him to stand in, and fetch the Colonel off in the Night, which he fortunately effected. Towards Day-Light it blew very strong, and before Ten o'Clock quite a Storm, which made it prudent for me to bear up for Porto Ferrara, which I had a fair Prospect of getting to before Night; but in the Afternoon, when we were within Five Leagues of Elba, the Weather was so extremely thick, that the Pilot declined the Charge of the Ship; consequently I was driven to Leeward of the Island, where I passed Three very disagreeable Nights, having had Two Main Topsails blown to Rags, and the Topsail Yard rendered totally unserviceable. However we got safe to Porto Ferrara on the 29th; and having got all the Ships set to rights, and sent for Bread and Wine from Leghorn, I put to Sea again on the 6th Instant: Commodore Linzee, with most of the Transports, got out the Evening before. On the 7th the Commodore, having the Direction of disembarking the Troops at the Time and in the Manner Lieutenant-General Dundas should desire, anchored in a Bay to the Westward of Mortella Point, with the several Ships and Transports under his Command. The Troops were mostly landed that Evening, and Possession taken of a Height which overlooks the Tower of Mortella. The next Day the General and Commodore being of Opinion that it was adviseable to attack the Tower from the Bay, the Fortitude and Juno were ordered against it, without making the least Impression by a continued Cannonade of Two Hours and a Half; and the former Ship being very much damaged by red-hot Shot, both hauled off. The Walls of the Tower were of a prodigious Thickness, and the Parapet, where there were Two Eighteen-Pounders, was lined with Bass Junk Five Feet from the Walls, and filled up with Sand; and, although it was cannonaded from the Height for Two Days, within 150 Yards, and appeared in a very shattered State, the Enemy still held out; but a few hot Shot setting Fire to the Bass, made them call for Quarter. The Number of Men in the Tower were Thirty-three only Two were wounded, and those mortally.

On the 11th I was again forced from the Gulph by a strong westerly Gale, and took Shelter under Cape Corse; and, upon the Wind abating, it fell at once calm, which prevented my Return off St. Fiorenzo until the Morning of the 17th. At Nine that Evening the Enemy's Works were stormed and taken, with inconsiderable Loss on the Part of His Majesty, but the French suffered much; and on the 19th in the Evening the empty Town of Fiorenzo was taken Possession of, the Whole of the Garrison having gone off towards Bastia in the Two preceding Days.

The cool and intrepid Conduct of Captain Young cannot be too much admired, or that of Captain Woodley of the Alcide, who, from having a correct Knowledge of the Bay, nobly offered his Service to place the Fortitude, which he did with the greatest Judgment; and the handsome Testimony Captain Young bears of it, makes it unnecessary for me to say a Word in his Praise; but I felt it very much my Duty to write Commodore Linzee the Letter I also herewith transmit a Copy of, as well as Copies of Letters the Commodore and I have been honoured with from Lieutenant-General Dundas, which will shew that Exertions were not wanting in the Officers and Seamen of His Majesty's Navy.

I should be wanting in Gratitude as well as Justice to Lieutenant-Colonel Moore and Major Koehler was I to omit acquainting you how much I feel myself indebted for their very great Zeal and Exertion and informing themselves of the State of the Country and the Neighbourhood of Fornelli, and cannot help attributing much to both for our Success. With respect to their Conduct in the Field, I leave Lieutenant-General Dundas to speak of it, but I understand it has been highly meritorious, as has that of the Whole of the Troops.

Captain Woodley will be the Bearer of this Letter, to whom I beg to refer you for such Particulars as you wish to be informed of, as he is perfectly well acquainted with every Transaction from the Landing of the Troops to this Hour.

I have the Honor to be, &c.
HOOD

Alcide, in the Bay to the Westward of Mortella,
February 9, 1794.

MY LORD,

I Have the Honor to inform your Lordship, that it being the Opinion of Lieutenant-General Dundas, as well as my own, that an Attack, both by Sea and Land, should be made as speedily as possible on the Tower of Mortella, in order to secure the Anchorage in that Bay for His Majesty's Ships, and to have easy Communication with the Troops on Shore, I immediately directed His Majesty's Ships Fortitude and Juno for that Service. The Land Wind in the Morning was too faint for them to weigh; at One o'Clock P. M. the Sea Breeze came in, and they immediately got under Sail, and both Ships (with the Assistance of Captain Woodley, who, with great Zeal and Activity, voluntarily undertook to assist Captain Young in placing the Ships against the Tower, he having a very good Knowledge of the Bay, and which he executed with great Skill and Judgment) when a very severe and well-directed Fire was kept up by both Ships for Two Hours and a Half. Captain Young, whose cool, steady and gallant Conduct was very conspicuous, deserves the highest Encomiums, and by his Exertion the Flames, which at several Times broke out by the red hot Shot lodged in the Ship's Side, were extinguished, which would otherwise have inevitably destroyed her: His Officers and Ship's Company have their Share of Merit on the Occasion.

Captain Hood of the Juno, who fortunately received no Damage, did every Thing that this Situation could admit of, and conducted himself like an experienced and good Officer.

I have the Honor, &c.
ROBERT LINZEE.

Fortitude, Feb. 9, 1794.

SIR,

IN Obedience to your Orders, I went Yesterday in His Majesty's Ship Fortitude, which I command, against the Tower of Mortella, where I remained Two Hours and a Half; when finding that neither the Fire of the Fortitude nor that of the Juno (who was extremely well placed to batter the Tower) had made any material Impression; and the Main-Mast of the Ship being much wounded, many of the Shrowds cut away, Three of the Lower Deck Guns dismounted, several hot Shot in the Hull, and a great many Men blown up by the Explosion of Powder from a Powder-Box that was struck by a hot Shot; and being so near the Tower and the Rocks, that if the Wind should die away it would be difficult, and if it should change so as to blow on Shore it might be impossible to get away, I thought it prudent to haul off. Soon after I had done so, the Ship was perceived to be on Fire from the Main Deck to the upper Part of the Quick Work on the Quarter Deck, occasioned by a hot Shot that had lodged in the Side; but after cutting out the Shot, and opening the Side in different Places, the Fire was extinguished without having done any material Damage.

I had infinite Pleasure in observing, during the whole of the Action, the most cool, intrepid Courage in all the Officers and Men of the Fortitude; and I am particularly pleased to have this Opportunity of doing them Justice, by saying, that I do not think any Men could do their Duty better; and I have only to regret, with them, that their Exertions were not attended with better Success.

And if Captain Woodley will allow me, I shall be happy also in having this Opportunity of thanking him for the very great Assistances received in placing the Ship, from his Knowledge of the Place, and from the Coolness and Clearness with which he gave his Directions, as well as for the Advantages I reaped from his Skill and Presence of Mind during the whole of the Action.

SIR, &c.
WILLIAM YOUNG.

5

Capture Of Martinique

Whitehall, April 21.

MAJOR Grey arrived this Morning at the Office of the Right Honourable Henry Dundas, His Majesty's Principal Secretary of State for the Home Department, with Dispatches from Sir Charles Grey, K.B. of which the following is a Copy.

Fort Royal, Martinico, March 25, 1794.

SIR,

I Have the Happiness to acquaint you of the complete Conquest of this very valuable Island, the last and most important Fortress of Fort Bourbon having surrendered to His Majesty's Arms at Four o'Clock in the Afternoon of the 23d Instant; at which Time His Royal Highness Prince Edward, Major-General of His Majesty's Forces, took Possession of both Gates with the First and Third Battalions of Grenadiers and the First and Third Light Infantry: And I have the Honor to transmit to you the Articles of Capitulation, together with a List of the Killed and Wounded, and a Return of the Ordnance, &c. taken since my Dispatch of the 16th Instant, in which I communicated the Transactions and Progress of this Army to that Period.

 Having concerted Measures with the Admiral for a combined Attack by the Naval and Land Forces upon the Fort and Town of Fort Royal, and the Batteries of my Second Parallel being ready those on Morne Tortenson and Carriere kept up an incessant Fire upon Fort Royal, and all the other Batteries on Fort Bourbon, during the Day and Night of the 19th Instant, and on the Morning of the 20th following, till the Ships destined for this Service had taken their Stations. The Asia of 64 Guns, Captain Browne and the Zebra Sloop of 16 Guns, Captain Faulknor, with Captain Rogers, and a Body of Seamen in Flat Boats, the Whole under Commodore Thompson, composed the Naval Force; and the Land Force consisted of the First Battalion of Grenadiers, under Lieutenant-Colonel Stewart, and the Third Light Infantry, under Lieutenant-Colonel Close, from Prince Edward's Camp at La Coste; with the Third Grenadiers, under Lieutenant-Colonel Buckeridge, and the First Light

Infantry under Lieutenant-Colonel Coote, from Lieutenant-General Prescott's Camp at Soururie.

The Navy acquitted themselves with their usual Gallantry, (particularly Captain Faulknor, whose Conduct justifiably gained him the Admiration of the Whole Army) carrying the Fort by Escalade about Twelve o'clock of the 20th Instant, under the able Conduct of Commodore Thompson, whose judicious Disposition of the Gun and Flat Boats, assisted by that spirited and active Officer Captain Rogers, contributed materially to our Success, at the same Time that the Land Forces, commanded by that excellent Officer Colonel Symes, critically advancing with equal Ardor, forced and entered the Town triumphantly, hoisting the British Colours, and changing the Name to Fort Edward.

Immediately after this General Rochambeau, who commanded in Fort Bourbon, sent his Aide de Camp with a Flag, offering to surrender on Capitulation, and the Terms were finally adjusted and agreed to on the 22d Instant, by Three Commissioners on each Side, the Ratifications thereof being signed by the Commanders in Chief, on the 23d following; and the Garrison, amounting to 900 Men, marched out this Morning Prisoners of War, laying down their Arms on the Parade of Fort Royal, and were embarked for France immediately.

His Majesty's Troops having marched in, struck the French and hoisted the British Colours, and changed the Name from Bourbon to that of Fort George.

I consider myself under great Obligations to Lieutenant-General Prescott for the Zeal and Ability with which he has assisted me throughout this arduous Service, now brought to so fortunate a Conclusion, and to all the Generals and other Officers. Colonel Durnford, with the Corps of Engineers, and Lieutenant-Colonels Paterson and Sowerby and Major Manley, with the Royal Artillery, have also a Claim to my warmest Approbation, for their Exertions in placing and constructing of the Batteries, and the well directed Fire of the Artillery. The Bravery, Regularity, and good Behaviour of the Troops on every Occasion has been most meritorious and exemplary.

Forts Bourbon and Royal have suffered greatly from our Fire during the Siege, and we are diligently employed to put them in a proper State of Defence, effectually to secure this important Acquisition of Territory to the Crown of Great Britain. I am restoring Order as fast as possible, from the Confusion naturally occasioned by a Siege, and have the Pleasure to observe that every Thing in the Forts is as tranquil and well-regulated as could be expected in the Time. I shall not lose a Moment in embarking Ordnance and Ordnance Stores, with Troops, &c. to prosecute with Vigor the Execution of such other Objects and Services as His Majesty has been pleased to entrust to me; and hope to be enabled to proceed before much Time can elapse, after regulating the Garrisons of these Forts, and all such other Matters as require immediate Attention. Major Grey, Deputy Quartermaster-General, will have the Honor to deliver this Dispatch, and can communicate any other Particulars or Information you may wish to have.

I have the Honor, &c.
CHARLES GREY.

P.S. At the Commencement of the Siege, the Garrison of Fort Bourbon consisted of about 1200.

I send Five Stand of Colours, laid down by the Garrison, together with the Two Colours of Fort Bourbon, to be presented to His Majesty.

The gallant Defence made by General Rochambeau and his Garrison was strongly manifested on entering Fort Bourbon, as there was scarce an Inch of Ground untouched by our Shot and Shells, and it is but Justice to say that it does them the highest Honor.

6

Capture Of St Lucia

Admiralty-Office, May 16, 1794.

CAPTAIN Parker, late of His Majesty's Ship Blanche, arrived this Morning with Dispatches from Vice-Admiral Sir John Jervis, K.B. Commander in Chief of His Majesty's Ships and Vessels at Barbados and the Leeward Islands, to Mr. Stephens, dated Barrington Bay, (late Grand Cul de Sac) St. Lucia, April 4, 1794, of which the following is an Extract.

SIR,

ON the 29th and 30th of March I directed such Troops and Artillery as the General thought necessary for the Reduction of St. Lucia to be embarked on board the Ships of War and Coppersheathed Transports; and on the 31st at Noon I sailed with the Squadron of His Majesty's Ships under my Command, and the Day following landed the Light Infantry and Grenadiers in the following Order: Major-General Dundas, with a Part of his Corps, embarked on board the Solebay, Winchelsea, and London Transport, about Three o'Clock, at Ance de Becune, a little within Point du Cap, and One Mile and Quarter distant from Gros Islet.

    This Service was performed with Neatness and Precision under the Direction of Lord Viscount Garlies, Captain Kelly being ill of a Fever. The other Part of Major-General Dundas's Corps embarked on board the Vengeance, Irresistible and Rattlesnake; were landed in Choc Bay, by Signal from the Boyne, at Five o'Clock; and the Corps of Grenadiers under the Command of His Royal Highness Prince Edward, (embarked in the Santa Margaritta, Rose and Woolwich) were landed under the judicious Direction of Captain Harvey, at Marigot des Rofeaux, before Sun-set; as were the Corps of Light Infantry embarked in the Boyne and Veteran, under the Command of Colonel Coote, near the Grand Cul de Sac, after the Close of the Day.

    In ranging the Coast to these different Points of Debarkation the Ships were obliged to hug the Shore, and received many Shot in their Hulls, Yards, Sails and Rigging, from the numerous Batteries along the Coast, but happily, though the Ships were so much crowded with Men, not a Drop of Blood was spilt.

    The Grenadiers and Light Infantry having carried all the Out-Posts and Batteries the Night before last, with some Loss on the Part of the Enemy, the General and myself thought proper to summons the Morne Fortunée to surrender Yesterday

Morning, to which an equivocal Answer being returned, a Disposition was made for landing the Battalions of Seamen from the different shps, and ther Terms of Surrender were instantly dispatched, to which the Garrison has acceded, and marched out at Nine o'Clock this Morning, grounding their Arms at a Place appointed for that Purpose.

The same Spirit of Enterprize, which inspired every Breast in the Reduction of Martinique, has shone in full Lustre here.

I am much obliged to Captain Salisbury for serving a Voluntier on board the Boyne upon this Service, whose critical Pilot Knowledge has been very useful.

To Captain Parker, the Bearer of this Dispatch, (who commanded these Seas with great Reputation previous to my arrival) I beg leave to refer the Lords Commissioners of the Admiralty for further particulars.

J. JERVIS.

7

Siege Of Bastia

Whitehall. June 10.

THE Dispatch, of which the following Is a Copy Was received on Sunday last from Admiral Lord Hood, by the Right Honourable Henry Dundas, One of His Majesty's Principal Secretaries of State.

Victory, off Bastia, May 24, 1794.

SIR,

I Have the Honor to acquaint you, that the Town and Citadel of Bastia, with the several Posts upon the Heights, surrendered to the Arms of His Majesty on the 22nd. On the 19th I received a Message, that the Garrison was desirous of capitulating upon honourable Terms; in consequence of which I sent the inclosed Note on Shore. This brought on Board the Victory Three Officers, who informed me that Gentili, the Commandant, would assemble the Officers of the several Corps, and of the Municipality, if a Truce took Place, which I agreed to, a little before Sun-set. The next Day I received a Note from Gentili, which I also inclose, and sent Captain Young on Shore, on the Morning of the 21st, who soon returned to the Victory, with Two Officers and Two of the Administrative Bodies, which, with Vice-Admiral Goodall, Captain Young, Captain Inglefield, and my Secretary, Mr. M. Arthur, settled the Articles of Capitulation which were signed the following Morning, when His Majesty's Troops took Possession of all the Posts above the Town, the Troops in each retiring to the Citadel, from whence they marched to the Mole Head, where they grounded their Arms, and were embarked. You will receive herewith the Articles of Capitulation which I hope His Majesty will approve.

I am unable to give due Praise to the unremitting Zeal, Exertion and judicious Conduct of Lieutenant-Colonel Villettes, who had the Honor of commanding His Majesty's Troops; never was either more conspicuous. Major Brereton, and every Officer and Soldier under the Lieutenant-Colonel's Orders, are justly entitled to my warmest Acknowledgments; their persevering Ardour and Desire to distinguish themselves cannot be too highly spoken of, and which it will be my Pride to remember to the latest Period of my Life.

Captain Nelson, of His Majesty's Ship Agamemnon who had the Command and Directions of the Seamen, in landing the Guns, Mortars and Stores; and Captain Hunt, who commanded at the Batteries, very ably assisted by Captain Buller and Captain Serocold, and the Lieutenants Gore, Hotham, Stiles, Andrews and Brisbane, have an equal Claim to my Gratitude, as the Seamen under their Management worked the Guns with great judgment and Alacrity.

Never was an higher Spirit or greater Perseverance exhibited, and I am happy to say, that no other Contention was at any Time known, than who should be most forward and indefatigable for promoting His Majesty's Service; for, although the Difficulties they had to struggle with were many and various, the perfect Harmony and good Humour that universally prevailed throughout the Siege overcame them all.

I cannot but express, in the strongest Terms, the meritorious Conduct of Captain Duncan and Lieutenant Alexander Duncan, of the Royal Artillery, and Lieutenant De Butts, of the Royal Engineers; but my Obligation is particularly great to Captain Duncan, as more Zeal, Ability and Judgment was never shewn by any Officer than were displayed by him; and I take the Liberty of mentioning him as an Officer highly entitled to His Majesty's Notice.

I feel myself very much indebted for the Vigilance and Attention of Captain Wolseley, of the Imperuse, and of Captain Hallowell, who became a Volunteer wherever he could be useful, after being superseded in the Command of the Courageux by Captain Waldegrave. The former kept a diligent Watch upon the Island of Capraia, where the Enemy have Magazines of Provisions and Stores and the Latter did the same, by guarding the Harbour's Mouth of Bastia with Gun-Boats and Launches well armed, the whole of every Night, whilst the smaller Boats were very judiciously placed in the Intervals between, and rather without the Ships (which were moored in a Crescent just out of Reach of the Enemy's Guns) by Captain Young, of the Fortitude, the Center Ship, on Board of which every Boat assembled at Sun-set for Orders; and the Chearfulness with which the Officers and Men performed this nightly Duty is very much to be admired, and afforded me the most heartfelt Satisfaction and Pleasure.

The very great and effectual Assistance I received from Vice-Admiral Goodall, Captain Inglefield and Captain Knight, as well as from every Captain and Officer of His Majesty's Ships under my Command, have a just Claim to my most particular Thanks, not only in carrying into Execution my Orders afloat, but in attending to.and supplying the Wants of the little Army on Shore: It is to the very cordial and decided Support alone I had the Honor to receive from the Whole, that the innumerable Difficulties we had to contend with were so happily surmounted.

Major Smith and Ensign Vigonreux, of the 25th Regiment, and Captain Radsdale and Lieutenant St. George of the 11th, not embarking with their respective Regiments, having Civil Employments on Shore; it is to their Honor I mention, that they relinquished those Employments, and joined their Corps, soon after the Troops were landed.

It is very much my Duty to inform you, that I am extremly obliged, to General

Petrecono, Mr. Frediani and all the Officers of the Corsicans, serving with the Army, for their great Zeal, Ardour and Attention, in forwarding the Reduction of Bastia by every Means in their Power, who were of infinite Service by preserving good Order in the Troops.

I transmit an Account of the Loss on the Part of His Majesty, in Killed and Wounded, which, I am happy to say, is inconsiderable; but the Enemy suffered much, their Hospitals being full.

At the Commencement of the Siege, the Number of the Enemy bearing Arms was 3000.

By the first Ship that sails for England, I shall have the Honor of sending, to be laid at His Majesty's Feet, the several Stand of Colours taken at Bastia.

Captain Hunt, who was on Shore in the Command of the Batteries from the Hour the Troops landed to the Surrender of the Town, will be the Bearer of this Dispatch, and can give any further Information you may wish to know respecting the Siege.

I have the Honor, &c.
HOOD

8

Capture Of Guadeloupe

Whitehall May 19, 1794.

A Dispatch, dated Pointe à Pitre, Guadaloupe, April 12, 1794 of which the following is an Extract, was this Day received from General Sir Charles Grey, K. B. by the Right Honourable Henry Dundas, His Majesty's Principal Secretary of State for the Home Department.

IN my Dispatch of the 4th Instant, I had the Honor to acquaint you with the Success of His Majesty's Arms in the Conquest of the Island of St. Lucia.

Having left Colonel Sir Charles Gordon to command in that Island, I reembarked the same Day, and returned to Martinico the 5th Instant, where we shifted the Troops from the King's Ships back to the Transports, took on Board, during the 6th and 7th, the heavy Ordinance and Stores, Provisions, &c and sailed again in the Morning of the 8th following: The Admiral detaching Captain Rogers with the Quebec, Captain Faulkner with the Blanche, Captain Incledon with the Ceres, and Captain Scott with the Rose, to attack the small Islands called the Saints, which they executed with infinite Gallantry and good Conduct, having landed Part of their Seamen and Marines, and carried them early in the Morning without Loss. The Boyne, in which I sailed with the Admiral, and the Veteran, anchored off this Place about Noon the 10th Instant, and some more of the Fleet in the Course of that Afternoon; but a fresh Wind and Lee Current prevented most of the Transports from getting in till Yesterday, and some of them until this Day.

Without waiting, however, for the Arrival of all the Troops, I made a Landing at Gosier-Bay, at One o'Clock in the Morning of the 11th Instant, under the Fire of Fort Gosier and Fort Fleur d'Epée, with Part of the 1st and 2nd Battalions of Grenadiers, One Company of the 43d Regiment, and 506 Seamen and Marines, detached by the Admiral, under the Command of Captain George Grey, of the Boyne; the Whole under the Conduct and Command of that able and vigilant Officer Colonel Symes, who had infinite Merit in the Execution of it, and the Landing, was covered by Lord Garlies in the Winchelsea his Lordship having with infinite judgment, and Intrepidity, placed his Ship so well and laid it so close to their Batteries, that they could not stand to their Guns, which were soon silenced.

In effecting this essential Service Lord Garlies was slightly wounded, and we did not suffer materially in any other respect. Some more of the Troops being arrived, and perceiving the Enemy in considerable Force and Number at the strong Situation of Fort Fleur d'Epée, I determined that no Time should be lost in attacking them, and carried those Posts by Storm at Five o'Clock this Morning, under a heavy fire of Cannon and Musquetry, although they were found infinitely strong, and changed the Name of Fort d'Epée to that of Fort Prince of Wales our Troops being ordered, which was strictly obeyed, not to fire, but to execute every Thing with the Bayonet, having previously made the following Disposition: The First Division, under the Command of His Royal Highness Prince Edward, consisting of the 1st and 2d Battalions of Grenadiers, and 100 of the Naval Battalion, to attack the Post on Morne Marcot. The Second, commanded by Major-General Dundas, consisting of the 1st and 2d Battalions of Light Infantry, and 100 of the Naval Battalion, to attack the Fort of Fleur d'Epée in the Rear, and to cut off its Communication with Fort Louis and Pointe à Pitre. The Third, commanded by Colonel Symes, consisting of the 3d Battalion of Grenadiers, and the 3d. Battalion of Light Infantry, and the Remainder of the Naval Battalion, to proceed by the Road on the Sea Side, to co-operate with Major-General Dundas. The Detachments of the Naval Battalion, who were of most essential Service in those brilliant Actions, were very ably commanded by Captain Nugent and Captain Faulknor. The Signal given for the Whole to commence the Attack, was a Gun from the Boyne by the Admiral, at Five o'Clock this Morning. The several Divisions having marched earlier according to the Distance they had to go, to be ready to combine and commence the Attack at the same Instant; and this Service was performed with such Exactitude, superior Ability, Spirit and good Conduct by the Officers who severally commanded those Divisions, and every Officer and Soldier under them, as do them more Honor than I can find Words to convey an adequate Idea of, or to express the high Sense I entertain of their extraordinary Merit on the Occasion. The Success we have already had puts us in Possession of Grande Terre, and we shall use our utmost Exertions to get in Possession of Basse Terre also, with all possible Expedition, to complete the Conquest of this Island.

(Signed) Fra. Dundas,
Adjutant General.

Whitehall, May 21.

Letter (of which the following is an Extract) from Sir Charles Grey, K.B. dated Basfeterre, Guadaloupe, April 22, 1794, was Yesterday received by the Right Honourable Henry Dundas, His Majesty's Principal Secretary of State for the Home Department.

SIR,

IN my Dispatch of the 12th Instant, by the Sea Flower, I had the Honor to acquaint you with the Capture of that Part of the Island of Guadaloupe denominated Grand

Terre. The 43d Regiment being landed to garrison Fort Prince of Wales (late Fort Fleur d'Epée) the Town of Pointe à Pitre, &c. and the other Troops re-embarked, at Twelve o'Clock the 14th, the Quebec, with several other Frigates and some Transports, dropped down opposite to Petit Bourg, with Grenadiers and Light Infantry, commanded by Prince Edward, and began landing at Five o'Clock in the Afternoon, at which Time I joined them, and was received with great Demonstrations of Joy by the French People on Marquis de Bouillie's Estate; and I returned on Board the Boyne at Ten o'Clock the same Evening. At Day-Break in the Morning of the 15th I went to St. Mary's, where I found Lieutenant-Colonel Coote, with the First Light Infantry, having got there before Day, from Petit Bourg; and the Second Battalion of Grenadiers joined at Ten o'Clock. The Troops advancing, (April the 16th) reached Trou Chien, which the Enemy had abandoned, although very strong, and before Dark we halted on the high Ground over Trois Rivierre, forn whence we saw the Enemy's Two Redoubts and their strong Post of Palmiste. I intended to have attacked the Enemy that Night, but the Troops were too much fatigued, from the difficult March they had just finished. Major-General Dundas landed at Vieux Habitant at Eleven o'Clock in the Night of the 17th, with the Third Battalion of Grenadiers, and the Second and Third Battalions of Light Infantry, with little Opposition and no Loss, (having sailed from Pointe à Pitre the 15th preceding) taking Postition of Morne Magdaline, and destroying Two Batteries: Then detaching Lieutenant-Colonel Blundell, with the Second Battalion of Light Infantry, he forced several very difficult Posts of the Enemy during the Night. I made a Disposition for the Attack of the Enemy's Redoubt d'Arbaud, at Grande Ance, and their Battery d'Anet, to be executed during that night; but at Eight o'Clock in the Evening they evacuated the former, setting Fire to every Thing in and about it; and I ordered the Attack of the latter to proceed, which was well executed by Lieutenant-Colonel Coote and the First Light Infantry, who were in Possession of it by Day-Break of the 18th, having killed, wounded, or taken every one of those who were defending it, without any Loss. At Twelve o'Clock on the Night of the 19th I moved forward, with the First and Second Battalions of Grenadiers and the First Light Infantry, from Trois Rivierre and Grande Ance, and took their famous Post of Palmiste, with all their Batteries, at Day-Break of the 20th, commanding Fort St. Charles and Basseterre; and communicating with Major-General Dundas's Division on the Morning of the 21st, who had made his Approach by Morne Howel; after which General Collot capitulated, surrendering Guadaloupe and all its Dependencies, comprehending the Islands of Marigalante, Disseada, the Saints, &c on the same Terms that were allowed to Rochambeau at Martinique, and Ricard at St. Lucia, to march out with the Honors of War, and lay down their Arms, to be sent to France and not to serve against the British Forces or their Allies during the War. Accordingly at Eight o'Clock this Morning the French Garrison of Fort St. Charles marched out, consisting of 55 Regulars of the Regiments of Guadaloupe, and the 14th of France, and 818 National Guards and others. Prince Edward, with the Grenadiers and Light Infantry, taking Possession, immediately hoisting the British Colours, and changing the Name of it to Fort Matilda. The Terms of Capitulation are transmitted herewith, but the Forts and

Batteries are so numerous, and some of them at such Distance, that a Return of the Ordnance, Stores, &c. cannot be obtained in Time for the sailing of this Vessel, as I am unwilling to detain her so long as would be necessary for that Purpose. From a Return found amongst General Collot's Papers, it appears that the Number of Men able to carry Arms in Guadaloupe, is 5877, and the Number of Fire Arms actually delivered out to them is 4044. In former Dispatches I have mentioned that Lieutenant-General Prescott was left to command at Martinico, and Colonel Sir Charles Gordon at St. Lucia; and the Conquest of Guadaloupe and its Dependencies being now also completely accomplished, I have placed Major-General Dundas in the Command of this Island, with a proper Garrison; and His Majesty may place the firmest Reliance on the Ability, Experience and Zeal for the good of his Service and their Country, of those excellent Officers. Although I have not been wanting in my several Dispatches to you, Sir, to bestow just Praise on the Forces I have the Honor to command, yet I conceive it a Duty, which I embrace with infinite Pleasure, to repeat, that, to the Unanimity and extraordinary Exertions of the Navy and Army on this Service, under Fatigues and Difficulties never exceeded, His Majesty and their Country are indebted for the rapid Success which, in so short a Space of Time, has extended the British Empire, by adding to it the valuable Islands of Martinique, St. Lucia, Guadaloupe, the Saints, Marigalante, and Disseada. Captain Thomas Grey, one of my Aides de Camp, will have the Honor to deliver this Dispatch, and can communicate any other Particulars or Information you may desire.

(Signed) Fra. Dundas,
Adjutant General.

9

The Battle Of Beaumont-en-Cambrésis

Whitehall, April 30.

THE Letters, of which the following are Copies, were this Morning received from His Royal Highness the Duke of York, by the Right Honourable Henry Dundas, His Majesty's Principal Secretary of State for the Home Department.

Heights above Cateau,
April 26, 1794.

SIR,

IT is from the Field of Battle that I have the Satisfaction to acquaint you, for His Majesty's Information, with the glorious Success which the Army under my Command have had this Day.

At Day-Break this Morning the Enemy attacked me on all Sides. After a short but severe Conflict we succeeded in repulsing him, with considerable Slaughter. The Enemy's General, Chapuy, is taken Prisoner, and we are Masters of Thirty-five Pieces of the Enemy's Cannon.

The Behaviour of the British Cavalry has been beyond all Praise.

It is impossible for me as yet to give any Account of the Loss sustained by His Majesty's Troops. I have Reason to believe that it is not considerable.

The only Officers of whom I have any Account as yet, and who I believe are all who have fallen upon this Occasion, are, Major-General Mansel, Captain Pigot, and Captain Fellows of the Third Dragoon Guards.

The Army under His Imperial Majesty was attacked at the same Time, and the only Particulars with which I am acquainted at present are, that the Enemy were likewise repulsed with great Loss.

I shall not fail to send you a more full Account by the first Opportunity.

FREDERICK.

P.S. This Letter will be delivered to you by my Aide de Camp, Capt. Murray, who will be able to give you any further Information that you may wish to receive.

Whitehall, May 3.

A Dispatch from His Royal Highness the Duke of York, of which the following is a Copy, was Yesterday received by the Right Honourable Henry Dundas, His Majesty's Principal Secretary of State for the Home Department.

Cateau, April 28, 1794.

SIR,

AS I thought His Majesty might wish to be informed, as soon as possible, of the Success which the Combined Troops under my Command had had on the 26th Instant, I dispatched my Aide-de-Camp, Captain Murray, from the Field of Battle, and take this Opportunity of giving you some further Details concerning the Action.

It appears that the Attack of the Enemy was intended to be general, along the whole Frontier, from Treves to the Sea.

The Corps, which attacked that under my Command, consisted of a Column of Eight and Twenty Thousand Men, and Seventy-nine Pieces of Cannon, which marched out of Cambrai the preceding night at Twelve o'Clock, and a smaller one, whose Force I am not justly acquainted with, which moved forwards by the Way of Premont and Marets. The Enemy formed their Line at Day-Break in the Morning, and, under Favour of a Fog, advanced to the Attack of the Villages in my Front, which, being occupied by Light Troops only, they possessed themselves of without much Resistance; and advancing, formed their Attack upon the Village of Troisville, Into which they had actually entered, but were dislodged again by the well-directed Fire of Grape Shot from Two British Six-Pounders, under the Command of Lieutenant-Colonel Congreve.

Their Movements being now plainly seen, and their Left appearing to be unprotected, I determined to detach the Cavalry of the Right Wing, consisting of the Austrian Cuirassier Regiment of Zetchwitz, of the Blues, 1st, 3d, 5th Dragoon Guard, and Royals, under the Command of Lieutenant-General Otto, and to turn them on that Flank; whilst, by a severe Cannonade from our Front, I endeavored to divert their Attention from this Movement. Some Light Troops likewise were directed to turn, if possible, their Right Flank; but having received a very severe Fire from a Wood, which they imprudently approached too near, they were obliged to retire. They however immediately rallied, and, after driving the Enemy back, took from them Two Pieces of Cannon.

General Otto completely succeeded in his Movements. The Enemy were attacked in their Flank, and Rear, and, although they at first attempted to resist, they were soon thrown into Confusion, and the Slaughter was immense. Twenty-two Pieces of Cannon, and a very great Quantity of Ammunition, fell into our Hands.

Lieutenant-General Chapuy, who commanded this Corps, with Three Hundred and Fifty Officers and Privates, were taken.

While this was passing on the Right, we were not less fortunate on our Left.

The Cavalry of the Left Wing having moved forwards to observe the Enemy's Column, which was advancing from Premont and Marets, the 7th and 11th Regiments of Light Dragoons, with Two Squadrons of Arch-Duke Ferdinand's Hussars, under the Command of Major Stephanitz, attacked their Advanced Guard with so much Spirit and Impetuosity, as to defeat them completely. Twelve Hundred Men were left dead on this Part of the Field; Ten Pieces of Cannon, and Eleven Tumbrils filled with Ammunition, were taken.

I cannot sufficiently express my Thanks to Lieutenant-General Otto for the Manner in which he conducted the Movements of the Cavalry of the Right Wing, as well as to Prince Schwartzenberg and Colonel Vyfe, (the latter of whom commanded the Two Brigades of British Cavalry after General Mansel's Death) for the Spirit and Gallantry with which they led on the Troops.

The Coolness and Courage manifested by all the Officers and Soldiers of His Majesty's Troops, demand my highest Acknowledgements; and it is a Duty I owe to them, to desire that you will lay my humble Recommendation of them before His Majesty.

The Enemy, in Three Columns, attacked likewise the Army under His Imperial Majesty: They were, however, repulsed with considerable Loss, and driven back under the Cannon of Guise.

I am, Sir,
Your's,
FREDERICK

10

The Battle Of Tourcoing

Whitehall, May 23.

A Dispatch, of which the following is a Copy, was this Morning received from His Royal Highness the Duke of York, by the Right Honourable Henry Dundas, His Majesty's Principal Secretary of State for the Home Department.

Tournay, May 19, 1794.

IN my last Letter I mentioned to you His Imperial Majesty's Intention of making a general Attack With his whole Force, in order, by a joint Co-operation with the Troops under the Command of General Clairfayt to compel the Enemy to evacuate Flanders.

On the 16th at Night the Army moved forward, for this Purpose, in Five Columns.

The Two Columns on the Left were intended to force the Passages of the Marque, and, by a vigorous Attack on the Enemy's Posts along the River, to cover the Operations of the Three remaining Columns: These were destined to force the Enemy's Posts by Roubaix, Waterloo and Moucron, thus to favor General Clairfayt's Passage of the Lys, and then, by a Junction with his Corps, to have cut off the Communication between Lisle and Courtray.

Unfortunately the Two Columns on the Left forced the Passage of the Marque so late, and were so much fatigued by the Length of their March, that they were not able to accomplish the Remainder of the proposed Plan, while the Column on the Right, under General Busche, finding the Enemy at Moucron in much greater Numbers than had been expected, was under the Necessity of relinquishing its Attack, and of retreating to its former Position at Turcoing.

Lieutenant-General Otto proceeded with his Column through Leers to Waterloo, from whence, after some Resistance, he drove the Enemy, and pushed on to Tourcoing.

My Column consisted of Seven Battalions of British, Five of Austrians, and Two of Hessians, with Six Squadrons of Light Dragoons, and Four of Hussars. We moved forward from Tempieuve to Lannoy, which we forced the Enemy to evacuate, after a short Cannonade, in which I had the Misfortune to lose Major Wright, of the Royal Artillery, a brave and deserving Officer.

Having left the Two Hessian Battalions at Lannoy, I proceeded to Roubaix, where we found the Enemy in great Strength both of Men and Cannon. The Resistance was proportionably stronger, but equally unavailing, as the Enemy soon found themselves compelled to retire, which they did towards Moucron.

Having at this Time no Intelligence of the Two Columns on my Right and Left, notwithstanding I had made every Effort to obtain it, I did not think it prudent to advance any further, but was resolved to have left my Advanced Guard, under the Command of Lieutenant-General Abercromby, at Roubaix, and, with the Remainder of my Corps to have taken a Position on the Heights behind Lannoy. The Orders for this Purpose were given, but having acquainted His Imperial Majesty, who had advanced to Lannoy, with my Intention, the Necessity of co-operating with General Clairfayt induced His Majesty to direct that I should proceed to the Attack of Mouveaux.

I accordingly directed the Attack to be made by Lieutenant-General Abercromby with the Four Battalions of Guards. He found the Enemy strongly intrenched, but having cannonaded it for some Time, the good Countenance of the Flank Battalion of Guards, who advanced to storm it with the utmost Order, supported by the First Battalion, and seconded by the 7th and 15th Light Dragoons, under Lieutenant-Colonel Churchill, compelled the Enemy to retire, with the Loss of Three Pieces of Cannon and of a considerable Number of Men, who were cut down by the Light Dragoons in the Pursuit, which was continued as far as Bouderes.

Upon maturely, considering the Nature of our Situation, I directed Lieutenant-General Abercromby to remain at Mouveaux with the Four Battalions of Guards; and having posted Four Austrian Battalions to cover Roubaix, I detached the Second Brigade of British Infantry, under the Command of Major-General Fox, to take Post on my Left, on the great Road leading From Lisle to Roubaix. The Cavalry was divided, with these several Corps, for the Purpose of patroling, the Nature of the Country not admitting of their being of any other Use. My Advanced Posts communicated with those of General Otto, on my Right, who I now found had got Possession of Turcoing.

Early the next Morning the Enemy attacked the Post of Turcoing in great Force, and I received an Application from Colonel Devay, who commanded there, to make a Diversion in his Favor; for which Purpose I sent Two Battalions of Austrians giving them express Direction, if they should be pressed, to fall back upon me, but, by some Mistake, instead of doing so, they joined Colonel Devay. From this Circumstance, an Opening was left on my Right, of which the Enemy availed himself in the Attack upon my Corps, which took Place soon after, and, by so doing, obliged me to employ the only Battalion I had left, to secure a Point which was of the utmost Consequence to us.

At this Period a very considerable Column of the Enemy, which we have since learnt amounted to 15,000 Men, appeared advancing from Lisle, whilst another Corps, having forced its Way through General Otto's Position by Waterloo, attacked us on the Rear. The few Troops that remained with me, soon gave Way before such superior Numbers, nor was it in my Power, with every Effort I could use, assisted by those of the Officers who were about me, to rally them. At that Moment the advanced Parties of the Column from Lisle shewed themselves also upon the Road between Roubaix and Mouveaux, and I found it impossible to succeed in the Attempt which I made to join the Brigade of Guards.

Thus circumstanced, I turned my Attention to join General Fox's Brigade, but upon proceeding to Roubaix for that Purpose, I found it in the Possession of the Enemy.

Thus completely cut off from every Part of my Corps, nothing remained for me to do, but to force my Way to that of General Otto, and to concert Measures with him to free my own Troops.

This I effected, accompanied by a few Dragoons of the 16th Regiment, with great Difficulty; but the Project of marching upon Lannoy, to which General Otto had consented, as a Measure which would greatly facilitate the Retreat of my Corps, being given up, upon finding that the Hessians had been obliged to abandon that Place, I found myself under the painful Necessity of continuing with General Otto's Column the remainder of the Day.

Previous to this, I had sent Orders to General Abercromby to retire from Mouveaux to the Heights behind Roubaix, where it was my Intention to have assembled my Corps; and the Coldstream Battalion had been posted to cover the Communication till he effected his Retreat. In consequence of these Directions, General Abercromby began his Retreat, and on his Arrival upon the Heights at Roubaix, finding himself surrounded upon all Sides without a Possibility of assembling the Corps, he determined to continue it to Lannoy. This he effected amidst the repeated Attacks of the Enemy, who poured upon him from all Parts. General Abercromby found Lannoy also in Possession of the Enemy, but he avoided the Town by marching round it under a very heavy Fire, and soon after reached Templeuve.

Major-General Fox, after sustaining, with great Resolution, a very vigorous Attack from the principal Part of the Column which came from Lisle, began his Retreat also, and finding himself cut off from the Brigade of Guards, and Lanrioy occupied by the Enemy, he directed his March upon the Village of Leers, at which Place he joined the Column of Lieutenant-General Otto.

I inclose you a Return of our Loss upon this Occasion. I regret that it is so great, but when the Nature of the Action is considered, and that it was conducted in a Country the most favourable to the Views of the Enemy that they could have wished for while their perfect Knowledge of these Parts enabled them to take every Advantage of it, it might have been expected to have been still more considerable. From the Badness of the Roads, the Loss of the Horses, and the Timidity of the Drivers, the leaving a Part of our Artillery became inevitable.

I am to desire that you will assure His Majesty, that the Officers and Men shewed all the Firmness and Resolution on this Occasion that could be expected from them; and it would be an Injustice done to the Rest to distinguish any particular Corps. The Abilities and Coolness with which Lieutenant-General Abercromby and Major-General Fox conducted their different Corps under these trying Circumstances, require, however, that I should particularly notice them.

It is a peculiar Consolation to me that the Column under my Command executed to the full Extent their intended Part of the Operation; and that in the Check which they afterwards sustained, the Conduct of the British Troops has entitled them to the warmest Expressions of Gratitude and Admiration on the Part of His Imperial Majesty.

I am, &c.
FREDERICK.

11
Battle Of Tournay

Whitehall, May 25.

A Dispatch, of which the following is a Copy, was received this Afternoon from His Royal Highness the Duke of York by the Right Honourable Henry Dundas, His Majesty's Principal Secretary of State for the Home Department.

Tournay, May 23, 1794.

SIR,

I Have the Satisfaction to acquaint you, for His Majesty's Information, that Yesterday Morning the Enemy, having made an Attack upon the Combined Army under the Command of His Imperial Majesty, were repulsed, after a long and obstinate Engagement.

The Attack began at Five o'Clock, but did not appear to be serious till towards Nine, when the Whole Force of the Enemy (consisting, according to every Account, of upwards of One Hundred Thousand Men) was brought against the Right Wing, with the Intention of forcing, if possible, the Passage of the Scheldt, in order to invest Tournay.

At first they drove in the Out-Posts, and obliged General Busche's Corps, which was posted at Espierres, to fall back upon the Main Army; but Upon Succour being sent, General Wallmoden, who, though unwell, had retaken the Command of the Hanoverians, maintained his Position. The Enemy, by constantly bringing up fresh Troops, were enabled to continue the Attack, without Intermission, till Nine o'Clock at Night.

The Troops of the Right Wing being greatly fatigued, it became necessary to support them from my Wing; for which Purpose, besides Seven Austrian Battalions, I detached the Second Brigade of British, under the Command of Major-General Fox. Nothing could exceed the Spirit and Gallantry with which they conducted themselves, particularly in the Storm of the Village of Pontechin, which they forced with the Bayonet. The Enemy immediately began to retreat, and during the Night withdrew all their Posts, and, according to every Information, have fallen back upon Lisle.

Seven Pieces of Cannon and about 500 Prisoners have fallen into Our Hands, and the Enemy's Loss, in Killed and Wounded, is said to amount to little short of Twelve Thousand Men, which is by no Means improbable, as they were exposed to an incessant Fire of Cannon and Musquetry for upwards of Twelve Hours.

The Manner in which General Fox conducted the Brigade of British Infantry of the Line merits my warmest Approbation.

      I am, &c.
      FREDERICK

12

The Glorious First Of June (Second Battle Of Ushant)

Admiralty-Office, June 10.

SIR Roger Curtis, First Captain to the Admiral Earl Howe, arrived this Evening with a Dispatch from his Lordship to Mr. Stephens, of which the following is a Copy.

Queen Charlotte at Sea, June 2, 1794, Ushant, E. Half N. 140 Leagues.

SIR,

THINKING it may not be necessary to make a more particular Report of my Proceedings with the Fleet, for the present Information of the Lords Commissioners of the Admiralty, I confine my Communications chiefly, in this Dispatch, to the Occurrences when in Presence of the Enemy Yesterday.

Finding, on my Return off of Brest on the 19th past, that the French Fleet had, a few Days before, put to Sea; and receiving, on the same Evening, Advices from Rear-Admiral Montagu, I deemed it requisite to endeavour to form a Junction with the Rear-Admiral as soon as possible, and proceeded immediately for the Station on which he meant to wait for the Return of the Venus.

But, having gained very credible Intelligence, on the 21st of the same Month, whereby I had Reason to suppose the French Fleet was then but a few Leagues farther to the Westward, the Course before steered was altered accordingly.

On the Morning of the 28th the Enemy were discovered far to Windward, and partial Actions were engaged with them that Evening and the next Day.

The Weather Gage having been obtained, in the Progress of the last mentioned Day, and the Fleet being in á Situation for bringing the Enemy to close Action the 1st Instant, the Ships bore up together for that Purpose, between Seven and Eight o'Clock in the Morning.

The French, their Force consisting of Twenty-six Ships of the Line, opposed to His Majesty's Fleet of Twenty-five (the Audacious having parted Company with the sternmost Ship of the Enemy's Line, captured in the Night of the 28th) waited for the Action, and sustained the Attack with their customary Resolution.

In less than an Hour after the close Action commenced in the Centre, the French Admiral, engaged by the Queen Charlotte, crowded off, and was followed by most of the Ships of his Van in Condition to carry Sail after him, leaving with us about Ten or Twelve of his crippled or totally dismasted Ships, exclusive of One sunk in the Engagement. The Queen Charlotte had then lost her Fore Topmast, and the Main Topmast fell over the Side very soon after.

The greater Number of the other Ships of the British Fleet were, at this Time, so much disabled or widely separated, and under such Circumstances with respect to those Ships of the Enemy in a State for Action, and with which the Firing was still continued, that Two or Three, even of their dismantled Ships, attempting to get away under a Spritsail singly, or smaller Sail raised on the Stump of the Foremast, could not be detained.

Seven remained in our Possession, One of which, however, sunk before the adequate Assistance could be given to her Crew; but many were saved.

The Brunswick, having lost her Mizen Mast in she Action, and drifted to Leeward of the French retreating Ships, was obliged to put away large to the Northward from them. Not seeing her chased by the Enemy, in that Predicament, I flatter myself she may arrive in Safety, at Plymouth. All the other Twenty-four Ships of His Majesty's Fleet re-assembled later in the Day; and I am preparing to return with them, as soon as the captured Ships of the Enemy are secured, for Spithead.

The material Injury to His Majesty's Ships, I understand, is confined principally to their Masts and Yards, which I conclude will be speedily replaced.

I have not been yet able to collect regular Accounts of the Killed and Wounded in the different Ships. Captain Montague is the only Officer of his Rank who fell in the Action. The Numbers of both Descriptions I hope will prove small, the Nature of the Service considered; but I have the Concern of being to add, on the same Subject, that Admiral Graves has received a Wound in the Arm, and that Rear-Admirals Bowyer aud Pasley, and Captain Hutt of the Queen, have each had a Leg taken off; they are, however, (I have the Satisfaction to hear) in a favorable State under those Misfortunes. In the captured Ships the Numbers of Killed and Wounded appear to be very considerable.

Though I shall have, on the Subject of these different Actions with the Enemy, distinguished Examples hereafter to report, I presume the determined Bravery of the several Ranks, of Officers and the Ships Companies employed under my Authority, will have been already sufficiently denoted by the Effect of their spirited Exertions; and, I trust, I shall be excused for postponing the more detailed Narrative of the other Transactions of the Fleet thereon, for being communicated at a future Opportunity; more especially as my first Captain Sir Roger Curtis, who is charged with this Dispatch, will be able to give the farther Information the Lords Commissioners of the Admiralty may at this Time require. It is incumbent on me, nevertheless, now to add, that I am greatly indebted to him for his Councils as well as Conduct in every

Branch of my Official Duties: And I have similar Assistance, in the late Occurrences, to acknowledge of my Second Captain, Sir Andrew Douglas.

I am, with great Consideration

SIR,
Your most obedient Servant,
HOWE

P.S. The Names and Force of the captured French Ships with the Fleet is transmitted herewith.

List of French Ships captured on the 1st Day of June 1794,
La Juste 80 Guns
Sans Pareille 80
L'America 74
L'Achille 74
Northumberland 74
L'Impetueux 74
Vengeur 74, sunk almost immediately upon being taken Possession of.

N.B. The Ship stated to have been captured on the Evening of the 28th of last Month, is said by the Prisoners to be the Revolutionaire of 120 Guns.

13

Siege Of Calvi

Whitehall September 1.

A Dispatch, of which the following is a Copy was last Night received from Lieutenant-General the Honourable Charles Stuart by the Right Honourable Henry Dundas, one of His Majesty's Principal Secretaries of State.

Calvi, August 10, 1794.

SIR,

I HAVE the Satisfaction to inform you, that the Town of Calvi surrendered to His Majesty's Forces on the 10th Instant, after a Siege of Fifty-one Days.

As I perfectly agreed with Lord Hood in Opinion that the utmost Dispatch was necessary, in order to enable the Troops selected for the Siege of Calvi to begin their Operations before the Commencement of the unhealthy Season, every Effort was used to forward the necessary Preparations; and so effectual were the Exertions of the different Departments, that in the Course of a very few Days, these Regiments embarked at Bastia; and Captain Nelson, of His Majesty's Ship Agamemnon, consented, in Lord Hood's Absence, to proceed to Port Agra, where a Landing was effected on the 19th of June; and, in the Course of the same Day, the Army encamped, in a strong Position, upon the Serra del Capuccine, a Ridge of Mountains, Three Miles distant from the Town of Calvi.

From many of the Out-Posts, and particularly from those the friendly Corsicans were ordered to occupy, I could distinctly discover that the Town of Calvi was strong in Point of Situation, well fortified, and amply supplied with heavy Artillery; the exterior Defences, on which the Enemy had bestowed a considerable Labour, consisted in the Bomb Proof Stone Star Fort Mozello, mounting Ten Pieces of Ordnance, with a Battery of Six Guns on it's Right, flanked by a small Entrenchment. In the Rear of this Line (which covered the Town to the Westward) On a rocky Hill to the East, Was placed a Battery of Three Guns. Considerably advanced on the Plain to the South West, the Fort Mollinochesco, on a steep Rock, commanded the Communication between Calvi and the Province of Balagni, supported by Two

Frigates moored in the Bay, for the Purpose of raking the intermediate Country; But the principal Difficulties in approaching the Enemy's Works, did not so much arise from the Strength of the Defences, as from the Height of the Mountains and rugged rocky Surface of the Country it was necessary to penetrate; and so considerable were these Obstacles against the usual Mode of Attack, that it was judged expedient to adopt rapid and forward Movements, instead of regular Approaches. In conformity to this Plan of Proceeding, the Seamen and Soldiers were laboriously employed in making Roads, dragging Guns to the Tops of the Mountains, and collecting Military Stores for the Purpose of erecting Two Mortar and Four separate Gun Batteries on the same Night. One of these was intended against the Mollinochesco; the Second to be constructed on Rocks to cover the principal one of Six Guns; which, by a sudden March, and the Exertions of the whole Army, was to be erected within Seven Hundred and Fifty Yards of the Mozello.

From some Mistake, the Battery proposed against the Mollinochesco was built and opened Two Days before the appointed Time, and considerably damaged that Fort. Observing, however, that it was the Determination of the Enemy to repair, and not to evacuate it, the Royal Irish Regiment was ordered, on the Evening of the 6th of July, to move towards their Left, exposing the Men to the Fire of their Artillery. This Diversion was seconded at Sun-set, and during the greater Part of the Night, by a feigned Attack of the Corsicans, which so effectually deceived the Enemy, that they withdrew a considerable Piquet from the Spot where the principal Battery was to be constructed, in order to support the Mollinochesco, and directing the Whole of their Fire to that Point, enabled the Troops to complete their Work. This important Position established, the Enemy was compelled to evacuate the Mollinochesco, and to withdraw the Shipping under the Protection of the Town. A very heavy Fire immediately commenced on both Sides, and continued, with little Intermission until the 18th of that Month, when, observing that their Batteries were considerably damaged, and a Breach appearing practicable on the West Side of the Mozello, a Disposition was made for a general Attack upon the Out-Works, under Cover of Two Batteries, ordered to be erected that Night, which, from their Position, would, in the Event of a Check, appear the principal Object of the Movement.

From the Zeal of Lieutenant-Colonel Bauchope, and the great Exertions of the 50th Regiment, the Battery, which he undertook to construct within Three Hundred Yards of the Mozello, was completed an Hour before Day-Break, without Discovery: A Signal Gun was then fired from it for the troops to advance. Lieutenant Newhoule, of the Royal Artillery, with Two Field Pieces, covered the Approach; and the Grenadiers, Light Infantry and 2d Battalion of the Royals, under the Command of Lieutenant-Colonel Moore of the 51st Regiment, and Major Brereton of the 30th Regiment, proceeded with a cool, steady Confidence, and unloaded Arms towards the Enemy, forced their Way through a smart Fire of Musquetry, and, regardless of live Shells flung into the Breach, or the additional Defence of Pikes, stormed the Mozello; while Lieutenant-Colonel Wemyss, with the Royal Irish Regiment, and Two Pieces of Cannon, under the Direction of Lieutenant Lemoine of the Royal Artillery, equally regardless of Opposition, carried the Enemy's Battery on the Left, and forced their Trenches without firing a Shot.

The Possession of these very important Posts, which the Troops maintained under the heaviest Fire of Shells, Shot and Grape, induced me to offer to consider such Terms as the Garrison of Calvi might be inclined to propose; but receiving an unfavourable Answer, the Navy and Army once more United their Efforts, and, in Nine Days, Batteries of Thirteen Guns, Four Mortars and Three Howitzers, were completed within Six Hundred Yards of the Town, and opened with so well-directed a Fire, that the Enemy were unable to remain at their Guns; and in Eighteen Hours sent Proposals, which terminated in a Capitulation, and the Expulsion of the French from Corsica.

It is with sincere Regret that I have to mention the Loss of Captain Serocold of the Navy, who was killed by a Cannon Shot when actively employed on the Batteries. The Assistance and Co-operation of Captain Nelson, the Activity of Captain Hallowell, and the Exertions of the Navy, have greatly contributed to the Success of these Movements.

The Spirit, Zeal and Willingness with which this Army has undergone the greatest Labour and Fatigue in the most oppressive Weather, is hardly to be described; and such has been the determined Animation of both Officers and Men, that, the smallest Murmur has never been heard, unless Illness deprived them from making their Services useful to their Country.

I am much indebted to Lieutenant-Colonel Moore for his Assistance upon every Occasion; and it is only a tribute due to his Worth to mention, that he has distinguished himself upon this Expedition for his Bravery, Conduct and Military Talent.

It is with the utmost Confidence I presume to recommend to His Majesty my Aide du Camp, Captain Duncan, of the Royal Artillery, whose Activity, Zeal and Ability, in his own and the Engineer Department, merits the highest Commendation and Advancement; Captain Stephens, the Officers and Men of the Royal Artillery, have distinguished themselves with their usual Ability in the Management of the Batteries, and their Attention to the different Branches of that Line.

Sir James Erskine and Major Oakes have been essentially useful in their different Departments; and permit me to assure you, that a Cordiality subsists throughout the Army, which promises the most signal Success on any future Undertaking.

I have the Happiness to inform you, that Captains Macdonald and Mackenzie, and the other wounded Officers and Soldiers, are in a fair Way of Recovery.

Captain Stewart, an Officer of great Merit and my Aide du Camp, will have the Honor of delivering this Dispatch.

> I have the Honor to be, &c.
> C. STUART, Lieut. Gen.

14

Battle Of Fleurus

Whitehall, July 1.

A Letter, of which the following is a Copy, has been this Morning received from His Royal Highness the Duke of York by the Right Honourable Henry Dundas, His Majesty's Principal Secretary of State for the Home Department.

Renaix, June 28, 1794.

SIR,

HAVING received Intelligence, on Tuesday Night, that the Enemy had moved forward in great Force upon General Clerfayt's Position, and that they had detached a Corps to attack Oudenarde, I found it absolutely necessary, for the Defence of the Scheldt, to march immediately to this Place, as from hence I could, with greater Facility, support that Place, and move upon any Point at which they might attempt to force a Passage.

The Enemy obliged General Clerfayt to abandon his Position at Deynse, and fall back upon Ghent on Wednesday, where they again attacked him the next Day, but were fortunately repulsed.

This Retreat of General Clairfayt rendered it impossible for General Walmoden to support himself with so small a Body of Troops as he had under his Command at Bruges. He therefore found it necessary to abandon that Place on Thursday, and to fall back to Landmarck, and join General Clerfayt's Right Flank.

The Consequences of these last Movements, though necessary, are exceedingly unpleasant, as all immediate Communication with Ostend is cut off.

Yesterday the Enemy made another Attempt upon Oudenarde, which they cannonaded the whole Day, and even carried in the Afternoon the Fauxbourg; but were driven out again in the Night, and have now retreated to a small Distance.

Yesterday Evening I received the disagreeable Intelligence of the Prince of Coburg's having failed in his Attack upon the French Army at Gosselies and Fleurus, as well as of the Surrender of Charleroi.

Report of the Action of the 26th of June, 1794, near Fleurus.
Marbais, June 26, 1794.

Although there was great Reason to suspect that Charleroi was already in the Hands of the Enemy, yet, as no certain Intelligence could possibly be procured, the Attack, which had been determined upon for it's Relief, became necessary, to prevent the Fate of so important a Place as Charleroi being left to Chance.

In consequence, the Army marched on the 25th in Five Columns, and early on the Morning of the 26th attacked the Enemy's entrenched Position between Lambusart, Espinies and Gosselies.

The Attack, which was executed with great Resolution, was everywhere successful, and the Enemy's advanced Corps, although protected by Strong Redoubts, were driven back. In the Evening the Left Wing arrived at the principal Heights on this Side the Sambre.

The Ground here forms a gentle Declivity, which the Enemy had fortified by a very extensive Line of Redoubts, in which they had brought an immense Number of Cannon. Notwithstanding these Obstacles, the Left Wing attempted to force the Enemy's Position with fixed Bayonets. But the Surrender of Charleroi, which took Place on the Evening of the 25th, having enabled the Enemy to reinforce themselves with the Besieging Army, and thus to bring the greatest Part of their Force against our Left Wing, this Advantage, added to those of their Situation, and of the Quantity of heavy Artillery, enabled them to repulse our Attack. The Troops, nervertheless, formed again under the Fire of the Enemy's Guns, and would have renewed the Attack with the same Resolution, had not the Certainty of the Fall of Charleroi, now confirmed by the Reports of Prisoners, and by several other Circumstances, determined our General Officers not to expose their brave Troops any further. They halted to remove the Wounded, and to give the Infantry Time to rest, and then begun the Retreat, which was effected, with the greatest Order, as far as Marbais, where the Army Passes this Night, and will march to Nivelles To-morrow, to cover the Country as far as is possible, and to protect Namur.

Our Loss is not very considerable, and may perhaps amount to 1500 Men. No Cannon have been lost, but a Howitzer and One Colour have been taken from the Enemy.

I am, &c.
FREDERICK

15

Battle Of Boxtel

Horse-Guards, September 21.

A Dispatch, of which the following is a Copy, was this Morning received from His Royal Highness the Duke of York by the Right Honourable Henry Dundas, One of His Majesty's Principal Secretaries of State.

Head Quarters, at Grave, September 17, 1794.

SIR,

IN my last Letter of the 13th Instant I acquainted you, for His Majesty's Information, with a Report, which I had just received, of the Enemy's having made a Movement towards Oosterwych. It appeared, however, by the Account of the next Day, that this Corps had fallen back in the Night. The same Accounts, confirmed by the Reports of Deserters, assured us, that a very considerable Detachment, amounting to Fifteen Thousand Men, had been made towards Maastricht. On Sunday Afternoon a sudden Attack, in which it appeared that the Enemy were in great Force, was made upon all my Posts of the Right; and that of Boxtel, which was the most advanced, was forced, with considerable Loss to the Hesse Darmstadt Troops, who occupied it.

As the Line of Outposts upon the Dommel could not be maintained, while the Enemy were in Possession of Boxtel it appeared necessary to regain it; at the same Time the Degree of Resistance which the Enemy would make, would serve to ascertain whether this Attack was supported by their Army, with a View, to a general Attack, or was merely an Affair of Outposts.

I therefore ordered Lieutenant-General Abercromby to march with the Reserve during the Night, with Directions to reconnoitre the Post at Day-Light, and to act as he should judge best, from what he should discover of the Force of the Enemy.

Lieutenant-General Abercromby having advanced as directed, found the Enemy in such Strength as left little Room to doubt of the Proximity of their Army, and he accordingly retired, but in such good Order as prevented the Enemy from making any Impression, although they followed him for some Distance.

About this Time I received private Information, upon which I could rely, and which was confirmed by the Observation of my Patroles, and the Reports of Deserters, that the Enemy had been reinforced by The Corps which had hitherto been acting in West Flanders, as well as by a Column of the Army which had been employed before Valenciennes and Conde. The same Information assured me, also, that the Column, which had been marching toward Maestricht, had suddenly returned towards us.

From these Accounts, and what I knew of the previous Strength of the Enemy, it appeared that the actual Force now advancing against me, and whose Object could only be an Attack upon my Army could scarcely be less than Eighty Thousand Men.

The Hazard of an Action with such a very great Disparity of Numbers, could not but become a Matter of the most serious Consideration; and, after the most mature Deliberation, I did not think myself at Liberty to risk, in so unequal a Contest, His Majejsty's Troops, or those of His Allies serving with them. I had the utmost Reliance on their Courage and Discipline, and I had no Doubt but that these would have enabled me to resist the first Efforts of the Enemy; but it could scarcely be expected that even by the utmost Exertion of these Qualities they would be able to withstand the repeated Attacks, which the vast Superiority of the Enemy would enable them to make, and which we know, from Experience, is a general Principle upon which they act.

Actuated by these Reasons, and the further Information which I received about Noon, that the Enemy were marching considerable Columns towards my Left in which Part of my Position was most vulnerable, I determined on retreating across the Meuse. The Army accordingly marched at Three o'Clock, and, without any Loss whatever, took up a Position, which had been previously reconnoitred, about Three Miles in Front of this Place, from which they crossed the River Yesterday Morning.

The Loss in the Attack upon the Out-Posts has fallen chiefly upon the Hesse Darmstadt Troops, with some of the Foreign Troops newly raised for His Majesty's Service. I have not as yet, however, received the Returns.

I am, &c.
(Signed) FREDERICK

16

Battle Of Genoa

Admiralty-Office, April 6.

A Dispatch, of which the following is a Copy, was this Evening received from Vice-Admiral Hotham, Commander of His Majesty's Ships and Vessels in the Mediterranean.

Britannia, at Sea, March 16, 1795.

SIR,

YOU will be pleased to inform their Lordships, that on the 8th Instant, being then in Leghorn Road, I received an Express from Genoa, that the French Fleet, consisting of Fifteen Sail of the Line and Three Frigates, were seen Two Days before off the Isle of Marguerite, which Intelligence corresponding with a Signal made from the Mozelle, then in the Offing, for a Fleet in the North-West Quarter, I immediately caused the Squadron to be unmoored, and at Day-Break the following Morning we put to Sea with a strong Breeze from the East-North-East.

The Mozelle previously returned to me, with the Information, that the Fleet he had seen were steering to the Southward, and supposed to be the Enemy; in consequence of which I shaped my Course for Corsica, lest their Destination should be against that Island, and dispatched the Tarleton Brig to St. Fiorenzo, with Orders for the Berwick to join me with all possible Expedition off Cape Corse; but, in the Course of the Night, she returned to me with the unwelcome Intelligence of that Ship having been captured Two Days before by the Enemy's Fleet.

To trespass as little as possible upon their Lordships Time, I shall not enter into a Detail of our Proceedings until the Two Squadrons got Sight of each other, and the Prospect opened of forcing the Enemy to Action, every Movement which was made being directed to that Object, and that alone.

Although the French Ships were seen by our advanced Frigates daily, yet the Two Squadrons did not get Sight of each other until the 12th, when that of the Enemy was discovered to Windward.

Observing them on the Morning following still in that Direction, without any apparent Intention of coming down, the Signal was made for a general Chace, in the Course of which, the Weather being squally, and blowing very fresh, we discovered one of their Line of Battle Ships to be without her Topmasts, which afforded to Captain Freemantle, of the Inconstant Frigate, (who was then far advanced on the Chace) an Opportunity of shewing a good Proof of British Enterprize, by his attacking; raking, and harrassing her Until the coming up of the Agamemnon, when he was most ably seconded by Captain Nelson, who did her so much Damage as to disable her from putting herself again to rights; but they were at this Time so far detached from our own Fleet, that they were obliged to quit her, as other Ships of the Enemy were coming up to her Assistance, by one of which he was soon afterwards taken in tow.

Finding that our heavy Ships did not gain On the Enemy during the Chace, I made the Signal for the Squadron to form upon the Larboard Line of Bearing, in which Order we continued for the Night.

At Day-Light the next Morning (the 14th) being about Six or Seven Leagues to the South-West of Genoa, we observed the Enemy's disabled Ship, with the one that had her in tow, to be so far to Leeward, and separated from their own Squadron, as to afford a probable Chance of our cutting them off. The Opportunity was not lost; all Sail was made to effect that Purpose, which reduced the Enemy to the Alternative of abandoning those Ships, or coming to Battle.

Although the latter did not appear to be their Choice, they yet came down (on the contrary Tack to which we were) with the View of supporting them; but the Captain and Bedford, whose Signals were made to attack the Enemy's disabled Ship and her Companion, were so far advanced, and so closely supported by the other Ships of our Van, as to cut them off effectually from any Assistance that could be given to them; the Conflict ended in the Enemy's abandoning them, and firing upon our Line as they passed with a light Air of Wind.

The Two Ships that fell proved to be the Ca-ira (formerly the Couronne) of 80 Guns, and the Censeur of 74.

Our Van Ships suffered so much by this Attack, particularly the Illustrious and Courageux (having each lost their Main and Mizen Masts) that it became impossible for any Thing further to be effected.

I have, however, good Reason to hope, from the Enemy's steering to the Westward, after having passed our Fleet, that, whatever might have been their Design, their Intentions are for the present frustrated.

The French Fleet were loaded with Troops; the Ca-ira having Thirteen Hundred Men on Board, and the Censeur One Thousand, of whom, by their obstinate Defence, they lost in Killed and Wounded between Three and Four Hundred Men.

The Efforts of our Squadron to second my Wishes for an immediate and effectual Attack upon the Enemy, were so spirited and unanimous, that I feel peculiar Satisfaction in offering to their Lordships my cordial Commendation of all Ranks collectively. It is difficult to specify particular Desert, where Emulation was common to all, and Zeal for His Majesty's Service the general Description of the Fleet.

It is, however, an Act of Justice To express the Sense I entertain of the Services of

Captain Holloway, of the Britannia: During a long Friendship with that Officer I have had repeated Proofs of his personal and professional Talents; and on this recent Demand for Experience and Information, his Zeal afforded me the most beneficial and satisfactory Assistance.

I understand from some I have to lament the loss of Captain Littlejohn, of the Berwick (who, I understand from some of her Men that were retaken in the Ca-ira) was unfortunately killed the Morning of the Ship being captured; by which Misfortune His Majesty has lost a most valuable and experienced Officer, and I have only to add that he has left a Widow and Four small Children.

I am, SIR,
Your most obedient humble Servant,
W. HOTHAM.

P.S. I am now on the Way with the Prizes to St. Fiorenzo, but doubt much whether it will be possible to get them in, as they are dismasted, greatly shattered, and very leaky, particularly the Ca-ira.

17

Battle Of Île De Groix

Admiralty-Office, June 27.

THE following Dispatch was this Morning received from Admiral Lord Bridport, K.B.

Royal George, at Sea, June 24, 1795.

SIR,

IT is with sincere Satisfaction I acquaint you, for the Information of the Lords Commissioners of the Admiralty, that His Majesty's Squadron under my Command attacked the Enemy's Fleet, consisting of Twelve Ships of the Line, attended with Eleven Frigates and some smaller Cruizers, on the 23d Instant, close in with Port L'Orient. The Ships which struck are the Alexander, Le Formidable, and Le Tigre, which were with Difficulty retained. If the Enemy had not been protected and sheltered by the Land, I have every Reason to believe that a much greater Number, if not all the Line of Battle Ships, would have been taken or destroyed.

In detailing the Particulars of this Service, I am to state, that at the Dawn of Day on the 22d Instant, the Nymphe and Astræa, being the Look-out Frigates ahead, made the Signal for the Enemy's Fleet. I soon perceived that there was no Intention to meet me in Battle; consequently I made the Signal for Four of the best sailing Ships, the Sans Pareil, Orion, Russel, and Colossus, and soon afterwards for the whole Fleet, to chase, which continued all that Day, and during the Night, with very little Wind.

Early in the Morning on the 23d Instant, the headmost Ships, the Irresistible, Orion, Queen Charlotte, Russel, Colossus, and Sans Pareil, were pretty well up with the Enemy, and a little before Six o'Clock the Action began, and continued till near Nine o'Clock. When the Ships struck, the British Squadron was near to some Batteries, and in the Face of a strong Naval Port, which will manifest to the Publick the Zeal, Intrepidity and Skill of the Admirals, Captains, and all other Officers, Seamen and Soldiers employed upon this Service; and they are fully entitled to my warmest Acknowledgments.

I beg also to be allowed to mark my Approbation, in a particular Manner, of

Captain Domett's Conduct, serving under my Flag, for his manly Spirit, and for the Assistance I received from his active and attentive Mind. I feel likewise great Satisfaction in doing Justice to the meritorious Conduct of all the Officers of every Class, as well as to the Bravery of the Seamen and Soldiers in the Royal George, upon this Event, and upon former Occasions.

I judged it necessary, upon the Information I had received of the Force of the Enemy, to put the Robust, Thunderer and Standard into my Line of Battle; but their Distance from my Squadron, and under the Circumstance of little Wind, they could not join me till after the Action was over.

I shall proceed upon my Station as soon as I have ordered a Distribution of the Prisoners, and made other necessary Arrangements for the Squadron. It is my Intention to keep at Sea, in order to fulfil every Part of my Instructions.

I have judged it necessary to send Captain Domett with my Dispatches, who will give their Lordships such farther Particulars as shall have occurred to him on the Victory we have gained.

       I am, &c.
       BRIDPORT.

18

Battle Of Hiéres Islands

Admiralty Office, August 7, 1795.

Extract of a Letter from Admiral Hotham, Commander in Chief of His Majesty's Ships in the Mediterranean, to Mr. Nepean, dated Britannia, at Sea, July 14, 1795.

SIR,

YOU will be pleased to inform their Lordships that I dispatched on the 4th Instant, from St. Fiorenzo, the Ships named in the Margin*, under the Orders of Captain Nelson, whom I directed to call off Genoa for the Inconstant and Southampton Frigates that were laying there, and to take them with him, if, from the Intelligence he might there obtain, he should find it necessary.

On the Morning of the 7th I was much surprised to learn that the above Squadron was seen in the Offing, returning into Port, pursued by the Enemy's Fleet, which, by General De Vins's Letter, (the latest Account I had received) I, had Reason to suppose were certainly at Toulon.

Immediately on the Enemy's Appearance, I made every Preparation to put to Sea after them; and notwithstanding the unpleasant Predicament we were in, most of the Ships being in the Midst of watering and refitting, I was yet enabled, by the Zeal and extraordinary Exertions of the Officers and Men, to get the whole of the Fleet under Weigh that Night, as soon as the Land Wind permitted us to, move from which Time we neither saw or heard any thing of the Enemy till the 12th, when being, to the Eastward, and within Sight of the Hieres Islands, Two Vessels were spoken with by Captain Hotham of the Cyclops and Captain Boys of La Fleche, who acquainted them they had seen the French Fleet, not many Hours before, to the Southward of those Islands: Upon which Information I made the Signal before Night to prepare for Battle, as an Indication to our Fleet that the Enemy was near.

Yesterday, at Day-Break, we discovered them to Leeward of us, on the Larboard Tack, consisting of Twenty three Sail, Seventeen of which proved to be of the Line: The Wind at this Time blew very hard from the W. N. W. attended with a heavy Swell, and Six of our Ships had to bend Main-Topsails, in the room of those that were split by the Gale, in the Course of the Night.

I caused the Fleet, however, to be formed with all possible Expedition, on the Larboard Line of Bearing, carrying all Sail possible to preserve that Order, and to keep the Wind of the Enemy, in the Hopes of cutting them off from the Land from which we were only Five Leagues distant.

At Eight o'Clock, finding they had no other View but that of endeavouring to get from us, I made the Signal for a general Chace, and for the Ships to take suitable Stations for their mutual Support, and to engage the Enemy as arriving up with them in Succession; but the baffling Winds and vexatious Calms, which render every Naval Operation in this Country doubtful, soon afterwards took Place, and allowed a few only of our Van Ships to get up with the Enemy's Rear about Noon, which they attacked so warmly, that, in the Course of an Hour after, we had the Satisfaction to find one of their Sternmost Ships, viz. L'Alcide, of Seventy-four Guns, had struck; the Rest of their Fleet, favoured by a Shift of Wind to the Eastward, (that, placed them now to Windward of us) had got so far into Frejus Bay, whilst the major Part of our's was becalmed in the Offing, that it became impossible for any thing further to be effected; and those of our Ships which were engaged had approached so near to the Shore that I judged it proper to call them off by Signal.

If the Result of the Day was not so compleatly satisfactory as the Commencement promised, it is my Duty to state, that no Exertions, could be more unanimous than those of the Fleet under my Command; and it would be Injustice to the general Merit of all to select individual Instances of Commendation, had not Superiority of Sailing placed some of the Ships in an advanced Situation, of which they availed themselves in the most distinguished and honourable manner; and amongst the Number was the Victory, having Rear-Admiral Man on Board, who had shifted his Flag to that Ship upon this Occasion.

I am sorry to say that the Alcide, about Half an Hour after she had struck, by some Accident caught Fire in her Fore-Top, before she was taken Possession of, and the Flames spread with such Rapidity that the whole Ship was soon in a Blaze; several Boats from the Fleet were dispatched as quickly as possible to rescue as many of her People as they could save from the Destruction that awaited them, and Three Hundred of them were in consequence preserved, when the Ship blew up with the most awful and tremendous Explosion, and between Three and Four Hundred People are supposed to have perished.

Had we fortunately fallen in with the Enemy any Distance from the Land, I flatter myself we should have given a decisive Blow to their Naval Force in these Seas; and although, the Advantage of Yesterday may not appear to be of any great Moment, I yet hope it will have served as a Check upon their present Operations, be they what they may.

I am, Sir,

Your most obedient Servant,
W. HOTHAM.

*Agamemnon, Meleager, Ariadne, Moselle, Mutin (Cutter).

19

Re-Capture Of St Lucia (Morne Fortune)

Parliament-Street, July 4, 1796.

Dispatches, of which the following are Copies, have been received from Lieutenant-General Sir Ralph Abercromby, K.B., by the Right Honourable Henry Dundas, One of His Majesty's Principal Secretaries of State.

St. Lucia, May 22, 1796.

SIR,

IN my Letter of the 4th of May I had the Honor to acquaint you of the unsuccessful Attack on the Enemy's Batteries on the Side of the Grand Cul de Sac; and as it had been previously determined that the principal Attack on the Enemy's Works should be made on the North Side of Morne Fortune by the Ridge of Duchasseaux, every Exertion was made to complete the Road for erecting the necessary Batteries, and to bring forward the Artillery and Ammunition.

On the 16th Instant the Batteries, consisting of Eighteen Pieces of Ordnance, were opened. These could only be considered in the Light of a First Parallel. The Second Parallel is now nearly complete, and the Lodgment for the last or Third is to be made To-Morrow. If this Operation should be attended with the Effect expected from it, it is probable that we shall, in the Course of Ten or Twelve Days, be in Possession of the Enemy's Works upon Morne Fortune. It is difficult for me to give an adequate Idea of the Ground on which we are obliged to act. The natural Obstructions, as well as every Obstacle that the Enemy could throw in our Way, render the Post of Morne Fortune not only respectable, but in a high Degree difficult to be subdued.

As the Enemy still retained Possession of the Vigie, and as they only held it with a slender Force, it appeared of Consequence to get Possession of it, as it would shorten our Line of Attack, and cover our Right Flank; and also as it gave us in some Degree the Command of the Carenage. For this Purpose on the Night of the 17th Instant, the 31st Regiment, happening to be the Regiment nearest at Hand, was ordered to march immediately after it was dark to take Posession of the Vigie, where the Enemy had not apparently more than from One Hundred and Fifty to Two Hundred Men. The first Part of the Attack succeeded to our Wish; a Battery of Three Eighteen Pounders, which was feebly defended, was seized, the Guns spiked and thrown over the Precipice.

There remained on the Summit of the Hill One large Gun and a Field Piece, which the Regiment was ordered to take Possession of; unfortunately the Guide was wounded, and the Troops became uncertain of the right Approach to the Hill: While in this Situation the Enemy's Grape Shot took Effect to such a Degree, as induced Lieutenant-Colonel Hay to order the Regiment to retreat, which it did with considerable Loss. Lieutenant-Colonel Macdonald handsomely advanced with Part of the Grenadiers to cover the Retreat of the 31st Regiment, which he accomplished. It is proper to observe that a Night Attack on the Vigie was indispensably necessary, as Three Batteries of the Enemy flanked the Neck of Land which connects the Vigie with the Main; and in general in this Country, when you have to march to attack an Enemy's Post, who have Artillery, and where it is impossible for you to advance with any on your Part, it is almost a Matter of Necessity to attack at Night.

Hitherto the Troops continue healthy, notwithstanding their Exertions and Fatigue.

I am, &c.
(Signed) RALPH ABERCROMBY.

Head Quarters, St. Lucia, May 31, 1796.

SIR,

I HAVE the Honor to acknowledge the Receipt of your Letter of the 18th of March. In my Letter of the 22d of May I acquainted you that on the Day following we intended to make a Lodgement as near to the Enemy's Works as possible. This, however, was deferred from Necessity till the 24th.

The 27th, 53d, and 57th Regiments had been previously placed near the Point of Attack. On the Morning of the 24th the 27th Regiment lodged themselves upon Two different Points, the nearest of which was not more than Five Hundred Yards from the Fort. The Enemy made a vigorous Effort to dislodge them, but by the good Conduct and Spirit of Brigadier-General Moore, and the steady and intrepid Behaviour of the Officers and Men of the 27th Regiment, the Enemy were twice repulsed with considerable Loss, and before Night the Troops were compleatly under Cover: At the same Time the Communication to the Posts occupied by the 17th Regiment, was carried on with the utmost Vigour, and Two Batteries for Eight Pieces of Artillery were begun.

Upon the Evening of the 24th, the Enemy desired a Suspension of Arms until Noon the next Day, which was granted till Eight in the Morning: A Capitulation for the whole Island ensued, a Copy of which I have the Honor to enclose. On the 26th the Garrison, to the Amount of Two Thousand Men, marched out and laid down their

Arms, and are become Prisoners of War. Pidgeon Island is in our Possession: The 55th Regiment has been detached to Souffriere and Vieux Fort, to receive the Submission of the Garrisons of those Places. From Souffriere we have been informed that peaceable Possession has been given; from Vieux Fort there is no Report. The principal Object of the Blockade of Morne Fortune has been obtained. The Enemy has been prevented from escaping into the Woods; their Troops, whom they call Regulars, have been made Prisoners of War, and the armed Negroes have been in a considerable Degree disarmed.

Our Operations have been attended with considerable Labour and Fatigue, Roads were every where to be made through a mountainous and rugged Country, Artillery and Ammunition to be carried forward, and the Line of Investment, extending about Ten Miles, to be supplied with Provisions, without the Assistance of Carriages, and with few Horses.

It is but Justice to the Troops to say that their Conduct has been meritorious; that they have undergone an uncommon Share of Fatigue with Chearfulness, and in several Instances have given Proofs of the greatest Intrepidity. We are under great Obligations to Brigadier-General Knox for planning and executing the Road of Communication from Choc Bay, by Chabot, to Morne Duchasseaux. Brigadier-General Lloyd, of the Royal Artillery, and Captain Hay, the Chief Engineer, may justly claim their Share of Praise. Brigadier-General Hope has on all Occasions most willingly come forward and exerted himself in Times of Danger, to which he was not called from his Situation of Adjutant-General.

Rear-Admiral Sir Hugh Christian and the Royal Navy have never ceased to shew the utmost Alacrity in forwarding the Public Service. To their Skill and unremitting Labour the Success which has attended His Majesty's Arms is in a great Measure due. By their Efforts alone the Artillery was advanced to the Batteries, and every Co-operation, which could possibly be expected or desired, has been afforded in the fullest Manner. I have the Honor to enclose the Return of Killed and Wounded during our Operations in this Island, together with a Return of the Artillery, Stores and Ammunition, as far as we have been enabled to collect. This will be delivered to you by Major Forbes, my Aid de Camp, whom I beg Leave to recommend to your Protection.

I have the Honor to be, &c.
(Signed) RALPH ABERCROMBY.

20 & 21

The Capture Of St Vincent And Grenada

Parliament-Street, July 25, 1796.

DISPATCHES, of which the following are Copies, were this Day received by the Right Honourable Henry Dundas, one of His Majesty's principal Secretaries of State, from Lieutenant-General Sir Ralph Abcrcromby, K.B. Commander in Chief of His Majesty's Troops in the West Indies.

St. Vincent, June 21, 1796.

SIR,

THE last Letter which I had the Honor to write to you was on the 31st of May, from St. Lucia, wherein I acquainted you with the Reduction of that Island. Brigadier-General Moore informs me, in a Letter of the 12th of June, that every Thing remained quiet, and I have every Reason to hope that the Measures he has adopted will tend to insure Tranquillity, as far as it depends upon him.

 The Embarkation of the Artillery and Troops destined to act in St. Vincent and Grenada necessarily employed some Days, and at that Moment the Weather proved particularly unfavourable. The Whole, however, was embarked and ready to sail on the 3d of June, The St. Vincent Division was ordered to rendezvous at Kingston Bay, and that for Grenada at Cariacou, one of the Grenadines. While the Troops were assembling at the Rendezvous, Major-General Nicolls met me at Cariacou, where the Operations for Grenada were settled. On the 7th Instant, I returned to St. Vincent, and on the 8th in the Evening the Troops disembarked.

 The following Day they marched in One Column, by the Right, as far as Stubbs, about Eight Miles from Kingston; each Division Halted that Evening opposite to their respective Point of Attack. On the 10th in the Morning the Enemy's Flank was turned, Two Twelve Pounders, Two Six Pounders, and Two Howitzers, were advanced, with considerable Difficulty, within Six Hundred Yards of the Enemy's Works; but, notwithstanding our Efforts to drive the Enemy from their Post, on the Old Vigie, by

Means of a well-served Artillery, they maintained themselves from Seven in the morning until Two in the Afternoon. Major-General Morshead had very handsomely, early in the Day, offered to carry the Redoubt by Assault, but being willing to spare the Lives of the Troops, and observing that the Part of the Line which he commanded laboured under Disadvantage, the Assault was deferred until the Decline of the Day rendered it absolutely necessary.

From Major General Hunter's Division on the Right a Part of Lewenstein's Corps, and Two Companies of the 42d Regiment, with some Island Rangers, availed themselves of the Profile of the Hill, and lodged themselves within a very short Distance of the Fort. At Two o'Clock the Two remaining Companies of the 42d Regiment, from Major-General Hunter's Column, and the Buffs, supported by the York Rangers from Major-General Morshead's, were ordered to advance to the Attack. The Enemy, unable to withstand their Ardour, retired from their first, second, and third Redoubts, but rallied round the New Vigie, their principal Post. They were now fully in our Power, as Brigadier-General Knox had cut off their Communication with the Charib Country, and Lieutenant-Colonel Dickens, of the 34th Regiment, who had been previously ordered to make a Diversion with the Remains of his own and the 2d West India Regiments upon their Right, where the Charibs were posted, had succeeded beyond Expectation, having forced the Charibs to retire, and taken their Post. The Enemy, therefore, in the New Vigie, desired to capitulate, which was granted upon the Conditions herewith inclosed.

The Number of Prisoner about 700. At the first of the Attack, the Charibs, and, towards the Close of it, near 200 of the Insurgents of the Island, made their Escape into the Woods.

Lieutenant-Colonel Spencer, with 600 Men, was immediately detached to Mount Young, and Lieutenant-Colonel Gower, with 300 Men, embarked to go by Sea to Owia; but being unable to land, on Account of the Surf, he has returned, the Troops have been disembarked, and he has marched through the Charib Country.

I feel myself under great Obligations to Major-General Hunter, and to the Gentlemen of the Island, for the local Information which they gave me, and for the Zeal and Intelligence which they shewed in conducting the Columns. I have to thank Major-General Morshead for his Exertions; and I am highly satisfied with the spirited Behaviour of the Officers and Soldiers. The Corps of Island Rangers, Commanded by Lieutenant-Colonel Hassey and Major Jackson, rendered essential Service. Captain Douglas, of the Royal Engineers, was among the Wounded, and is since dead. He is a real Loss to the Service in this Country, as he was indefatigable in the Discharge of his Duty, and had acquired minute Knowledge of this Island.

Captain Woolley, of His Majesty's Ship the Arethusa, was intrusted by Rear-Admiral Sir Hugh Christian with the Command of the Navy acting with us in the Expeditions against St. Vincent and Grenada, in which I can say, with the greatest Truth, he has conducted himself with very great Judgment and Good-Will.

I have the Honor to be, &c.
R.A. ABERCROMBY

St. Vincent June 22, 1796.

SIR,

I Had the Honor to inform you, that in Concert with Major-General Nicolls at Cariacou, the Arrangement for the Attack of Grenada was settled.

The Troops were in consequence disembarked at Palmiste, near Goyave, where the Enemy had their principal Post, while Brigadier-General Campbell advanced from the Windward Side of the Island to attack the Enemy's Rear. Major-General Nicolls, in his Letter of the 11th of June, reports to me that the Commandant of the French Troops at Goyave had surrendered himself, with Part of the Force under his Command, and that the Remainder, under Fedon, had retired to their strong Hold in the high Mountains above Goyave. He likewise informs me that several of the most guilty of the old French Inhabitants had surrendered themselves. In this Part of our Operations we have to regret the Loss of Major De Ruvynes, of the Royal Artillery, who was killed immediately after the Disembarkation of the Troops at Goyave. The fortunate Issue of the Business at St. Vincent's permitted me to visit Grenada, where I found Fedon invested: His Force is supposed not to exceed 300 Men, without any regular Supply of Provisions, but in a Situation very difficult of Access. Major-General Nicolls was directed to straiten him as much as possible, and not to grant him any Terms short of unconditional Submission. The Atrocity of his Character, and the Crimes of which he has been guilty, render it impossible to treat with him upon any other Terms.

Before I left Grenada there appeared a general Disposition in the Revolted to submit; and to throw themselves upon the Mercy of the British Government.

I cannot forbear mentioning that Brigadier General Hope, with his usual Zeal, offered his Services in the Operations at Grenada, and very much contributed to the Success which followed. I have hitherto received no Return of the Killed and Wounded, but I am happy to say that the Number is inconsiderable.

Captain Scott, of His Majesty's Ship Hebe, conducted the Disembarkation, and gave general Satisfaction.

This Letter will be delivered to you by Captain Hay, of the Royal Engineers, who came out with the Expedition as a Volunteer; he has acted as my Aide de Camp, and as Chief Engineer at the Attack of St. Lucia.

I have the Honor to be, &c.
R.A. ABERCROMBY

St. Vincents, June 23, 1796.

SIR,

SINCE I had the Honor to write to you Yesterday, I have received the following Inclosures from Major-General Nicolls at Grenada, which contains an additional

Proof of the good Conduct and Spirit of the Officers and Men of His Majesty's Troops employed on this Service. We may now flatter ourselves that the Insurrection in the Island of Grenada is nearly, if not altogether, quelled.

I have the Honor to be, &c.
R.A. ABERCROMBY Lt. Gen.

Copy of a Letter from Major-General Nicolls to Lieutenant-General Sir Ralph Abercromby, dated Gouyave, 21 June, 1796.

SIR,

YOUR Excellency knew that the Weather being favourable the Morning of the 18th, Brigadier-General Campbell's Brigade, and the Brigade commanded by Colonel Count D'Heillimer, had marched from their Position on Mount St. John's and Chadeans; the former to force a Post the Enemy had established at Michells, and afterwards to proceed against their Camp at Aches; while the Count's Brigade were to try to get above the Enemy, and at the Back of their Redoubts on Morne Quaquo. Lieutenant-Colonel Gledslanes, who was posted with the 57th Regiment at the Head of Grand Roy Valley, (which is on the opposite Side of Morne Quaquo to that on which Count D'Heilliner was to attack) was desired to send a strong Detachment on the Back of the Mountain, and, if he found the Enemy's Redoubts assailable, instantly to attack them, but, if too strong to be entered without further Preparation, to take Post as near them as possible, and there wait further Instructions. Such was the general Disposition made for the Attack of their Two strong Positions on Morne Quaquo and Foret Noir, (commonly called Aches Camp) while a small Detachment of Three Companies of the Colonial Black Corps, and the Grenadiers of the 38th Regiment, went against a Post the Enemy had at the Head of Beau Sejour Valley.

The Troops were successful every where, and nearly at the same Hour on the Morning of the 19th, we were in full Possession of every established Post we heard the Enemy had in this Island. We were divided in Search of the Monsters in every Direction; I can call them by no other Name, as, when they saw our Men on the Point of forcing what they thought their impregnable Posts on Morne Quaquo, they led out a Number of White People they had Prisoners, shipped them, tied their Hands behind their Backs, end then murdered them. Above Twenty were put to Death in this barbarous Manner.

The Conduct of Brigadier-General Campbell and Count D'Heillimer has been Officer-like and meritorious, and, as such, I take the Liberty of mentioning them to your Excellency; indeed Count D'Heillimer's Disposition for the Attack was so judiciously made, and so well executed by Lewenstein's Yagers in particular, and the Royal Etrangers, who got up to the Top of the Mountain in the Night, that when the Enemy saw them, soon after Day-light, in Possession of their upper small Post at the Vigie, their Resistance was afterwards feeble, and as our Troops advanced they abandoned their Works, and fled into the Woods, where the Yagers soon followed them. I cannot speak with any Certainty of the Enemy's Loss on the 19th, but Yesterday Count D'Heillimer informed me his different Parties in the Woods killed 109 Brigands.

The French Inhabitants who, through Fear or Compulsion, as some of them say, or through Inclination, as is generally believed here, had joined the Insurgents, have come in, and given themselves up to me. I have sent them all to the Lieutenant-Governor's, to be tried by the Civil power.

If we have a few Days of dry Weather, we hope to clear the Country so far as to enable me to put the Troops in comfortable Quarters, agreeably to your Excellency's Orders.

We have taken, in their different Posts, since the 9th Instant, above Twenty Pieces of Cannon, many of them so bad that, though they used them, our Artillery Men would not think it safe to do so.

The Ammunition we found in their Batteries was chiefly Calculated for close Attack, being Grape and Cannister, made of Pieces of cut Iron; they had but a few Round Shot.

Captain Rutherford, of the Engineers, wishes to go to St. Vincent, and returns by the Vessel that carries this. And I send my Major of Brigade, Captain Drew, who is an intelligent Officer, and is perfectly acquainted with every Thing that has been done here, and able to answer any Questions your Excellency may wish to ask and where I have not been particular or explicit enough.

I have the Honor to be, &c.
OL. NICOLLS,
Maj. Gen.

22

The Battle Of Cape St Vincent

Admiralty-Office, March 3, 1797.

ROBERT CALDER, Esq; First Captain to Admiral Sir John Jervis, K.B. arrived this Morning with Dispatches from him to Mr. Nepean, of which the following are Copies.

HMS Victory, in Lagos Bay February 16th 1797.

SIR,

The Hopes of falling in with the Spanish Fleet, expressed in my Letter to you of the 13th Instant, were confirmed, that Night, by our distinctly hearing, the Report of their Signal Guns, and by Intelligence received from Captain Foote, of His Majesty's Ship the Niger, who had, with equal Judgment and Perseverance, kept Company with them for several Days, on my prescribed Rendezvous, (which, from the strong South-East Winds, I had never been able to reach) and that they were not more than the Distance of Three or Four Leagues from us. I anxiously awaited the Dawn of Day, when, being on the Starboard Tack, Cape St. Vincent bearing East by North Eight Leagues, I had the Satisfaction of seeing a Number of Ships extending from South-West to South, the Wind then at West and by South. At Forty-nine Minutes past Ten, the Weather being extremely hazy; La Bonne Citoyenne made the Signal that the Ships seen were of the Line, Twenty-five in Number. His Majesty's Squadron under my Command, consisting of the Fifteen Ships of the Line named in the Margin* happily formed In the most compact Order of Sailing; in Two Lines. By carrying a Press of Sail I was fortunate in getting in with the Enemy's Fleet at Half past Eleven o'Clock, before it had Time to connect, and form a regular Order of Battle. Such a Moment was not to be lost; and, Confident in the Skill, Valour and Discipline of the Officers and Men, I had the Happiness to command, and, judging that the Honor of His Majesty's Arms and the Circumstances of the War in these Seas required a considerable Degree of Enterprize, I felt myself justified in departing front the regular System of passing through their Fleet, in a Line formed with the utmost Celerity, tacked, and thereby separated one third from the main Body, after a partial Connonade, which prevented their Rejunction till the Evening; and by the very great Exertions of the Ships which

Had the good Fortune to arrive up with the Enemy on the Larboard Tack, the Ships named in the Margin were captured** and the action ceased about Five o'Clock in the Evening.

I enclose the most complete list I have been able to obtain of the Spanish Fleet opposed to me amounting to Twenty-seven Sail of the Line, and an Account of the Killed and Wounded in His Majesty's Ships, as well as in those taken from the Enemy. The Moment the latter (almost totally dismasted) and His Majesty's Ships the Captain and Culloden are in a State to put to Sea I shall avail myself of the first favourable Wind to proceed off Cape St. Vincent on my Way to Lisbon.

Captain Calder, whose able Assistance has greatly contributed to the Publick Service during my Command, is the Bearer, of this, and will more particularly describe to the Lords Commissioners of the Admiralty the Movements of the Squadron on the 14th, and the present State of it.

I am, Sir, &c.
J. JERVIS.

* *Victory, Britannia, Barfleur, Prince Orange, Blenheim, Captain, Goliath, Namur, Excellent, Orion, Colossus, Egmont, Culloden, Irresistible, Diadem*

***Salvador del Mundo, San Josef, San Nicolas, San Pablo.*

*List of the Spanish Fleet opposed to the British,
the 14th of February, 1797.*

	Guns.
Santissima Trinidad	130 .
Mexicana	112
Principe de Asturias	112
Concepcion	112
Conde de Regla	112
Salvador del Mundo	112 taken
San Josef	112 taken
San Nicolas	84 taken
Oriente	74
Glorioso	74
Atlante	74
Conquestador	74
Soberano	74
Fiane	74
Pelayo	74
San Genaro	74
San Ildephonso	74
San Juan Nepomuceno	74
San Francisco de Paula	74
San Isidro	74 taken
San Antonio	74
San Pablo	74
San Firmin	74
Neptuna	74
Bahama	74
Name unknown	74
Name unknown	74

J. JERVIS.

23

The Capture Of Trinidad

Parliament-Street,
March 27, 1797.

EARLY this Morning; Captain Drew, of the 45th Regiment, arrived from the Island of Trinidad, with a Dispatch from Lieutenant-General Sir R. Abercromby, K.B. to the Right Honourable Henry Dundas, of which the following is a Copy.

Head Quarters, Trinidad,
February 27, 1797.

SIR,

ON my Arrival in this Country, I did not fail to lay before the Admiral my Instructions, and to consult with him upon the Means to carry them into Execution. I found in him every Desire to cooperate in the Execution of the Views to which they are directed. The Arrival of Part of the Convoy from England enabled us to proceed with Confidence in our Operations; therefore, as soon as the Troops could be collected from the different Islands, which were ordered to rendezvous at Cariacou, the Admiral sailed from Martinique, which Island he left with his Squadron on the 12th Instant.

The Precision with which the Admiral had given his Orders to assemble the Ships of War and Transports, left us not a Moment of Delay. On the 15th, in the Morning, the Fleet sailed from Cariacou.

On the 16th, in the Afternoon, it passed through the Bocas, or Entrance into the Gulph of Paria, where we found the Spanish Admiral with Four Sail of the Line and a Frigate, at Anchor under Cover of the Island of Gaspargrande, which was fortified.

Our Squadron worked up, and came to Anchor opposite to, and nearly, within Gunshot of the Spanish Ships, The Frigates and Transports were ordered to anchor higher up in the Bay, and at the Distance nearly of Five Miles from the Town of Port D'Espagne. The Disposition was immediately made for Landing at Day-light next Morning, and for a general Attack upon the Town and Ships of War.

At Two o'Clock in the Morning of the 17th we perceived the Spanish Squadron to be on Fire; the Ships burnt with great Fury, One Line of Battle Ship excepted, which escaped the Conflagration, and was taken Possession of at Day-Light in the Morning, by the Boats from our Fleet; the Enemy at the same Time evacuated the Island, and abandoned that Quarter.

This unexpected Turn of Affairs directed our whole Attention to the Attack of the Town. The Troops were immediately ordered to land, and, as soon as a few Hundred Men could be got on Shore, about Four Miles to the Westward of it, we advanced, meeting with little or no Resistance. Before Night we were Masters of Port D'Espagne and the Neighbourhood, Two small Forts excepted. In the Morning a Capitulation was entered into with the Governor Don Chacon, and in the Evening all the Spanish Troops laid down their Arms, and the whole Colony passed under the Dominion of His Britannick Majesty.

It is a peculiar Satisfaction to me that there is no List of Killed or Wounded; Lieutenant Villeneuve, of the 8th Regiment of Foot, who was Brigade Major to Brigadier-General Hompesch, being the only Person who was wounded, and he is since dead of his Wounds.

From the Admiral I have experienced every possible Co-operation. Captain Woolley, of His Majesty's Ship the Arethusa, and Captain Wood, of the Favorite Sloop of War, who had been sent to reconnoitre in the Gulph of Paria, afforded us minute Information of the Situation of the Enemy previous to our Arrival. Captain Woolley, who directed the Disembarkation, shewed all the Zeal and Intelligence which I have experienced from him on former Occasions.

To Lord Craven, who begged to attend the Expedition, I am indebted for great Zeal and Exertion.

Lieutenant-Colonel Soter, who is intimately acquainted with this Country, has been, and continues to be, of very great Use to me. I should not do Justice, to his general Character, if I did not take this Opportunity to express it. My Aide-de-Camp, Captain Drew, of the 45th Regiment, will have the Honor to deliver this Letter: He has served long in this Country, and is capable to give such further Information as may be required. I humbly beg Leave to recommend him to His Majesty's Favor.

I have the Honor to be, etc.
R.A. ABERCROMBY, K.B.

Off Port D'Espagne, in the Gulph of Paria,
February 21, 1797.

SIR,

I Have the Honor to acquaint you, for the Information of their Lordships, that it having been determined an Attack should be made on the Island Trinidad, both with a View to that Colony, and to the Spanish Squadron which had been there for some Time past, the Troops intended for this Expedition from Martinique were accordingly embarked in the Ships of War and Transports, and I sailed from Fort Royal Bay the 12th Instant, with the Ships and Vessels of His Majesty's Squadron under my Command, as per Margin*. Lieutenant-General Sir Ralph Abercromby embarked with me in the Prince of Wales.

The Invincible had previously sailed for Barbadoes, with Two Transports, to embark a Part of the 14th Regiment, and the Thorn and Zebra were ordered to receive the Detachment from Tobago.

The Favorite was sent to St. Vincent to collect some Troops from that Island, and the Whole were ordered to rendezvous at the Island of Cariacou, One of the Grenadines, on or before the 13th; and, on my Arrival at that Island, the 14th, I found all the Ships and Transports were assembled.

On the 15th, in the Morning, I sailed with the Squadron and Transports, passing between Cariacou and Grenada; and on the 16th arrived off Trinidad, and stood toward the Gulph of Paria, when, having passed through the Great Bocas Channel, at Half past Three in the Afternoon, the Spanish Squadron were discovered at Anchor in Shagaramus Bay, consisting of Four Sail of the Line, under the Flag of a Rear Admiral, and One Frigate.

As the Day was well advanced before I approached the Bay, and the Enemy appeared in Strength on Gasparaux Island, which commanded the Anchorage, by Batteries erected for that Purpose, I ordered the Arethusa, Thorn, and Zebra, to proceed a little farther up the Gulph, and anchor with all the Transports. The Alarm, Favorite, and Victorieuse were ordered to keep under Sail above the Transports during the Night, and prevent any Vessels sailing from Port Espagne.

In the Evening, just before Dark, I anchored with the Ships of the Line in Order of Battle, opposite the Enemy's Squadron, within Random-Shot of their Ships and Batteries, and in constant Readiness to prevent their Escape during the Night, which I suspected they might attempt, as all their Sails were bent, and they appeared perfectly ready for sailing.

At Two o'Clock in the Morning of the 17th we discovered One of their Ships on Fire, and soon after Three others, all of which burnt with great Fury until near Daylight, when they were entirely consumed.

One of them having escaped the Conflagration, the Boats were sent from the Squadron, and she was brought out without having received any Damage.

I have great Satisfaction in acquainting their Lordships, that this Squadron of the Enemy, commanded by Rear-Admiral Don Sebastian Ruiz de Apodaca, were destroyed or captured according to the List I herewith enclose; and although this Service was effected without any other Act, on the Part of His Majesty's Squadron under my Command, than being placed in such a Situation as to prevent their Escape, I am fully convinced that, had they remained at their Anchorage until the next Day, the Officers and Men whom I have the Honor to command would have completed, by their Exertion and Zeal, the Capture of the Whole, notwithstanding the Advantage of their Situation, under the Cover of about Twenty Pieces of Cannon and Three Mortars, which were mounted on Gasparaux Island, and had been placed there for the sole Purpose of defending the Ships in the Bay: That Island, which, like the Ships, had been abandoned during the Night, was taken Possession of soon after Day-light by a Party of the Queen's Regiment.

General Abercromby, early in the Morning, joined the Arethusa, and the Troops were all landed, in the Course of the Day, under the Direction of Captain Wolley, covered by the Favorite Sloop, about Three Miles from the Town, without Opposition: The General took Possession of the Town the same Evening, and the 18th the Governor desired to capitulate for the whole Island, and the Articles were agreed to, and signed the same Day.

Captain Harvey, of His Majesty's Ship Prince of Wales, will have the Honor to deliver this Dispatch, from whom I have always experienced the greatest Zeal and Attention to His Majesty's Service.

I have the Honor to be,

SIR,
Your most obedient humble Servant,
HENRY HARVEY.

* Prince of Wales, Bellona, Vengeance, Scipio, Favorite, Zephyr, Terror Bomb.

24

Battle Of Fishguard

Whitehall, February 27, 1797.

A LETTER, of which the following is a Copy, has been this Day received from the Right Honourable Lord Cawdor by His Grace the Duke of Portland, His Majesty's Principal Secretary of State for the Home Department.

Fishguard, Friday, February 24, 1797.

MY LORD,

IN consequence of having received Information, on Wednesday Night at Eleven o'Clock, that Three large Ships of War and a Lugger had anchored in a small Roadsted, upon the Coast in the Neighbourhood of this Town, I proceeded immediately, with a Detachment of the Cardigan Militia and all the Provincial Force I could collect, to the Place. I soon gained positive Intelligence they had disembarked about 1200 Men, but no Cannon. Upon the Night's setting in, a French Officer, whom I found to be the Second in Command, came in with a Letter, a Copy of which I have the Honor to inclose to your Grace, together with my Answer: In consequence of which they determined to surrender themselves Prisoners of War, and accordingly laid down their Arms this Day at Two o'Clock.

I cannot at this Moment inform your Grace of the exact Number of Prisoners, but I believe it to be their whole Force: It is my Intention to march them this Night to Haverfordwest, where I shall make the best Distribution in my Power. The Frigates, Corvette, and Lugger, got under Weigh Yesterday Evening, and were this Morning entirely out of Sight.

The Fatigue we have experienced will, I trust, excuse me to your Grace for not giving a more particular Detail; but my Anxiety to do Justice to the Officers and Men I had the Honor to command, will induce me to attend your Grace with as little Delay as possible to state their Merits, and at the same Time to give you every Information in my Power upon this Subject.

The Spirit of Loyalty which has pervaded all Ranks throughout this Country is infinitely beyond what I can express.

I am, &c. CAWDOR.

Cardigan Bay, 5th of Ventose,
5th Year of the Republic.

SIR,

THE Circumstances under which the Body of the French Troops under my Command were landed at this Place renders it unnecessary to attempt any Military Operations, as they would tend only to Bloodshed and Pillage. The Officers of the whole Corps have therefore intimated their Desire of entering into a Negotiation, upon Principles of Humanity, for a Surrender. If you are influenced by similar Considerations you may signify the same by the Bearer, and in the mean Time Hostilities shall cease.

Salut and Respect,
TATE,
Chef de Brigade.

Fishguard,
February 23, 1797

SIR,

THE Superiority of the Force under my Command, which is hourly increasing, must prevent my treating upon any Terms short of your surrendering your whole Force Prisoners of War.

I enter fully into your Wish of preventing an unnecessary Effusion of Blood, which your speedy Surrender can alone prevent, and which will entitle you to that Consideration it is ever the Wish of British Troops to shew an Enemy, whose Numbers are inferior.

My Major will deliver you this Letter, and I shall expect your Determination by Ten o'Clock, by your Officer, whom I have furnished with an Escort, that will conduct him to me without Molestation.

I am, &c.
CAWDOR.

25

Battle Of San Juan (Puerto Rico)

Parliament-Street, June 6, 1796.

A DISPATCH, of which the following is a Copy, has been received by the Right Honourable Henry Dundas, one of His Majesty's Principal Secretaries of State, from Sir Ralph Abercromby, K.B. Commander in Chief of His Majesty's Forces in the West Indies.

His Majesty's Ship Prince of Wales, off Porto Rico, May 2, 1797

SIR,

AFTER the Reduction of Trinidad, the Force destined for the Expediton against Porto Rico being assembled, on the 8th of April the Fleet sailed from Martinico and arrived at St. Kitt's on the 10th, where we waited the Arrival of Captain Woolley of His Majesty's Ship Arethusa who had been sent to Tortola and St. Thomas to procure Pilots and Guides. This occasioned the Delay of a few Days.

On Monday the 17th we made the Island of Porto Rico, and came to an Anchor off Congrejos Point. The Whole of the North Side of this Island is bounded by a Reef, and it was with much Difficulty that a narrow Channel was discovered, about Three Leagues to the Eastward of the Town, through which His Majesty's Sloops the Beaver and Fury, with the lighter Vessels, passed into a small Bay, in which the Troops, on the next Morning, were disembarked with little Opposition from about a Hundred of the Enemy, who were concealed in the Bushes at the Landing Place. In the Afternoon of the same Day the Troops advanced, and took a Position very favourable for our Numbers, with our Right to the Sea, and the Left to a Lagoon, which extends far into the Country. The Artillery was brought up without Loss of Time, and every Preparation made to force a Passage into the Island on which the Town of Porto Rico is situated. It is necessary here to observe, that as the Moro Castle completely commands the Passage into the Harbour, the Enemy kept open their Communication

A Young Captain John Jervis, later Admiral of the Fleet John Jervis, 1st Earl of St Vincent, 1735-1823, by Francis Cotes.

Lord Howe's action, or the Glorious First of June, by Philippe-Jacques de Loutherbourg.

Vice Admiral Horatio Lord Nelson, by Lemuel Francis Abbott.

The Battle of Camperdown, 11 October 1797, by Thomas Whitcombe.

Sir Ralph Abercromby, 1734-1801, by John Hoppner.

Admiral Sir Robert Calder's action off Cape Finisterre, 23 July 1805, by William Anderson.

Above: Major General Wellesley (mounted) commanding his troops at the Battle of Assaye, by J.C. Stadler after W. Heath.

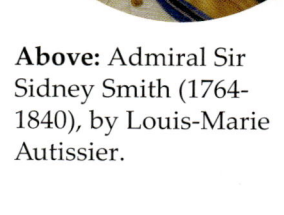

Above: Admiral Sir Sidney Smith (1764-1840), by Louis-Marie Autissier.

Right: The Destruction of L'Orient at the Battle of the Nile, by George Arnald.

Frederick, Duke of York (1763-1827), by Sir Thomas Lawrence.

Admiral of the Fleet Howe (1726-1799), 1st Earl Howe, by John Singleton Copley.

Action off San Domingo, 6 February 1806, by Nicholas Pocock.

Adam Duncan, 1st Viscount Duncan (1731-1804), by John Hoppner.

Charles Cornwallis, First Marquis of Cornwallis (1738 - 1805), by John Singleton Copley.

The "Last Effort and Fall of Tippoo Sultaun", by Henry Singleton.

Battle of Cape St. Vincent (1797), by Robert Cleverley.

The Battle of Copenhagen, 2 April 1801, by Nicholas Pocock.

The Battle of Trafalgar, as seen from the mizen starboard shrouds of HMS *Victory*, by J.M.W. Turner.

with the Southern and Western Part of the Island, and even teazed and harrassed our Left Flank with their numerous Gun-Boats. The only Point, therefore, on which we could attack the Town was on the Eastern Side, where it is defended by the Castle and Lines of St. Christopher, to approach which it was necessary to force our Way over the Lagoon, which forms this Side of the Island. This Passage was strongly defended by Two Redoubts and Gun-Boats, and the Enemy had destroyed the Bridge which connects in the narrowest Channel the Island with the Main Land.

After every Effort on our Part, we never could sufficiently silence the Fire of the Enemy, (who had likewise entrenched themselves in the Rear of these Redoubts) to hazard forcing the Passage into the Island with so small a Force; and this indeed would have been in vain, as the Enemy could support a Fire ten Times more powerful than we could have brought against them. The only Thing left was to endeavour to bombard the Town from a Point to the Southward of it, near to a large Magazine abandoned by the Enemy. This was tried for several Days without any great Effect on Account of the Distance.

It appearing, therefore, that no Act of Vigour on our Part, nor that any combined Operation between the Sea and Land Service, could in any Manner avail, I determined to withdraw, and to re-embark the Troops, which, was done on the Night of the 30th of April, with the greatest Order and Regularity.

All our Artillery and Stores were brought off, except Seven Iron Guns, Four Iron Mortars, and Two Brass Howitzers, which were rendered unserviceable, it being impossible to remove them. Not a sick or wounded Soldier was left behind, and nothing of any Value fell into the Hands of the Enemy.

During the Whole of our Operations, I have experienced from Admiral Harvey the most cordial Co-operation, and every Act of personal Kindness. At my Request he landed Three Hundred Seamen, under Captains Toddy and Browne, of the Royal Navy to whose Exertions while on Shore we are under the greatest Obligations. From the Arrangements of the Admiral, the Landing and Re-embarkation of the Troops were conducted in the best Order. To Captain Renou, of the Royal Navy, principal Agent of the Transports, I desire to express the Sense I have of his good Conduct upon all Occasions.

I beg Leave to assure you, that the Behaviour of the Troops has been meritorious; they were patient under Labour, regular and orderly in their Conduct, and spirited when an Opportunity to shew it occurred.

All the Departments of the Army exerted themselves to my Satisfaction.

I have the Honor to be, &c.
R.A. ABERCROMBY.

P.S. I have omitted to say, that Four Spanish Brass Field Pieces fell into our Hands, which were brought off.

26

Battle Of Santa Cruz De Tenerife

Admiralty-Office, September 2, 1797.

CAPTAIN Waller, of His Majesty's Ship Emerald, arrived here Yesterday with Dispatches from Admiral Lord St. Vincent to Evan Nepean, Esq; Secretary of the Admiralty, of which the following are Extracts.

Ville de Paris, off Cadiz, August 16, 1797.

SIR,

I Desire you will acquaint the Lords Commissioners of the Admiralty that I detached Rear-Admiral Nelson, and the Squadron named in the Margin* with Orders to make an Attempt upon the Town of Santa Cruz in the Island of Teneriffe, which, from a Variety of Intelligence, I conceived was vulnerable.

On Saturday the 15th of July the Rear-Admiral parted Company, and on Tuesday the 18th the Leander having joined from Lisbon, I sent her after the Rear-Admiral, under Instructions left by him.

The Emerald joined Yesterday, with the inclosed Dispatch and Reports from the Rear-Admiral; and although the Enterprize has not succeeded, His Majesty's Arms have acquired a very great Degree of Lustre: Nothing from my Pen can add to the Eloge the Rear-Admiral gives of the Gallantry of the Officers and Men employed under him. I have greatly to lament the heavy Loss the Country has sustained in the severe Wound of Rear-Admiral Nelson, and the Death of Captain Richard Bowen, Lieutenant Gibson, and the other brave Officers and Men who fell in this vigorous and persevering Assault.

The Moment the Rear-Admiral joins, it is my Intention to send the Seahorse to England with him, the Wound Captain Fremantle has received in his Arm also requiring Change of Climate; and I hope that both of them will live to render important Services to their King and Country.

I am, Sir,
Your most obedient humble Servant,

ST. VINCENT.

Theseus, Culloden, Zealous, Seahorse, Emerald, Terpsichore, Fox (1st) Cutter.

Theseus, off Santa Cruz, July 27, 1797.

SIR.

IN Obedience to your Orders to make a vigorous Attack on the Town of Santa Cruz in the Island of Teneriffe, I directed, from the Ships under my Command, One Thousand Men, including Marines, to be prepared for Landing, under the Direction of Captain Troubridge of His Majesty's Ship Culloden, and Captains Hood, Thompson, Fremantle, Bowen, Miller and Waller, who very handsomely voluntiered their Services; and although I am under the painful Necessity of acquainting you that we have not been able to succeed in our Attack, yet it is my Duty to state, that I believe more daring Intrepidity never was shewn than by the Captains, Officers and Men you did me the Honour to place under my Command.

I have the Honour to be, &c.
HORATIO NELSON.

27

The Battle Of Camperdown

Admiralty-Office, October 16, 1797.

CAPTAIN Fairfax, of the Venerable, arrived early this Morning with Dispatches from Adam Duncan, Esq; Admiral of the Blue, Commander in Chief of His Majesty's Ships, &c. employed in the North Sea, to Evan Nepean, Esq; Secretary of the Admiralty, of which the following are Copies.

Venerable, at Sea, 13th October, 1797 off the Coast of Holland.

SIR,

BE pleased to acquaint the Lords Commissioners of the Admiralty, that, judging it of Consequence their Lordships should have as early Information as possible of the Defeat of the Dutch Fleet under the Command of Admiral De Winter, I dispatched the Rose Cutter at Three P. M. on the 12th (11th) Instant, with a short Letter to you immediately after the Action was ended. I have now farther to acquaint you, for their Lordships' Information, that in the Night of the 10th Instant, after I had sent away my Letter to you, of that Date, I placed my Squadron in such Situation as to prevent the Enemy from returning to the Texel without my falling in with them. At Nine o'Clock in the Morning of the 11th I got Sight of Captain Trollope's Squadron, with Signals flying for an Enemy to Leeward; I immediately bore up, and made the Signal for a general Chase, and soon got Sight of them, forming in a Line on the Larboard Tack to receive us, the Wind at N. W. As we approached near I made the Signal for the Squadron to shorten Sail, in order to connect them; soon after I saw the Land between Camperdown and Egmont, about Nine Miles to Leeward of the Enemy, and finding there was no Time to be lost in making the Attack, I made the Signal to bear up, break the Enemy's Line, and engage them to Leeward, each Ship her Opponent, by which I got between them and the Land, whither they were fast approaching. My Signals were obeyed with great Promptitude, and Vice-Admiral Onslow, in the Monarch, bore down on the Enemy's Rear in the most gallant Manner, his Division following his Example, and the Action commenced about Forty Minutes past Twelve o'Clock. The Venerable soon got through the Enemy's Line, and I began a close

Action, with my Division on their Van, which lasted near Two Hours and a Half, when I observed all the Masts of the Dutch Admiral's Ship to go by the Board; she was, however, defended for some Time in a most gallant Manner; but being overpressed by Numbers, her Colours were struck, and Admiral De Winter was soon brought on Board the Venerable. On looking around me I observed the Ship bearing the Vice-Admiral's Flag was also dismasted, and had surrendered to Vice-Admiral Onslow; and that many others had likewise struck. Finding we were in Nine Fathoms Water, and not farther than Five Miles from the Land, my Attention was so much taken up in getting the Heads of the disabled Ships off Shore, that I was not able to distinguish the Number of Ships captured; and the Wind having been constantly on the Land since, we have unavoidably been much dispersed, so that I have not been able to gain an exact Account of them, but we have taken Possession of Eight or Nine; more of them had struck, but taking Advantage of the Night, and being so near their own Coast, they succeeded in getting off, and some of them were seen going into the Texel the next Morning.

It is with the greatest Pleasure and Satisfaction I make known to their Lordships the very gallant Behaviour of Vice-Admiral Onslow, the Captains, Officers, Seamen and Marines of the Squadron, who all appeared actuated with the truly British Spirit, at least those that I had an Opportunity of seeing.

One of the Enemy's Ships caught Fire in the Action, and drove very near the Venerable; but I have the Pleasure to say it was extinguished, and she is one of the Ships in our Possession. The Squadron has suffered much in their Masts, Yards, and Rigging, and many of them have lost a Number of Men; however, in no Proportion to that of the Enemy. The Carnage on Board the Two Ships that bore the Admirals Flags has been beyond all Description; they have had no less than Two Hundred and Fifty Men killed and wounded on Board of each Ship; and here I have to lament the Loss of Captain Burgess, of His Majesty's Ship the Ardent, who brought that Ship into Action in the most gallant and masterly Manner, but was unfortunately killed soon after. However, the Ship continued the Action close, until quite disabled. The Public have lost a good and gallant Officer in Captain Burgess, and I, with others, a sincere Friend.

Captain Trollope's Exertions and active good Conduct in keeping Sight of the Enemy's Fleet until I came up, have been truly meritorious, and, I trust, will meet a just Reward.

I send this by Captain Fairfax, by whose able Advice I profited much during the Action, and who will give their Lordships any further Particulars they may wish to know.

As most of the Ships of the Squadron are much disabled, and several of the Prizes dismasted, I shall make the best of my Way with them to the Nore.

I am SIR,
Your most obedient humble Servant,
ADAM DUNCAN.

28

Raid On Ostend

Admiralty-Office, May 22.

CAPTAIN Winthrop, of His Majesty's Ship Circe, arrived here this Day with a Dispatch from Captain Home Riggs Popham, of His Majesty's Ship Expedition, to Evan Nepean, Esq; Secretary of the Admiralty, of which the following is a Copy.

His Majesty's Ship Expedition, Ostend Roads, May 20 1798.

SIR,

I BEG you will do me the Honor to inform my Lords Commissioners of the Admiralty, that, in pursuance of their Orders of the 8th Instant, I proceeded to Sea the 14th, with the Ships and Vessels named in the Margin* having on Board the Troops, under the Command of Major-General Coote, for the Purpose of blowing up the Bason Gates and Sluices of the Bruges Canal, and destroying the internal Navigation between Holland, Flanders, and France. On the 18th, P. M. I spoke the Fairy, when Captain Hotten told me he had taken a Cutter from Flushing to Ostend, and he understood from the People on Board, that the Transport Schuyts fitting at Flushing were to go round immediately by the Canals to Dunkirk and Ostend; and although it was impossible that any Information could give additional Spirit to the Troops forming this Enterprize or encrease the Energy and Exertion of the Officers and Seamen under my Command, yet it convinced Major-General Coote and myself that it was of the greatest Importance not to lose any Time, but to attempt, even under an encreased Degree of Risk, an Object of such Magnitude as the one in Question; and as the Weather appeared more favourable than it had been, I made the Signal for Captain Bazely, in the Harpy, to go ahead, with the Vessels appointed to lie as Beacons N. W. Of the Town of Ostend, and for Captain Bradby in the Ariadne, to keep between the Expedition and Harpy, that we might approach as near the Coast as possible, without the Chance of being discovered from the Shore.

At One A. M. We anchored; soon afterwards the Wind shifted to West, and threatened so much to blow, that the General and myself were deliberating whether it would not be better to go to Sea and wait a more favorable Opportunity, when a

Boat from the Vigilant brought a Vessel alongside, which she had cut out from under the Light-House Battery and the Information obtained from the Persons who were on Board her, under separate Examinations, so convinced us of the small Force at Ostend, Newport and Bruges, that Major-General Coote begged he might be landed to accomplish the great Object of destroying the Canals, even if the Surf should prevent his Retreat being so successful as he could wish. I of Course acceded to his spirited Propositions, and ordered the Troops to be landed as fast as possible, without waiting for the regular Order of Debarkation.

Many of the Troops were on Shore before we were discovered and it was not till a Quarter past Four that the Batteries opened on the Ships, which was instantly returned in a most spirited Manner by Captain Mortlock, of the Wolverene, Lieutenant Edmonds, of the Asp, and Lieutenant Norman, of the Biter. The Hecla and Tartarus Bombs very soon opened their Mortars and threw their Shells with great Quickness, and Precision. The Town was on Fire several Times, and much Damage was done to the Ships in the Bason. By Five o'Clock all the Troops ordered to land, except those from the Minerva were on Shore with their Artillery, Miners, wooden Petards, Tools and Gunpowder; and before Six o'Clock I heard from General Coote that he had no Doubt of blowing up the Works. I now became very anxious for the Situation of the Major-General, from the State of the Weather, and I ordered all the Gun-Boats that had anchored to the Eastward of the Town to get as near the Shore as possible, to cover and assist the Troops in their Embarkation.

The Batteries at the Town continued their Fire on the Wolverene, Asp and Biter, and as the Wolverene had received much Damage, and the Asp had been laying near Four Hours within 300 Yards of the Battery, I made their Signal to move, and soon after directed the Dart, Harpy and Kite to take their Stations, that the Enemy might be prevented from turning their Guns against our Troops; but it being low Water, they could not get so near as their Commanders wished. At Half past Nine the Minerva came in, and as I thought an additional Number of Troops would only add to the Anxiety of the General, from the little Probability of being able to embark them, I sent Captain Mackellar on Shore to report his Arrival with Four Light Companies of the Guards. In his Absence, Colonel Ward filled Two flat Boats with his Officers and Men, and was proceeding with every Zeal to join the Battalion of Guards, without considering the Danger he was exposed to in crossing the Surf, when Captain Bradby fortunately saw him, and advised him to return immediately to his Ship. At Twenty Minutes past Ten I had the Pleasure of seeing the Explosion take place; and soon after the Troops assembled on the Sand Hills near the Shore; but the Sea ran so high that it was impossible to embark a single Man therefore I could only make every Arrangement against the Wind moderating; and this Morning at Day-Light I went in Shore, in the Kite, for the Purpose of giving every Assistance, but I had the Mortification to see our Army surrounded by the Enemy's Troops; and as I had no Doubt the General had capitulated, I ordered all the Ships to anchor farther out, and I sent in a Flag of Truce, by Colonel Boone of the Guards and Captain Brown of the Kite, with a Letter to the Commandant, a Copy of which I inclose for their Lordships Information. At Ten this Morning the General's Aid-de-Camp, Captain Williamson, came on Board, and though it was very painful to hear General Coote was wounded, after all his Exertions, yet it was very satisfactory to learn, that, Under many disadvantageous Circumstances, and after performing a Service of such Consequence to our Country, the Loss, killed and wounded, was only between Fifty and Sixty Officers and Privates; and that the General capitulated in consequence of being surrounded by several Thousands of the National Troops.

I inclose, for their Lordships Information, a Copy of such Minutes as were left me by Captain Wilson, from which their Lordships will see the Sluice Gates and Works are completely destroyed, and several Vessels, intended for Transports, burnt.

I this Morning learnt that the Canal was quite dry, and that the Works destroyed Yesterday had taken the States of Bruges Five Years to finish.

I hope their Lordships will be satisfied that the Enemy was surprised, and every Thing they wished was accomplished, although the Loss of the Troops far exceeded any Calculation, except under the particular Circumstances of the Winds coming to the Northward, and blowing very hard. If the Weather had continued fine the Troops would have been embarked by Twelve, at which Time the Return of killed and wounded did not exceed Four Rank and File.

I cannot help again noticing the particular good Conduct of Captain Mortlock, Lieutenant Edmond and Lieutenant Norman, and beg to recommend them to their Lordships Protection.

General Coote sent to inform me that he was highly pleased with the uncommon Exertions of Captains Winthrop and Bradby, and Lieutenant Bradby, who had acted on Shore as his Aide de Camp: He also noticed the Assistance he had derived from Captain Mackellar, after his Landing.

I take the Liberty of sending this Dispatch by Captain Winthrop, of the Circe, who commanded the Seamen landed from the different Ships, and as he had the particular Charge of getting the Powder and Mines up for the Destruction of the Works, in which he so ably succeeded, he will be enabled to inform their Lordships of every Circumstance.

Captain Mackellar, with the Officers and Men on Shore, were included in the Capitulation: But I have not yet been able to collect an exact Return of the Number of Seamen taken.

I have the Honor to be,

SIR,
Your most obedient humble Servant,
HOME POPHAM.

*To anchor, to the Eastward
Hecla Bomb, J. Oughton
Harpy, H. Bazely
Ariadne, J. Bradby
Expedition, H. Popham
Minerva, J. McKellar
Savage, N. Thompson
Blazer, D. Burgess

Lion, S. Bevel
Circe, R. Winthrop
Vestal, C. White
Hebe, W. Birchall
Druid, C. Apthorpe
Terrier, T. Lowen
Vesuve, W. Elliot
Furnace, M.W. Suckling

To Keep to the Westward, for the Purpose of making a feint to land there
Champion, H. Raper
Dart, R. Kaggett
Wolverine, L.M. Mortlock
Crash, P.M. Praid
Boxer, J. Gilbert
Acute, S. Seaver

Extract from the Minutes left on Board the Expedition by Captain Williamson, Aide de Camp to General Coote, dated 10 A. M. May 20th, Ostend Roads.

SLUICE-Gates destroyed in the most compleat Manner. Boats burnt, and every Thing done, and the Troops ready to embark by Twelve o'Clock. When we found it impossible to embark, took the strongest Position on the Sand-Hills, and about Four in the Morning were attacked by a Column of 600 Men to our Left, an immense Column in Front, with Cannon, and a very large Column on the Right.

The General and Troops would have all been off with the Loss of not more than Three or Four Men if the Wind had not come to the Northward soon after we landed, and made so high a Sea. We have not been able to ascertain the exact Number of Men killed and wounded, but it is supposed they amount to about Fifty or Sixty.

HOME POPHAM.

Parliament Street, May 22, 1798.

A DISPATCH, of which the following is a Copy has been this Day received by the Right Honourable Henry Dundas, one of His Majesty's Principal Secretaries of State, from Lieutenant-Colonel Warde of the 1st Regiment of Guards, dated on Board the Expedition Frigate, Eight o'Clock, P.M. May 20, 1798.

SIR,

IN consequence of the Minerva Frigate (on Board which were the Four Light Infantry Companies of the 1st Regiment of Foot Guards) having unfortunately lost her Situation in the Squadron under the Command of Captain Popham, of the Royal

Navy, during the Night of the 18th Instant, the Command of the Remainder of the Troops, from that Accident, has devolved upon me; and I have the Honour to transmit to you the most correct Account that I have been enabled to collect.

Early on the Morning of the 19th Instant the following Troops, under the Command of Major-General Coote, viz.

Two Companies, Light Infantry, Coldstream Guards,
Two Ditto, ditto, 3d Guards,
11th Regiment of Foot,
Flank Companies, 23rd & 49th

with Six Pieces of Ordnance, disembarked, and effected their Landing, at Three o'Clock in the Morning, to the Eastward of Ostend, and completed the Object of the Expedition, by burning a Number of Boats destined for the Invasion of England, and by so completely destroying the Locks and Basin Gates of the Bruges Canal, that it was this Morning without a Drop of Water; and as I understand all the Transports sitting out at Flushing were intended to be brought to Ostend and Dunkirk by the inland Navigation, to avoid our Cruizers, that Arrangement will be defeated, and it will be a long Time before the Works can be repaired, as they were five Years finishing, and were esteemed the most complete Works of the Kind in Europe. The Troops had retreated, and were ready to re-embark by Twelve o'Clock the same Morning, with the Loss of only one Rank and File killed, and one Seaman wounded, but found it impossible from the Wind having encreased, and the Surf running so high as entirely to prevent their regaining the Boats, upon which they took up a Position on the Sand Hills above the Beach, where they lay the whole of that Day and Night upon their Arms. The Enemy taking Advantage of the Length of Time and the Night, collected a very great Force, and soon after Day-Break this Morning, attacked them on every Side, when, after a most noble and gallant Defence, I am grieved to add, they were under the Necessity of capitulating, to a very great Superiority of Numbers.

I have the Honor to be, &c.
HENRY WARDE,
Capt, and Lieut. Col. 1st Guards.

29

The Battle Of The Nile

Admiralty-Office, October 2, 1798.

THE Honourable Captain Capel, of His Majesty's Sloop Mutine, arrived this Morning with Dispatches from Rear-Admiral Sir Horatio Nelson, K.B. to Evan Nepean, Esq; Secretary of the Admiralty, of which the following are Copies.

Vanguard, off the Mouth of the Nile, August 3, 1798.

MY LORD,

Almighty God has blessed His Majesty's Arms in the late Battle, by a great Victory over the Fleet of the Enemy, whom I attacked at Sun-set on the 1st of August off the Mouth of the Nile. The Enemy were moored in a Strong Line of Battle for defending the Entrance of the Bay (of Shoals), flanked by numerous Gun-Boats, Four Frigates, and a Battery of Guns and Mortars on an Island in their Van; but nothing could withstand the Squadron your Lordship did me the Honour to place under my Command. Their high State of Discipline is well known to you, and with the Judgement of the Captains, together with their Valour and that of the Officers and Men of every Description, it was absolutely irresistible.

Could any Thing from my Pen add to the Characters of the Captains, I would write it with Pleasure, but that is impossible.

I have to regret the Loss of Captain Westcott of the Majestic, who was killed early in the Action; but the Ship was continued to be so well fought by her First Lieutenant, Mr. Cuthbert, that I have given him an Order to command her till your Lordship's Pleasure is known.

The Ships of the Enemy, all but their Two Rear Ships, are nearly dismasted; and those Two, with Two Frigates, I am sorry to say, made their Escape; nor was it, I assure you, in my Power to prevent them. Captain Hood most handsomely endeavoured to do it, but I had no Ship in a Condition to support the Zealous, and I was obliged to call her in.

The Support and Assistance I have received from captain Berry cannot be sufficiently expressed. I was wounded in the Head, and obliged to be carried off the

Deck, but the Service suffered no Loss by that Event. Captain Berry was fully equal to the important Service then going on, and to him I must beg leave to refer you for every Information relative to this Victory. He will present you with the Flag of the Second in Command, that of the Commander in Chief being burnt in the L'Orient.

       I have the Honor to be, &c.
       HORATIO NELSON.

30

Battle Of St George's Caye

Whitehall, January 22, 1799.

LETTERS, of which the following are Copies, were Yesterday received from the Earl of Balcarras, by His Grace the Duke of Portland, one of His Majesty's Principal Secretaries of State.

Jamaica, November 7, 1798.

MY LORD, ON the 31st of October I received a Dispatch from the Bay of Honduras.

Lieutenant-Colonel Barrow informs me, that the Settlers had been attacked by a Flotilla consisting of Thirty-one Vessels, having on board Two Thousand Land Troops and Five Hundred Seamen: Arthur O'Neil, Governor-General of Yucatan, and a Field-Marshal in the Service of Spain, commanded in Person. I have great Satisfaction in transmitting the Letter of the Lieutenant-Colonel, by which, your Grace will be informed, that this Armament has been repulsed, and the Expedition entirely frustrated.

The Lieutenant-Colonel speaks in the handsomest Manner of the Conduct of Captain Moss, of His Majesty's Ship Merlin, and of the wonderful Exertions of the Settlers and their Negro Slaves, who manned the Gun-Boats.

The Conduct of Lieutenant-Colonel Barrow, and of the Settlers, in putting the Port of Honduras-Bay into a respectable State of Defence, as well as the gallant Manner in which it was maintained, gives me entire Satisfaction, and it is with Pleasure that I report their Services to your Grace.

I have the Honor to be, &c. &c. &c.
BALCARRAS.

To His Grace the Duke of Portland. Honduras,
Sept. 23, 1798.

MY LORD,

AFTER the Date of my last Dispatch of the 11th, 14th, and 21st August, by the Express Boat Swift, I continued to strengthen our Flotilla, which now consists of,

No. 1. Towser, 1 Gun, Eighteen-Pounder:
No. 2. Tickler, 1 Gun, Eighteen-Pounder:
No. 3. Mermaid, 1 Gun, Nine-Pounder:
No. 4. Swinger, 4 Guns, Six-Pounders, and 2 Guns, Four-Pounders:
No. 5. Teazer, 6 Guns, Four-Pounders:
Besides Eight Flat Gun-Boats, carrying each a Nine-Pounder in the Prow.

No. 1 and 2 are commanded by Mr. Gelston and Mr. Hofmer, Masters of Merchant Vessels, who, with some of their Crews, volunteered the Business in a very handsome Manner: to those Gentlemen I am much indebted for their able and active Services. The Masters and Crews of all the other Vessels consist entirely of Volunteers from the Colonial Troops, and together amount to Three Hundred and Fifty-four Men now on float. The Enemy was so well watched by Scout-Boats and Canoes, that not a single Movement could be made by him without our Knowledge; and finding that he aimed at the Possession of St. George's-Key, the Armed Vessels, No. 1, 4, and 5, were sent to that Place to guard the narrow Channels leading to that commodious Harbour.

On the 3d of September the Enemy endeavoured to force a Passage over Montego-Key-Shoal with Five Vessels, Two of which carried heavy Metal, but was repulsed; he renewed his Attempt on the following Day; but our little Squadron, being now reinforced by Six Gun-Boats, beat them off with great Ease, and the Five Vessels returned to the main Body of the Fleet, then at Anchor about Two Leagues to the Northward. This Movement gave our People an Opportunity of drawing and destroying all the Beacons and Stakes which the Enemy had placed in this narrow and crooked Channel, and without the Use of which nothing but Vessels of a very easy Draught of Water can pass. On the 5th, the same Vessels, accompanied by Two others, and a Number of Launches, endeavoured to get over this Shoal by another Passage, but were repulsed, apparently with Loss. On this, as well as on the Two preceding Days, the Spaniards expended an immense Quantity of Ammunition to no Manner of Purpose; while our People fired comparatively little, but with a Steadiness which surpassed my most sanguine Hopes.

Captain Moss, in his Majesty's Ship Merlin, left his Anchorage at Belize on the Evening of the 5th, and arrived at St. George's-Key about Noon on the 6th of September. The Spaniards having found a Passage through the Leeward Channels impracticable, had got under Weigh on the Morning of that Day with their whole Fleet, seemingly with a View of forcing a Passage through the Windward, a Sand-bore Passage, to the Eastward of Long-Key; but on seeing the Merlin beating into the Harbour of St. George's-Key, and that our Fleet was reinforced by the Armed Vessels No 2 and 3, and a large Gun-Boat, they Returned to their former Anchorage between Long-Key and Key-Chappel.

I was now of Opinion that the Enemy would alter his Mode of Attack, and endeavour to make a Landing on the Main Land to the Northward of our Posts at the Haul-over. Under this Idea, I began to prepare small Vessels and Gun-Boats, in which I meant to embark with 200 Men, including Detachments of His Majesty's 63d and 6th West India Regiments, and of the Royal Artillery, with One Howitzer and Two Field Pieces, Six-Pounders; with this Force it was my Intention to block up the Channel between the Main and the Western Point of Hicks's Keys, and to obstruct as much as possible a Landing in that Quarter; or, if foiled in both of these Objects, to throw the whole Strength into the Works at the Haul-over, and to defend that Post to the last Extremity; while a Body of experienced Bush-Men, all good Shots, and under Orders for that Purpose, should hang on the Flanks and Rear of the Enemy.

On the Morning of Monday the 10th of September, Fourteen of the largest Vessels of the Spanish Fleet weighed Anchor, and at Nine o'Clock brought to about a Mile and a Half distant from our Fleet. Captain Moss was then of Opinion that they meant to delay their Attack till the following Day; but Nine of them got under Weigh about Noon: these carried each Two Twenty-four Pounders in the Bow, and Two Eighteen Pounders in the Stern; One Schooner carried Twenty-two, and all the Rest from Eight to Fourteen Guns in their Waste; and every one of them, besides being crowded with Men, towed a large Launch full of Soldiers. The other Five Vessels, with several large Launches all full of Men, remained at this last Anchorage at the Distance of a Mile and a Half.

Our Fleet was drawn up with His Majesty's Ship Merlin in the Centre, and directly abreast of the Channel: the Sloops with heavy Guns, and the Gun-Boats in some Advance to the Northward, were on her Eastern and Western Flanks.

The Enemy came down in a very handsome Manner, and with a good Countenance, in a Line abreast, using both Sails and Oars. About Half after Two o'Clock Captain Moss made the Signal to engage, which was obeyed with a cool and determined Firmness, that, to use his own Expression to me on the Occasion, would have done Credit to Veterans. The Action lasted about Two Hours and a Half, when the Spaniards began to fall into Confusion, and soon afterwards cut their Cables, and sailed and rowed off, assisted by a great Number of Launches, which took them In Tow.

Captain Moss, on seeing them retreat, made the Signal for our Vessels to chace; but Night coming on, and rendering a Pursuit too dangerous in a narrow Channel and difficult Navigation, they were soon after recalled.

At Half after Three in the Afternoon, I received a Letter from Captain Moss, stating that the Enemy was preparing to attack him, and requiring all the Assistance which I could give. I immediately ordered as many Men to embark and proceed to his Assistance, as small Craft to carry them could be procured. The Alacrity shewn on this Occasion was great indeed; but as a Requisition of this Nature was by no Means expected, the necessary Arrangements had not been made for so speedily embarking the Troops, and of Consequence some Irregularity ensued; for the Cannonade being distinctly heard, and a Certainty of an Engagement having taken Place, it became impossible to restrain the Eagerness of the Colonial Troops, who, possessing Canoes,

Dories, and Pit-pans, without Thought or Retrospect to those left behind, hastened with Impetuosity to join their Companions, and share their Danger: hence arose Difficulty and Disappointment to the regular Troops, who being under Arms, and anxious to proceed with all Expedition, suffered Delay from Want of the necessary Boats and Craft to embark in.

As soon as I saw Seventeen Craft of different Descriptions, having on board Two Hundred Men, set off with Orders to rally round the Merlin, I immediately joined them in Hopes of assisting Captain Moss and harassing the Enemy; but although we were only Two Hours in getting on board the Merlin, a Distance of Three Leagues and a Half, in the Wind's-Eye, we were too late to have any Share in the Action. But I am of Opinion, that the Sight of so many Craft full of Men coming up with Velocity, hastened the Return of the Enemy, and that their Appearance on the following Day, as well as the Junction of Two Armed Ships, the Juba and Columbia, which I had ordered round to St. George's-Key on the 9th, induced the fleet to prepare for returning to their respective Posts. The Spaniards remained under Key-Chappel until the 15th; on the Morning of which they made various Movements, and in the Course of the Day some of them anchored under Key-Caulker. On the Morning of the 16th, it was discovered that they had stolen off; Eight of their largest Vessels got out to Sea, and stood to the Northward; the Remainder, being Twenty-three in Number, shaped their Course for Baccalar.

We have every Reason to believe that the Enemy suffered much in the Action of the 10th, as well in Killed and Wounded as in the Hulls and Rigging of the Vessels engaged; and I am happy to inform your Lordship that we had not a single Man hurt, and that no Injury was done to any of our Vessels deserving of Notice.

It would be unjust, my Lord, to mention the Names of any Officers, either of the Military or Militia, on Account of any particular Service performed by them; for the Conduct of all being such as to merit my best Thanks, no particular Distinction can be made.

It is also unnecessary for me to say any Thing respecting Captain Moss: his Penetration in discovering, and Activity in defeating, the Views of the Enemy; his Coolness and steady Conduct in Action, point him out as an Officer of very great Merit. He first suggested to me the very great Use which might be made of Gun-Boats against the Enemy, and gave me much Assistance by the Artificers belonging to his Ship in fitting them out; I am happy to say, that the most cordial Co-operation has always existed between us. On the 13th Instant, I sent out Two Scout Canoes well manned, with Orders to pass the Spanish Fleet in the Night; and, proceeding to the Northward, to board the first small Vessel they could fall in with. On the 16th they captured a small Packet-Boat with Five Hands, when taking out the Prisoners, Letters, &c and destroying the Boat, they returned hereon the 17th. At Day-Light of that Day the Canoes were entangled with the retreating Spanish Fleet near Savanna-Quay, and escaped with Difficulty.

The Expedition was commanded by Arthur O'Neil, a Field-Marshal in the Armies of Spain, and Captain-General of the Province of Yucatan. The Campeachy Fleet was commanded by Captain Bocco Negra: Two Thousand Soldiers were embarked and distributed in Proportion to the Dimensions of the Vessels, on board of the Fleet, which consisted of,

The Vessels which made the Attack, in Number, = 9
Reserve of equal Force, = 5

A very large Sloop of equal Force, and Six Schooners not so large, but armed in the same Manner as those which came down to the Attack, and drawing too much Water remained with the Transports and Victuallers, = 7

Transports, Victuallers, &c. all carrying Bow and Side Guns of different Calibres, = 11 Total = 32.

And navigated by Five Hundred Seamen, principally from the Havanna and Campeachy.

I am, &c. THO. BARROW,
Lieutenant-Colonel-Commandant.
BALCARRAS.

To the Earl of Balcarras. Admiralty-Office,
January 22, 1799.

Extract of a Letter from Vice-Admiral Sir Hyde Parker, Knt. Commander of His Majesty's Ships and Vessels at Jamaica, to Evan Nepean, Esq; dated on board His Majesty's Ship Abergavenny, in Port-Royal Harbour, the 6th November, 1798.

SIR,

YOU will be pleased to acquaint the Right Honourable the Lords Commissioners of the Admiralty, that I have received Dispatches from Captain Moss, of His Majesty's Sloop Merlin, dated Honduras, 27th September; a Copy of which, describing the Defeat of the Spanish Flotilla, is herewith enclosed.

Merlin, St. George's-Key,
September 27, 1798.

SIR,

MY Letters by the Swift Schooner, which sailed from Honduras express on the 21st of last August, have informed you of the Enemy's Force intended for the Reduction of this Settlement, and their Situation at that Time; since which our Look-out Canoes have watched them so closely, that all their Movements were known to me as they happened. On the 4th of this Month they were visible from our Mast-heads at Belize, and Look-outs reported to me Thirty-one Sail of all Descriptions, but their exact Force by no Means certain. The next Day Six of their heaviest Vessels attempted to force their Passage over Montego-Key Shoals, by putting their Provisions and Stores into other Vessels; had they effected this, it would have secured them all a Passage to

Belize over Shoal-Water, where I could by no Means act. I ordered Three of our Armed Vessels to annoy them in their Endeavours; which succeeded so far as to occasion their Removal at dark, and a small Channel they had marked by driving down Stakes was also taken up by our Canoes. I now clearly saw that their next Effort would be to get Possession of St. George's-Key, from which Place (only Nine Miles from Belize) they might go down through the different Channels leading to it, and continue to harass the Inhabitants and destroy the Town at their Leisure, and drive me from my Anchorage there; this determined me to gain the Key before them, if possible; I therefore left Belize on the Evening of the 5th, and secured this Place, at the Instant Twelve of their heaviest Vessels were attempting the same; they hauled their Wind and returned to Long-Key, on my hauling my Wind towards them. They continued working and anchoring among the Shoals until the 11th, at the Distance of Three or Four Miles; when having made their Arrangements, at One P.M. Nine Sail of Sloops and Schooners, carrying from Twelve to Twenty Guns, including Two Twenty-four and Two Eighteen-Pounders each had in Prow and Stern, with a large Launch a-stern of each full of Men, bore down through the Channel leading to us in a very handsome cool Manner; Five smaller Vessels lay to Windward out of Gun-shot, full of Troops, and the Remainder of their Squadron at Long-Key Spit to wait the Event, each of which carried small Prow-Guns, with Swivels fore and aft. At Half past One P.M. seeing their Intention to board the Two Sloops, and that they meant to come no nearer, but had anchored, I made the Signal to engage, which began and continued near Two Hours; they then cut their Cables and rowed and towed off by Signal in great Confusion over the Shoals. I had placed the Merlin as near the Edge of them as possible, and nothing that I had was equal to follow them unsupported by the Merlin.

At dark they regained their other Vessels, and continued in Sight till the 15th at Night, when they moved off with a light Southerly Wind: Some are gone to Bacalar, and some Prisoners taken report others to Campeche. I am happy to add that the Service was performed without a Man killed on our Side. The Enemy I think must have suffered much from the great Number of Men on board, and the precipitate Manner they made their Retreat. This Armament was commanded by General O'Neil, Governor of the Province; Troops and Sailors included, about Two Thousand Five Hundred Men: and so certain were the Spaniards of Success, that the Letters found in a Canoe taken were actually directed to Belize and St. George's-Key.

The Behaviour of the Officers and Crew of His Majesty's Ship gave me great Pleasure, and had we had deep Water to follow them in, I think many of them would have fallen into our Hands. The Spirit of the Negro Slaves that manned our small Crafts was wonderful, and the good Management of the different Commanders does them great Credit.

Our Force, besides the Merlin as follows:
Two Sloops, with 1 Eighteen-Pounder and 25 Men.
One Sloop, with 1 Short Nine-Pounder and 25 Men.
Two Schooners, with 6 Four-Pounders and 25 Men each.
Seven Gun-Flats, with 1 Nine-Pounder and 16 Men each.

I have the Honor to be Sir, &c. &c. &c.
 JNO. R. MOSS.

31

Battle Of Ballinamuck

Whitehall, September 14, 1798.

A DISPATCH, of which the following is a Copy, has been received this Morning from His Excellency the Lord Lieutenant of Ireland, by His Grace the Duke of Portland, One of His Majesty's Principal Secretaries of State.

Camp near St. Johnstown,
September 8, 1798.

MY LORD,

WHEN I wrote to your Grace on the 5th, I had every Reason to believe from the Enemy's Movement to Drumahain, that it was their Intention to march to the North; and it was natural to suppose that they might hope that a French Force would get into some of the Bays in that Part of the Country, without a Succour of which Kind every Point of Direction for their March seemed equally desperate.

I received, however, very early in the Morning of the 7th, Accounts from Lieutenant-General Lake, that they had turned to their Right to Drumkeirn, and that he had Reason to believe that it was their Intention to go to Boyle, or Carrick, or Shannon; in consequence of which I hastened the March of the Troops under my immediate Command, in order to arrive before the Enemy at Carrick, and directed Major-General Moore, who was at Tubercurry, to be prepared, in the Event of the Enemy's Movement to Boyle.

On my Arrival at Carrick, I found that the Enemy had passed the Shannon at Balintra, where they attempted to destroy the Bridge; but Lieutenant-General Lake followed them so closely, that they were not able to effect it.

Under these Circumstances I felt pretty confident, that one more March would bring this disagreeable Warfare to a Conclusion; and having obtained satisfactory Information that the Enemy had halted for the Night at Cloone, I moved with the Troops at Carrick, at Ten o'Clock on the Night of the 7th, to Mohill, and directed Lieutenant-General Lake to proceed at the same Time to Cloone, which is about Three Miles from Mohill; by which Movement I would be able either to join with

Lieutenant-General Lake in the Attack of the Enemy, if they should remain at Cloone, or to intercept their Retreat, if they should (as it was most probable) retire on the Approach of our Army.

On my Arrival at Mohill soon after Day-break, I found that the Enemy had begun to move towards Granard; I therefore proceeded with all possible Expedition to this Place, through which I was assured, on account of a broken Bridge, that the Enemy must pass in their Way to Granard, and directed Lieutenant-General Lake to attack the Enemy's Rear, and impede their March as much as possible, without bringing the Whole of his Corps into Action. Lieutenant-General Lake performed this Service with his usual Attention and Ability; and the inclosed Letter, which I have just received from him, will explain the Circumstances which produced the immediate Surrender of the Enemy's Army.

The Copy of my Orders, which I enclose [not present] will shew how much Reason I have to be satisfied with the Exertions of the Troops and I request that your Grace will be pleased to inform His Majesty, that I have received the greatest Assistance from the General and Staff Officers who have served with the Army.

I have the Honour to be, &c.
CORNWALLIS.

Letter received from Lieutenant-General Lake to Captain Taylor, Private Secretary to his Excellency the Lord Lieutenant, dated Camp near Ballinamuck, Sept. 8, 1798.

SIR,

I HAVE the Honour to acquaint you, for the Information of His Excellency the Lord Lieutenant, that finding upon my Arrival at Ballaghy, that the French Army had passed that Place from Castlebar, I immediately followed them to watch their Motions. Lieutenant-Colonel Crawfurd, who commanded my advanced Corps, composed of Detachments of Hompesch's and the First Fencible Cavalry, by great Vigilance and Activity, hung so close upon their Rear, that they could not escape from me, although they drove the Country, and carried with them all the Horses.

After Four Days and Nights most severe marching, my Column, consisting of the Carabineers, Detachments, of the 23d Light Dragoons, the First Fencible Light Dragoons, and the Roxburgh Fencible Dragoons, under the Command of Colonel Sir Thomas Chapman, Lieutenant-Colonel Maxwell, Earl of Roden, and Captain Kerr, the Third Battalion of Light Infantry, the Armagh, and Part of the Kerry Militia, the Reay, Northampton, and Prince of Wales's Fencible Regiments of Infantry, under the Command of Lieutenant-Colonel Innes, of the 64th Regiment, Lord Viscount Gosford, Earl of Glandore, Major Ross, Lieutenant-Colonel Bulkley, and Lieutenant-Colonel Macartney, arrived at Cloone about Seven o'Clock this Morning, where, having received Directions to follow the Enemy on the same Line, whilst his Excellency moved by the lower Road to intercept them, I advanced, having previously detached the Monaghan Light Company, mounted behind Dragoons, to harass their Rear.

Lieutenant-Colonel Crawfurd, on coming up with the French Rear Guard, summoned them to surrender; but as they did not attend to his Summons, he attacked them; upon which upwards of 200 French Infantry threw down their Arms, under the Idea that the Rest of the Corps would do the same Thing; Captain Packenham, Lieutenant-General of Ordnance, and Major-General Craddock, rode up to them. The Enemy, however, instantly commenced a Fire of Cannon and Musketry which wounded General Craddock; upon which I ordered up the third Battalion of Light Infantry, under the Command of Lieutenant-Colonel Innes, and commenced the Attack upon the Enemy's Position.

The Action lasted upwards of Half an Hour, when the Remainder of the Column making its Appearance, the French surrendered at Discretion. The Rebels, who fled in all Directions, suffered severely.

The Conduct of the Cavalry was highly conspicuous. The Third Light Battalion, and Part of the Armagh Militia (the only Infantry that were engaged) behaved most gallantly, and deserve my warmest Praise. Lieutenant-Colonel Innes's Spirit and Judgment contributed much to our Success.

To Brigadier-General Taylor I have to return my most sincere Thanks for his great Exertions and Assistance, particularly on this Day; also to Lord Roden, Sir Thomas Chapman, Major Kerr, and Captain Ferguson, whose Example contributed much to animate the Troops. I ought not to omit mentioning Lieutenant-Colonel Maxwell, Major Packenham, and Captain Kerr, whose Conduct was equally meritorious; and I feel infinitely thankful to all the commanding Officers of Corps, who, during so fatiguing a March, encouraged their Men to bear it with unremitting Perseverance.

To Captain Packenham, Lieutenant-Colonel Clinton (who came to me with Orders, from Lord Cornwallis), and Major-General Craddock (who joined me in the Morning), I am highly indebted for their spirited Support; the latter, though early wounded, would not retire from the Field during the Action.

I acknowledge with Gratitude the Zeal and Activity displayed on all Occasions by Lieutenant-Colonel Meade, Major Hardy, Assistant-Quarter-Master-General, Captains Taylor and Eustace of the Engineers, Captain Nicholson, and my other Aides-de-Camp.

I cannot conclude my Letter without expressing how much our Success is to be attributed to the Spirit and Activity of Lieutenant-Colonel Crawfurd, and I beg Leave to recommend him as a most deserving Officer.

I have the Honor to be, &c.
G. LAKE.

32

Battle Of Tory Island

Admiralty-Office, October 21, 1798.

LIEUTENANT WATERHOUSE arrived here late last Night with the Duplicate of a Dispatch from Sir John Borlase Warren, Bart, and K.B. Captain of His Majesty's Ship Canada, to Vice-Admiral Kingsmill, of which the following is a Copy.

Canada, Lough Swilly, Ireland,
16th October, 1798.

SIR,

IN pursuance of the Orders and Instructions I received by the Kangaroo, I proceeded with the Ships named in the Margin*, off Achill-Head, and on the 10th Instant I was joined by His Majesty's Ships Melampus and Doris, the latter of whom I directed to look out for the Enemy off Tory Island, and the Rosses; in the Evening of the same Day, the Amelia appeared in the Offing, when Captain Herbert informed me he had parted with the Ethalion, Anson, and Sylph, who, with great Attention, had continued to observe the French Squadron since their sailing on the 17th Ultimo. In the Morning of the 11th, however, these Two Ships also fell in with us, and at Noon the Enemy were discovered in the N.W. Quarter, consisting of One Ship of Eighty Guns, Eight Frigates, a Schooner, and a Brig. I immediately made the Signal for a general Chace, and to form in Succession as each Ship arrived up with the Enemy, who, from their great Distance to Windward, and a hollow Sea, it was impossible to come up with before the 12th.

The Chace was continued in very bad and boisterous Weather all Day of the 11th, and the following Night, when at Half past Five A. M. they were seen at a little Distance to Windward, the Line of Battle Ship having lost her Main Top Mast.

The Enemy bore down and formed their Line in close Order upon the Starboard Tack, and from the Length of the Chace, and our Ships being spread, it was impossible to close with them before Seven A. M. when I made the Robust's Signal to lead, which was obeyed with much Alacrity, and the Rest of the Ships to form in Succession in the Rear of the Van.

The Action commenced at Twenty Minutes past Seven o'Clock A. M. the Rosses bearing S. S. W. Five Leagues, and at Eleven, the Hoche, after a gallant Defence, struck; and the Frigates made Sail from us: the Signal to pursue the Enemy was made immediately, and in Five Hours afterwards Three of the Frigates hauled down their Colours also; but they, as well as the Hoche, were obstinately defended, all of them being heavy Frigates, and, as well as the Ship of the Line, entirely new, full of Troops and Stores, with every Necessary for the Establishment of their Views and Plans in Ireland. I am happy to say, that the Efforts and Conduct of every Officer and Man in the Squadron seemed to have been actuated by the same Spirit, Zeal, and Unanimity, in their King and Country's Cause; and I feel myself under great Obligations to them, as well as the Officers and Men of this Ship, for their Exertions upon this Occasion; which will, I hope, recommend them to their Lordships' Favour.

I left Captain Thornbrough after the Action; with the Magnanime, Ethalion, and Amelia, with the Prizes; and am sorry to find he is not arrived; but trust they will soon make their Appearance.

I have the Honor to remain, SIR,
Your most obedient humble Servant,
J.N. WARREN.

* Canada, Robust, Foudroyant and Magnanime.

33

Battle Of Seringapatam

Downing-Street, September 13, 1799.

A DISPATCH, of which the following is an Extract, was received this Morning by the Ship Sarah Christiana.

Fort Saint George, May 16, 1799.

YESTERDAY I received the enclosed Dispatch from Lieutenant-General Harris, containing the details of the Capture of Seringapatam; they require no Comment; and I am persuaded that no Solicitation is necessary to induce you to recommend the incomparable Army which has gained this glorious Triumph, to the particular Notice of His Majesty, and to the Applause and Gratitude of their Country.

Seringapatam, May 7, 1799.

MY LORD,

ON the 4th Instant, I had the Honor to address to your Lordship a hasty Note, containing in few Words the Sum of our Success, which I have now to report more in Detail.

The Fire of our Batteries, which began to batter in Breach on the 30th April, had on the Evening of the 3d Instant so much destroyed the Walls against which it was directed, that the Arrangement was then made for assaulting the Place on the following Day, when the Breach was reported practicable. The Troops intended to be employed were stationed in the Trenches early in the Morning of the 4th, that no extraordinary Movement might lead the Enemy to expect the Assault, which I had determined to make in the Heat of the Day, as the Time best calculated to ensure Success, as their Troops would then be least prepared to oppose us.

Ten Flank Companies of Europeans, taken from those Regiments necessarily left to guard our Camp and Out-Posts, followed by the 12th, 33d, 73d, and 74th

Regiments, and Three Corps of Grenadier Sepoys taken from the Troops of the Three Presidences, with Two Hundred of His Highness the Nizam's Troops, formed the Party for the Assault, accompanied by One Hundred of the Artillery and the Corps of Pioneers, and supported in the Trenches by the Battalion Companies of the Regiment de Meuron, and Four Battalions of Madras Sepoys. – Colonel Sherbrooke, and Lieutenant-Colonels Dunlop, Dalrymple, Gardiner, and Mignan, commanded the several Flank Corps; and Major-General Baird was entrusted with the Direction of this important Service.

At One o'Clock the Troops moved from the Trenches, crossed the rocky Bed of the Cavery under an extremely heavy Fire, passed the Glacis and Ditch, and ascended the Breaches in the Fausse Braye and Rampart of the Fort, surmounting in the most gallant Manner every Obstacle which the Difficulty of the Passage and the Resistance of the Enemy presented to oppose their Progress. Major-General Baird had divided his Force for the purpose of clearing the Ramparts to the Right and Left. One Division was commanded by Colonel Sherbrooke, the other by Lieutenant-Colonel Dunlop; the latter was disabled in the Breach; but both Corps, although strongly opposed, were completely successful. Resistance continued to be made from the Palace of Tippoo for some Time after all firing had ceased from the Works: Two of his Sons were there, who, on Assurance of Safety, surrendered to the Troops surrounding them; and Guards were placed for the Protection of the Family, most of whom were in the Palace. It was soon after reported that Tippoo Sultan had fallen. Syed Saheb, Meer Saduc, Syed Gofar, and many other of his Chiefs, were also slain. Measures were immediately adopted to stop the Confusion at first unavoidable in a City strongly garrisoned, crowded with Inhabitants and their Property, in Ruins from the Fire of a numerous Artillery, and taken by Assault. The Princes were removed to Camp.

It appeared to Major-General Baird so important to ascertain the Fate of the Sultan, that he caused immediate Search to be made for his Body, which, after much Difficulty, was found late in the Evening in one of the Gates under a Heap of Slain, and soon after placed in the Palace. The Corpse was the next Day recognised by the Family, and interred, with the Honors due to his Rank, in the Mausoleum of his Father.

The Strength of the Fort is such, both from its natural Position and the Stupendous Works by which it is surrounded, that all the Exertions of the brave Troops who attacked it, in whose Praise it is impossible to say too much, were required to place it in our Hands. Of the Merits of the Army I have expressed my Opinion in Orders, a Copy of which I have the Honor to enclose; and I trust your Lordship will point out their Services to the favourable Notice of their King and Country.

I am sorry to add that, on collecting the Returns of our Loss, it is found to be much heavier than I had at first imagined.

On the 5th Instant Abdul Khalie, the elder of the Princes formerly Hostages with Lord Cornwallis, surrendered himself at our Out-Posts, demanding Protection. Kerim Saheb, the Brother of Tippoo, had before sought Refuge with Meer Allum Behauder. A. Cowl Namah was Yesterday dispatched to Futteh Hyder, the eldest Son of Tippoo, inviting him to join his Brothers. Purneah and Meer Kummer ódeen Khan have also been summoned to Seringapatam: no Answers have yet been received, but I expect them shortly, as their Families are in the Fort.

This Moment Ali Reza, formerly one of the Vakeels from Tippoo Sultan to Lord Cornwallis, has arrived from Meer Kummer ódeen Khan, to ask my Orders for Four Thousand Horse now under his Command. Ali Reza was commissioned to declare, that Meer Kummer ódeen would make no Conditions, but rely on the Generosity of the English.

Monsieur Chapuy and most of the French are Prisoners; they have Commissions from the French Government.

I have the Honor, &c.
(Signed) GEORGE HARRIS.

34

Battle Of Callanstoog

Downing-Street, September 2, 1799.

A DISPATCH, of which the following is a Copy, was this Day received by the Right Honourable Henry Dundas, One of His Majesty's Principal Secretaries of State, from Lieutenant-General Sir R. Abercromby, K.B.

Helder, August 28, 1799.

SIR,

FROM the First Day after our Departure from England, we experienced such a Series of bad Weather, as is very uncommon at this Season of the Year.

The Ardour of Admiral Mitchell for the Service in which we were jointly engaged, left it only with me to follow his Example of Zeal and Perseverance, in which I was encouraged by the Manner that he kept a numerous Convoy collected.

It was our Determination not to depart from the Resolution of attacking the Helder, unless we should have been prevented by the Want of Water and Provisions.

On the Forenoon of the 21st Instant, the Weather proved so favourable that we stood in upon the Dutch Coast, and had made every Preparation to land on the 22d, when we were forced to Sea by a heavy Gale of Wind.

It was not until the Evening of the 25th that the Weather began once more to clear up.

On the 26th, we came to Anchor near the Shore of the Helder, and on the 27th, in the Morning, the Troops began to disembark at Day-light.

Although the Enemy did not oppose our Landing, yet the First Division had scarcely begun to move forward, before they got into Action, which continued from Five in the Morning until Three o'Clock in the Afternoon.

The Enemy had assembled a very considerable Body of Infantry, Cavalry, and Artillery, near Callanstoog, and made repeated Attacks on our Right with fresh Troops.

Our Position was on a Ridge of Sand Hills, stretching along the Coast from North to South. Our Right Flank was unavoidably exposed to the whole Force of the Enemy. We had nowhere sufficient Ground on our Right to form more than a Battalion in Line; yet, on the Whole, the Position, though singular, was not, in our Situation, disadvantageous, having neither Cavalry nor Artillery.

By the Courage and Perseverance of the Troops, the Enemy was fairly worn out and obliged to retire in the Evening to a Position Two Leagues in his Rear.

The Contest was arduous and the Loss has been considerable. We have to regret many valuable Officers lost to the Service, who have either fallen or been disabled by their Wounds. The Corps principally engaged were the Reserve under the Command of Colonel Macdonald, consisting of the Twenty-third and Fifty-fifth Regiments.

The Regiments of Major-General Coote's Brigade, which have been much engaged, were the Queen's, the Twenty-seventh, Twenty-ninth, and Eighty-fifth Regiments.

Major General Oyley's Brigade was brought into Action towards the Close of the Day, and has sustained some Loss.

As the Enemy still held the Helder with a Garrison of near Two Thousand Men, it was determined to attack it before Day-break on the Morning of the 28th, and the Brigade under Major-General Moore supported by Major-General Burrard's, were destined for this Service; but about Eight o'Clock Yesterday Evening, the Dutch Fleet in the Mars Diep got under Weigh, and the Garrison was withdrawn, taking their Route through the Marshes towards Medemblick, having previously spiked the Guns on the Batteries, and destroyed some of the Carriages. About Nine at Night Major-General Moore, with the Second Battalion of the Royals, and the Ninety-second Regiment, under the Command of Lord Huntley, took Possession of this important Post, in which he found a numerous Artillery of the best Kind, both of Heavy and Field Train.

All that Part of the Dutch Fleet in the Nieueve Diep, together with their Naval Magazine at Nieueve Werk, fell into our Hands this Morning; a full Detail of which it is not in my Power to send. This Day we have the Satisfaction to see the British Flag flying in the Mars Diep, and Part of the Five Thousand Men, under the Command of Major-General Don, disembarking under the Batteries of the Helder.

During the Course of the Action, I had the Misfortune to lose the Service of Lieutenant-General Sir James Pulteney, from a Wound he received in his Arm, but not before he had done himself the greatest Honor, and I was fully sensible of the Loss of him. Major-General Coote supplied his Place with Ability.

Colonel Macdonald, who commanded the Reserve, and who was very much engaged during the Course of the Day, though wounded, did not quit the Field.

Lieutenant-Colonel Maitland, returning to England, to go on another Service, and Major Kempt, my Aid-du-Camp and Bearer of this Letter, whom I beg leave to recommend to your Notice and Protection, will be able to give any further Information which may be required.

I have the honor to be, &c.

RALPH ABERCROMBY.

Admiralty-Office, September 2, 1799.

Captain Hope, of His Majesty's Ship Kent, and Captain Oughton, of His Majesty's Ship Isis, arrived this Afternoon, with a Dispatch from Admiral Lord Viscount Duncan, of which the following is a Copy.

Kent, off Aldborough, Sunday,
1st Sept. 1799.

SIR,

I Transmit, for the Information of my Lords Commissioners of the Admiralty, a Letter to me from Vice-Admiral Mitchell, giving a distinct Detail of the great Success with which it has pleased Almighty God to crown His Majesty's Arms. The Boldness of the Vice-Admiral in running in on an open Shore with so numerous a Fleet, and in so very unsettled Weather, could only be equalled by the Gallantry of Sir Ralph Abercromby and his brave Troops, landing in the Face of a most formidable Opposition. During the whole of the Conflict on Tuesday I could plainly perceive the vast Superiority of the British Troops over those of the Enemy, though opposed with Obstinacy; and, in Justice to both the Land and Sea Service, I must say that I never in my Life witnessed more Unanimity and Zeal than has pervaded all Ranks to bring the Expedition to its present happy Issue.

Finding the Kent with several of the Russian Seventy-four Gun Ships to draw too much Water to be able to get into the Harbour, I have returned with them to this Anchorage; but previous to my getting under Weigh at Eight o'Clock on Friday Morning, I had the Pleasure to see Vice-Admiral Mitchell, with the Men of War, Transports, and Armed Vessels in a fair Way of entering the Texel, with a fair Wind, and have not the least Doubt but the Whole of the Dutch Fleet were in our Possession by Noon on that Day.

These Dispatches will be delivered by Captains Hope and Oughton, both able and intelligent Officers, and who will give their Lordships more satisfactory Information relative to our successful Operations.

I shall now only add my sincere Congratulations to their Lordships on this great Event, which, I think, in its Consequences may be ranked among One of the greatest that has happened during the War.

I am, Sir, &c.
DUNCAN.

P.S. The Winds having proved unfavourable, has occasioned my anchoring here; but I shall proceed to Yarmouth as soon as the Weather moderates.

Isis, at Anchor off the Texel,
August the 29th, 1799.

MY LORD,

IN a former Letter I had the Honor to write your Lordship, I there mentioned the Reasons that had determined Sir Ralph Abercromby and myself not to persevere longer than the 26th in our Resolution to attack the Helder and Port of the Texel, unless the Wind became more moderate. Fortunately the Gale abated that Morning; and although a very heavy Swell continued to set in from the Northward, I thought a Moment was not to be lost in making the final Attempt. The Fleet therefore bore up to take the Anchorage, and I was happy to see the Transports and all the Bombs, Sloops, and Gun-Vessels in their Stations to cover the Landing of the Troops by Three in the Afternoon of that Day, when the Signal was made to prepare for Landing. The General, however, not thinking it prudent to begin disembarking so late on that Day, it was determined to delay it until Two in the Morning on the 27th. The intervening Time was occupied in making the former Arrangements more complete, and by explaining to all the Captains individually my ideas fully to them, that the Service might profit by their united Exertions. The Troops were accordingly all in the Boats by Three o'Clock; and the Signal being made to row towards the Shore, the Line of Gun-Brigs, Sloops of War, and Bombs opened a warm and well-directed Fire to scour the Beach, and a Landing was effected with little Loss. After the First Party had gained the Shore, I went with Sir Ralph Abercromby, that I might superintend the Landing of the Rest, and with the Aid of the different Captains, who appeared animated but with one Mind, the Whole were disembarked with as great Regularity as possible. The Ardour and glorious Intrepidity which the Troops displayed, soon drove the Enemy from the nearest Sand Hills, and the Presence of Sir Ralph Abercromby himself, whose Appearance gave Confidence to all, secured to us, after a long and very warm Contest, the Possession of the Whole Neck of Land between Kiek Down and the Road leading to Alkmaar, and near to the Village of Callanstoog. Late that Night the Helder Point was evacuated by the Enemy, and taken Possession of by our Troops quietly in the Morning, as were the Men of War named in the enclosed List, and many large Transports and Indiamen by us the next Day. I dispatched Captain Oughton, my own Captain, to the Helder Point last Evening to bring off the Pilots, and he has returned with enough to take in all the Ships necessary to reducing the remaining Force of the Dutch Fleet, which I am determined to follow to the Walls of Amsterdam, until they surrender or capitulate for His Serene Highness the Prince of Orange's Service.

I must now, my Lord, acknowledge in the warmest Manner the high Degree of Obligation I am under to your Lordship for the liberal Manner in which you continued to entrust to my Directions the Service I have had the Honor to execute under your immediate Eye; a Behaviour which added to my Wish to do all in my Power to forward the Views of Sir Ralph Abercromby.

It is impossible for me sufficiently to express my Admiration of the Bravery and Conduct of the General and the whole Army, or the Unanimity with which our whole

Operations were carried on; the Army and Navy on this Occasion having (to use a Seaman's Phrase) pulled heartily together.

Where the Exertions of all you did me the Honor to put under my Orders have been so great, it is almost impossible to particularize any; but Captain Oughton has had so much to do, from the first embarking of the Troops to the present Moment, and has shewn himself so strenuous in his Exertions for the good of the Expedition; as well as given me much Assistance from his Advice on every Occasion, that I cannot but mention him in the highest Manner to your Lordship; and at the same Time express my Wish that your Lordship will suffer him to accompany whoever may bear your Dispatches to England, as I think the local Knowledge he has gained may be highly useful to be communicated to their Lordships of the Admiralty.

The Manner in which the Captains, Officers, and Seamen, landed from the Fleet behaved, while getting the Cannon and Ammunition along to the Army, requires my particular Thanks; and here let me include in a special Manner the Russian Detachment of Boats, from whose Aid and most orderly Behaviour the Service was much benefited indeed.

I am also much indebted to Captain Hope for the clear Manner in which he communicated to me your Lordship's Ideas at all Times, when sent to me by your Lordship for that Purpose, as every Thing was better understood from such Explanation than they could otherwise have been by Letter.

It is impossible for me to furnish your Lordship at present with any List of the killed, wounded, or missing Seamen, or of those that were unfortunately drowned on the Beach in landing the Troops, having as yet no Return made me, but I am very sorry to say, that I was myself Witness to several Boats oversetting in the Surf, in which I fear several Lives were lost.

I have the Honor to be, &c. &c. &c.
A. MITCHELL.

35

Battle Of Krabbendam

Downing-Street, September 16, 1799.

A DISPATCH, of which the following is a Copy, was this Morning received from Lieutenant-General Sir Ralph Abercromby, K.B. At the Office of the Right Honourable Henry Dundas, One of His Majesty's Principal Secretaries of State.

Head-Quarters, Schager Brug, September 11, 1799.

SIR,

HAVING fully considered the Position which the British Troops had occupied on the 1st Instant, and having in View the Certainty of speedy and powerful Reinforcements, I determined to remain until then on the defensive.

From the Information which we had received, we were apprized of the Enemy's Intention to attack us, and we were daily improving the Advantages of our Situation.

Yesterday Morning at Daybreak the Enemy commenced an Attack on our Centre and Right, from Saint Martin's to Petten, in Three Columns, and apparently with their whole Force.

The Column on the Right, composed of Dutch Troops, and under the Command of General Dandaels, directed its Attack on the Village of Saint Martin's.

The Centre Column of the Enemy, under the Orders of General de Monceau, likewise composed of Dutch Troops, marched on to Crabbendam and Zyper Sluys.

The Left Column of the Enemy, composed of French, directed itself on the Position occupied by Major-General Burrard, commanding the Second Brigade of Guards.

The Enemy advanced, particularly on their Left and Centre, with great Intrepidity, and penetrated with the Heads of their Columns to within a Hundred Yards of the Post occupied by the British Troops. They were, however, everywhere repulsed, owing to the Strength of our Position, and the determined Courage of the Troops. About Ten o'Clock the Enemy retired towards Alkmaar, leaving behind them many dead and some wounded Men, with One Piece of Cannon, a Number of Waggons, Pontoons, and portable Bridges. Colonel McDonald with the Reserve pursued them for some Time and quickened their Retreat.

It is impossible for me to do full Justice to the good Conduct of the Troops.

Colonel Spencer; who commanded in the Village of St. Martin's, defended his Post with great Spirit and Judgment.

Major-General Moore, who commanded on his Right, and who was wounded, though I am happy to say slightly, was no less judicious in the Management of the Troops under his Command.

The Two Battalions of the 20th Regiment, posted opposite to Crabbendam and Zyper Sluys did Credit to the high Reputation which that Regiment has always borne. Lieutenant-Colonel Smyth of that Corps, who had the particular Charge of that Post, received a severe Wound in his Leg, which will deprive us for a Time of his Services.

The Two Brigades of Guards repulsed with great Vigour the Column of French which had advanced to attack them, and where the Slaughter of the Enemy was great.

I continue to receive every Mark of Zeal and Intelligence from the Officers composing the staff of this Army.

It is difficult to state with any Precision the Loss of the Enemy, but it cannot be computed at less than Eight Hundred or One Thousand Men, and on our Side it does not exceed, in killed, wounded, and missing, Two Hundred Men.

I have the Honor to be, &c. &c. &c
(Signed) R. ABERCROMBY.

36

Battle Of Bergen

Downing-Street, September 24, 1799.

A DISPATCH, of which the following is a Copy, has been this Day received from Field-Marshal His Royal Highness the Duke of York, by the Right Honourable Henry Dundas, One of His Majesty's Principal Secretaries of State.

Head-Quarters, Schagen Brug, Sept. 20, 1799.

Sir,

IN my Dispatch of the 16th Instant I acquainted you with my Intention of making an Attack upon the Whole of the Enemy's Position, the Moment that the Reinforcements joined.

Upon the 19th, every necessary Arrangement being made, the Army moved forward in Four principal Columns in the following Order:

The Left Column, under the Command of Lieutenant-General Sir Ralph Abercromby, consisting of:

Two Squadrons of the 18th Light Dragoons,
Major-General the Earl of Chatham's Brigade,
Major-General Moore's Brigade,
Major-General the Earl of Cavan's Brigade,
First Battalion of British Grenadiers of the Line,
First Battalion of Light Infantry of the Line,
The 23d and 55th Regiments under Colonel Macdonald,

destined to turn the Enemy's Right on the Zuyder Zee, marched at Six o'Clock on the Evening of the 18th.

The Columns upon the Right, the First commanded by Lieutenant-General D'Hermann, consisting of:

The 7th Light Dragoons,
Twelve Battalions of Russians, and Major-General Manners' Brigade;
the Second, commanded by Lieutenant-General Dundas, consisting of:
Two Squadrons of the 11th Light Dragoons,

Two Brigades of Foot Guards, and
Major-General His Highness Prince William's Brigade;
the Third Column, commanded by Lieutenant-General Sir James Pulteney, consisting of:
Two Squadrons of the 11th Light Dragoons,
Major-General Don's Brigade,
Major-General Coote's Brigade;
marched from the Positions they occupied at Daybreak the Morning of the 19th. The Object of the First Column was, to drive the Enemy from the Heights of Camper Duyne, the Villages under these Heights, and finally to take Possession of Bergen: the Second was to force the Enemy's Position at Walmenhuysen and Schoreldam, and to co-operate with the Column under Lieutenant-General D'Hermann: and the Third, to take Possession of Ouds Carspel at the Head of the Lange Dyke, a great Road leading to Alkmaer.

It is necessary to observe, that the Country in which we had to act, presented in every Direction the most formidable Obstacles. The Enemy upon their Left occupied to great Advantage the High Sand-Hills which extend from the Sea in front of Petten to the Town of Bergen, and were entrenched in Three intermediate Villages. The Country over which the Columns under Lieutenant-Generals Dundas and Sir James Pulteney had to move for the Attack of the fortified Posts of Walmenhuysen, Schoreldam, and the Lange Dyke, is a Plain intersected every Three or Four Hundred Yards by broad deep wet Ditches and Canals. The Bridges across the only Two or Three Roads which led to these Places were destroyed, and Abbatis were laid at different Distances.

Lieutenant-General D'Hermann's Column commenced its Attack, which was conducted with the greatest Spirit and Gallantry, at Half past Three o'Clock in the Morning, and by Eight had succeeded in so great a Degree as to be in Possession of Bergen. In the wooded Country which surrounds this Village the principal Force of the Enemy was placed, and the Russian Troops, advancing with an Intrepidity which overlooked the formidable Resistance with which they were to meet, had not retained that Order which was necessary to preserve the Advantages they had gained; and they were, in consequence, after a most vigorous Resistance, obliged to retire from Bergen, (where, I am much concerned to state, Lieutenants-General D'Hermann and Tchertkoff were made Prisoners, the latter dangerously wounded,) and fell back upon Schorel, which Village they were also forced to abandon, but which was immediately retaken by Major-General Manners' Brigade, notwithstanding the very heavy Fire of the Enemy. Here this Brigade was immediately reinforced by Two Battalions of Russians, which had co-operated with Lieutenant-General Dundas in the Attack of Walmenhuysen, by Major-General D'Oyley's Brigade of Guards, and by the 35th Regiment under the Command of his Highness Prince William. The Action was renewed by these Troops for a considerable Time with Success; but the entire Want of Ammunition on the Part of the Russians, and the exhausted State of the whole Corps engaged in that particular Situation, obliged them to retire, which they did in good Order, upon Petten and the Zyper Sluys.

As soon as it was sufficiently light, the Attack upon the Village of Walmenhuysen, where the Enemy was strongly posted with Cannon, was made by Lieutenant-General Dundas. Three Battalions of Russians, who formed a separate Corps, destined to co-operate from Krabbendam in this Attack, commanded by Major-General Sedmoratzky, very gallantly stormed the Village on its Left Flank, while at the same Time it was entered on the Right by the 1st Regiment of Guards. The Grenadier Battalion of the Guards had been previously detached to march upon Schoreldam, on the Left of Lieutenant-General D'Hermann's Column, as was the 3d Regiment of Guards and the 2d Battalion of the 5th Regiment, to keep up the Communication with that under Lieutenant-General Sir James Pulteney.

The Remainder of Lieutenant-General Dundas's Column, which, after taking Possession of Walmenhuysen, had been joined by the First Battalion of the Fifth Regiment, marched against Schoreldam, which Place they maintained, under a very heavy and galling Fire, until the Troops engaged on their Right had retired at the Conclusion of the Action.

The Column under Lieutenant-General Sir James Pulteney proceeded to its Object of Attack at the Time appointed, and after overcoming the greatest Difficulties and the most determined Opposition, carried by Storm the principal Post of Ouds Carspel at the Head of the Lange Dyke; upon which Occasion the 40th Regiment, under the Command of Colonel Spencer, embraced a favorable Opportunity which presented itself of highly distinguishing themselves.

This Point was defended by the chief Force of the Batavian Army under the Command of General Daendels. The Circumstances, however, which occurred on the Right rendered it impossible to profit by this brilliant Exploit, which will ever reflect the highest Credit on the General Officers and Troops engaged in it; and made it necessary to withdraw Lieutenant-General Sir James Pulteney's Column from the Position which he had taken within a short Distance of Alkmaer. The same circumstances led to the Necessity of recalling the Corps under Lieutenant-General Sir Ralph Abercromby, who had proceeded without Interruption to Hoorne, of which City he had taken Possession, together with its Garrison.

The Whole of the Army has therefore re-occupied its former Position.

The well-grounded Hopes I had entertained of complete Success in this Operation, and which were fully justified by the Result of the Three [attacks], and by the First Success of the Fourth Attack upon the Right, add to the great Disappointment I must naturally feel on this Occasion; but the Circumstances which have occurred I should have considered of very little general Importance, had I not to lament the Loss of many brave Officers and Soldiers, both of His Majesty's and the Russian Troops, who have fallen.

The Gallantry displayed by the Troops engaged, the Spirit with which they overcame every Obstacle which Nature and Art opposed to them, add the Cheerfulness with which they maintained the Fatigues of an Action which lasted without Intermission from Half past Three o'Clock in the Morning until Five in the Afternoon, are beyond my Powers to describe or to extol. Their exertions fully entitle them to the Admiration and Gratitude of their King and Country.

Having thus faithfully detailed the Events of this First Attack, and paid the Tribute of Regret due to the distinguished Merit of those who fell, I have much Consolation in being enabled to state that the Efforts which have been made, although not crowned with immediate Success, so far from militating against the general Object of the Campaign, promise to be highly useful to our future Operations. The Capture of Sixty Officers and upwards of Three Thousand Men, and the Destruction of Sixteen Pieces of Cannon, with large Supplies of Ammunition, which the intersected Nature of the Country did not admit of being withdrawn, are convincing Proofs that the Loss of the Enemy in the Field has been far superior to our own; and in addition to this it is material to state that nearly Fifteen Thousand of the Allied Troops had unavoidably no Share in this Action.

In viewing the several Circumstances which occurred during this arduous Day, I cannot avoid expressing the Obligations I owe to Lieutenant-Generals Dundas and Sir James Pulteney for their able Assistance, and also to mention my great Satisfaction at the Conduct of Major-Generals His Highness Prince William, D'Oyley, Manners, Burrard, and Don, to whose spirited Exertions the Credit gained by the Brigades they commanded is greatly to be imputed.

Captain Sir Home Popham and the several Officers of my Staff exerted themselves to the utmost, and rendered me most essential Service. I feel also much indebted to the spirited Conduct of a Detachment of Seamen, under the Direction of Sir Home Popham and Captain Godfrey of the Navy, in the Conduct of Three Gun Boats, each carrying One 12 Pound Carronade, which acted with considerable Effect on the Alkmaer Canal; nor must I omit expressing my Acknowledgments to the Russian Major-Generals Essen, Sedmoratzky, and Schutorss.

I am, Sir, yours,
FREDERICK.

37

Battle Of Alkmaar

Downing-Street, October 7, 1799.

A DISPATCH, of which the following is a Copy, was received late this Evening from Field-Marshal His Royal Highness the Duke of York, by the Right Honourable Henry Dundas, One of His Majesty's Principal Secretaries of State.

Head-Quarters, Zuyper Zluys,
October 4,1799.

SIR,

THE Inclemency of the Weather which prevailed at the Time of writing my last Dispatch, and which, as I therein explained, alone prevented me from putting the Army in Motion, having in some Measure subsided, and the necessary previous Arrangements having been made, the Attack was commenced on the whole of the Enemy's Line on the Morning of the 2d; and I have now the Happiness to Inform you, that after a severe and obstinate Action, which lasted from Six in the Morning until the same Hour at Night, the distinguished Valour of His Majesty's and the Russian Troops prevailed throughout; and the Enemy, being entirely defeated, retired in the Night from the Positions which he occupied on the Lange Dyke, the Koe Dyke at Bergen, and upon the extensive Range of Sand Hills between the latter Place and Egmont-op-Zee. The Points where this well fought Battle was principally contested, were from the Sea Store in Front of Egmont, extending along the Sandy Desert or Hills to the Heights above Bergen, and it was sustained by the British Columns under the Command of those highly distinguished Officers General Sir Ralph Abercromby and Lieutenant-General Dundas whose Exertions, as well as the Gallantry of the brave Troops they led cannot have been surpassed by any former Instance of British Valour.

On the Night of this memorable Day, the Army lay upon their Arms, and Yesterday moved forward and occupied the Positions of the Lange Dyke, Alkmaar, Bergen, Egmont-op-Hoof, and Egmont-op-Zee.

The Enemy's Forces according to the best Information I have been able to obtain, consisted of between Twenty-five and Thirty Thousand Men, of whom a very small

Proportion only were Dutch, General Daendals, who commanded the latter, is wounded. The French Troops, who have been continually reinforcing themselves, and whose Loss has been very great, were commanded by Generals Brune, Vandamme, and Boulet.

From the Continuance of the Action, and the Obstinacy with which it was contested, the Victory has not been gained without serious Loss. At present I am not in Possession of particular Returns; but I have the Satisfaction to say that no Officer of Rank has fallen. The British Army has to regret Major-Gefferal Moore's being wounded in Two Places; and the Russian Army, Major-General Emme's being also wounded; but I am happy to say that their Wounds are not of a Nature to lead me to apprehend that I shall long be deprived of the Assistance of their Abilities and Gallantry. It is impossible for me at this Moment to do Justice to the Merits of the other Generals and Officers of the Allied Army who distinguished themselves, as I must defer until To-morrow paying my Tribute of Praise to them and to the Troops generally, as well as giving the Details of the Battle of the 2d Instant.

My Attention is seriously engaged in making the Arrangements which are necessary for occupying a forward Position in Front of Beverwyck and Wyck-op-Zee, to which Line the Enemy has retreated. I entertain no Doubt that the Extent of Country which will now be under the Protection of the Allied Army, and rescued from French Tyranny, will afford an Opportunity to its Loyal Inhabitants of declaring themselves. The Town of Alkmaar, which is the Seat of the States of North Holland, has opened its Gates to our Troops, and a considerable Number of the Dutch Troops have come over to the Prince of Orange's Standard.

In order that you may be in Possession of such Information as Want of Time will not at present allow me to detail, I charge my Aid-de-Camp Captain Fitzgerald with this Dispatch. He is entirely In my Confidence, and I request Leave to recommend him to His Majesty as an Officer of superior Merit and Intelligence.

I am, Sir, yours,
FREDERICK

Downing-Street, October 13, 1799.

Dispatches, of which the following are Copies, were this Afternoon received from Field-Marshal His Royal Highness the Duke of York, by the Right Honourable Henry Dundas, One of His Majesty's Principal Secretaries of State.

Head-Quarters, Alkmaar,
October 6, 1799.

SIR,

I dispatched my Aid-de-Camp Captain Fitzgerald, on the 4th Instant, with an Account of the Success obtained over the Enemy on the 2d; and Circumstances at that Moment not enabling me to give the Particulars of that Day's Action, I shall now enter into a Detail of the Occurrences which then took place.

The Disposition I have already transmitted to you of the intended Attack will shew that it was determined that a vigorous Effort should be made on the Left of the Enemy, where the French Troops were posted and concentred about Bergen, a large Village surrounded by extensive Woods, through which passes the great Road leading to Haarlem, and between which and the Sea lies an extensive Region of high Sand Hills, impassable for Artillery or Carriages, difficult and very embarrassing from their Depth and broken Surface for Cavalry, and exceedingly forbidding from all these and other Circumstances to any Movements being attempted in them by a large Body of Infantry. Behind these Sand Hills, and to the Enemy's Right, through the whole Extent of North Holland, lies a wet and low Country, everywhere intersected with Dykes, Canals, and Ditches, which it rested with the Enemy to occupy and strengthen in whatever Manner and in whatever Points he pleased, and thereby to prevent our making any successful Attempt against his Right. His centre was supported by the Town of Alkmaar; and Water Communications gave him in every Direction the Advantage of drawing from and profiting by the Resources of the Country. The Delays which the unusual Severity of the Weather at this Season and the Whole of our Situation rendered inevitable enabled him to improve his Position by new Works, which bore a formidable Appearance and threatened much Resistance.

Under all Circumstances it was evident, that it was only by a great Advantage gained on the Enemy's Left that we could drive him back, and force him to evacuate North Holland, thereby materially bettering our Situation by opening the Sphere of our Resources and future Exertions.

The combined Attacks were therefore made in Four principal Columns:
The First on the Right, under General Sir Ralph Abercromby, consisting of
Major-General D'Oyley's Brigade,
Major-General Moore's Ditto,
Major-General Earl of Cavan's Ditto,
Colonel McDonald's Reserve,
Nine Squadrons of Light Dragoons commanded by Colonel Lord Paget, And One Troop of Horse Artillery, marched by the Sea-Beach against Egmont-op-Zee with a View to turn the Enemy's Left Flank.

Of the Second, consisting of Russian Troops commanded by Major-General D'Essen, the greater Proportion marched by the Slaper Dyke through the Villages of Groete and Schorel upon Bergen, by the Road which all the Way skirts the Foot of the Sand Hills of Camperdown, about Three Hundred Feet high, presenting a steep Face to the Country much wooded, but from their Summit more gradually sloping towards the Sea. Part of this Column, under Major-General Sedmoratsky, debouchéd from the Zuyper Sluys, and were destined to cover the Left Flank of the Remainder of the Russian Troops moving under the Sand Hills, to co-operate with the Brigade under Major-General Burrard in the Attack of Schoreldam, and to combine their Attack upon Burgen with the Troops upon their Right.

The Third Column, under the Command of Lieutenant-General Dundas, consisted of
Major-General Earl of Chatham's Brigade,
Major-General Coote's Ditto,
Major-General Burrard's Ditto,
And One Squadron of the 11th Light Dragoons.

Major-General Coote's Brigade was ordered to follow the Advanced Guard of Sir Ralph Abercromby's Column from Petten, to turn to the Left at the Village of Campe, and proceeding under the Hills to take the Slaper Dyke in Reserve and clear the Road to Groete and the Heights above it, for that Part of the Russian Column which marched by the Slaper Dyke, whose Right Major-General Coote was to cover, during its Progress towards Bergen, by detaching the required Number of Troops into the Sand Hills. Major-General Lord Chatham's Brigade was to follow that Part of the Russian Column which marched from the Zuyper Sluys, to turn to the Right, and falling into the Road in the Rear of Major-General D'Essen's Corps, to join such. Part of Major-General Coote's as moved along that Road, to proceed in Support of the Russian Column, covering its Right upon the Sand Hills, and from them ultimately to combine with that Column in its Attack upon Bergen; for which Purpose these Two Brigades were to extend as much as possible to the Right, and endeavour to connect themselves with the Right Column. Major-General Burrard's Brigade was ordered to move from Tutenhoorn and Crabbendam upon the Left of the Alkmaar Canal, to combine with the Corps under Major-General Sedmoratsky, its Attack from Schoreldam, which was further supported by Seven Gun-Boats moving along the above Canal. Major-General Burrard was to communicate upon his Left with the Fourth Column under Lieutenant-General Sir James Pulteney, consisting of
Major-General His Highness Prince William's Brigade,
Major-General Manners' Ditto,
Major-General Donn's Ditto,
Two Squadrons of the 18th Light Dragoons,
And Two Battalions of Russians.

This Column covered the whole of the Left of our Position to the Zuyder Zee, and was destined to threaten the Enemy's Right and to take Advantage of every favorable Circumstance that should offer.

Proportions of Artillery of Reserve were attached to each Column, and to the Russian Column about Two Hundred Cossacks and Hussars.

The Force of the Enemy was computed at Twenty-Five Thousand Men, much the greater Proportion of which were French.

The State of the Tide determined the March of the Right Column, which proceeded from Petten at Half past Six o'Clock in the Morning. Its Advanced Guard, composed of the Reserve under Colonel McDonald; *viz.*
1st Battalion of Grenadiers of the Line,
1st Battalion of Light Infantry of Ditto,
23d Regiment of Infantry,
And 55th Regiment of Infantry,
drove the Enemy from Campe and from the Sand Hills above that Village, and

continued its March upon the Ridge of those Hills inclining a little to the Left. Major-General Coote's Brigade, which next followed, turned to its Left at Campe, and advancing as far as the Extremity of the Slaper Dyke and the Village of Groete, cleared the Road for the Russian Column under Major-General D'Essen. Part of this Brigade, in Connexion with Colonel McDonald's Corps, drove the Enemy from the Sand Hills to the Right and Front of the Russian Column, and continued moving forward upon the Sand Hills a little in Advance of the Russian Troops, Major-General Sedmoratsky's Corps had marched from the Zuyper Sluys as soon as the Enemy had abandoned Groete, and advanced across the Plain between the Alkmaar Canal and the Road by which Major-General D'Essen moved, whose Left he joined, whilst his own Left was protected by the Fire of the Gun Boats and the Advance of Major-General Burrard's Corps.

The Enemy, who had gradually retired from Schorel, were now formed in considerable Force from Schorel to Schoreldam, and kept up a very warm Fire from the Cannon which they had posted at different Points of their Line. Major-General Lord Chatham's Brigade moved in the Rear of Major-General Sedmoratsky's Corps, close behind which it was formed in the Plain.

The Column under Major-General D'Essen proceeded along the Road upon Schorel, whilst Major-General Coote's Brigade was rapidly driving the Enemy from the Ridge of Sand Hills above that Village and to its Right. Colonel McDonald's Corps had moved considerably to the Right, with a View to connect itself with the Right Column, and continued warmly engaged with the Enemy who were in very considerable Force in the Sand Hills. After some Delay the Enemy were driven, about Eleven o'Clock by the Russian Troops, and by the Gun Boats and Major-General Burrard's Brigade upon their Left, from Schorel and Schoreldam, between which Major-Generals D'Essen's and Sedmoratsky's Corps took Post, and continued the Remainder of the Day engaged in a Cannonade with the Enemy posted in the Village of Bergen and between it and the Koe Dyke. Schoreldam was occupied by Major-General Burrard, whence he continued his Attack (in Conjunction with the Gun Boats) upon the Enemy, who was strongly posted on the Koe Dyke.

In this Situation it became necessary to make a great Effort to clear the Summit of the Sand Hills of the Enemy, who occupied them in great Numbers, and for a great visible Extent quite beyond Bergen. The Left of Major-General Coote's Brigade was then above Schorel, and the Regiments which composed it were separated by very considerable Intervals, and extended a long Way into the Sand Hills. The 85th Regiment being on the Right, and considerably advanced, was warmly engaged with the Enemy, who shewed a Disposition to come upon the Right of the Brigade.

I therefore directed Lieutenant-General Dundas to march Major-General Lord Chatham's Brigade from the Plain into the Sand Hills to the Right of Major General Coote's, leaving One Battalion (the 31st) to move close under the Hills parallel with the Left of Major-General Coote's Brigade. This Movement was admirably executed; and Major-General Lord Chatham's Brigade having arrived at some Distance behind the 85th Regiment, and outflanking it by about Two Battalions, the Line was formed, and the Whole was ordered to advance at a brisk Pace to gain the Heights about Three

Quarters of a Mile distant, across a Scrubby Wood, and then by a gradual Ascent to the Summit of the Sand Hills: the 85th Regiment at the same Time charged, and drove the Enemy before them, who, being thus taken in Flank and Rear, retired precipitately towards his Right, and took Post on the Summit of the Heights which hang over Bergen, whilst the Remainder of Major-General Coote's Brigade having also moved forward, joined the Left of Major-General Lord Chatham's. The 85th Regiment took Post in a favorable Situation below those Heights, so as to block up and command the Avenue and great Road which leads through Bergen.

From the Heights the Enemy were seen in the Village of Bergen and the Woods and Plains about it, wavering, and apparently in great Uncertainty; but Lieutenant-General Dundas's Corps not being able alone to undertake the Attack of the Village and Woods, or to bring Cannon into the Sand Hills, the Enemy re-occupied the Village in Force, and kept up a brisk Fire of Cannon and Musquetry on the Heights occupied by the British, and by which the latter were sheltered. A considerable Body of the Enemy advanced along the Avenue, and made a spirited Attack to regain the Heights on the Post of the 85th, but were driven back with Loss, and that Regiment gallantly maintained their Situation during the Rest of the Day against several other Attempts of the Enemy. – A large Body of the Enemy having been seen moving to their Left, Three Battalions of Major-General Coote's Brigade were marched beyond the Right of Lord Chatham's to support him and extend the Line. The 27th Regiment, posted at the Termination of another Avenue from Bergen, were attacked by a considerable Body issuing from the Woods; the Regiment having, however, by a spirited Charge driven the Enemy into the Wood, no further Attempt was made by them from that Time (about Half past Three P.M.) to dislodge Lieutenant-General Dundas's Corps. – The Extension of his Line had now brought its Right very near to the Reserve under Colonel McDonald, who had been advancing rapidly, notwithstanding the considerable Resistance he had experienced, and was now warmly engaged with a Body of the Enemy, lining a Sand Hill Ridge which crosses the Downs in a perpendicular Direction, and which Body had probably moved from Bergen and Egmont-op-te-Hooss with the View of turning Lieutenant-General Dundas's Right Flank. – Lieutenant-General Dundas, therefore, sent down the 29th Regiment on the Left of Colonel McDonald close to the Road leading from Bergen to Egmont; and although the Enemy's Position appeared steep and formidable, a general and rapid Attack was made. The Advance of the 29th Regiment was the Signal for the Whole on the Right of it to move forward briskly, which was done with such Spirit that they were soon at the Bottom of the Enemy's Position; and ascending the Hill without stopping, they pursued their Advantage with such Vigour as to drive the Enemy totally from the Sand Hills.

This was the last Event which took Place on the Side of Bergen; and as the Close of the Day was fast approaching, Colonel McDonald with Two Battalions, was sent to the Support of General Sir Ralph Abercromby. The Heights of the Sand Hills surrounding Bergen for about Three Miles remained crowned and possessed by Eleven British Battalions.

General Sir Ralph Abercromby had marched, according to the Disposition, along the Beach with Major-General D'Oyley's, Major-General Moore's and Major-General Lord Cavan's Brigades, the Cavalry and Horse Artillery (the Reserve under Colonel McDonald not having been able, owing to the great Extent of the Sand Hills, to rejoin him, after turning to the Left at Campe). The main Body of Sir Ralph Abercromby's Column had proceeded without meeting with much Resistance in the early Part of the Day, but was nevertheless much inconvenienced and his Troops harassed by the Necessity of detaching continually into the Sand Hills to his Left, to cover that Flank against the Troops whom the Enemy had placed in the Sand Hills. The admirable Disposition, however, which he made of his Troops, and their determined Spirit and Gallantry, enabled him to arrive within a Mile of Egmont. Here he was seriously opposed by a very considerable Corps of French Infantry, which occupied Egmont-op-Zee and the high Sand Hills in its Front, and who had formed a very strong Corps of Cavalry and Artillery to their Left upon the Beach. The Engagement was maintained during several Hours with the greatest Obstinacy; and in no Instance were the Abilities of a Commander, or the heroic Perseverance of Troops in so difficult and trying a Situation, more highly conspicuous. Animated by the Example of General Sir Ralph Abercromby, and the general and other Officers under him, the Troops sustained every Effort made upon them by an Enemy then superior in Number, and much favored by the Strength of his Position. Late in the Evening, the Enemy's Cavalry having been defeated in an Attempt which they made upon the British Horse Artillery on the Beach, and having been charged by the Cavalry under Colonel Lord Paget, was driven with considerable Loss nearly to Egmont-op-Zee: his Efforts then relaxed considerably upon the Right; and General Sir Ralph Abercromby having soon after been joined by the Reinforcement under Colonel McDonald, took Post upon the Sand Hills and the Beach within a very short Distance of Egmont-op-Zee, where the Troops lay upon their Arms during the Night.

Lieutenant-General Sir James Pulteney had assembled the greater Part of his Corps in Front of Drixhoorn, whence he threatened an Attack on Oudt Carspel, in and near which was placed the principal Force of the Enemy's Right, and could at the same Time have supported any Part of the Line which might be attempted. Lieutenant-General Sir James Pulteney, seconded by the active Exertions of the General Officers and Troops under his Command, executed with his usual Ability that Part of the Disposition with which he was entrusted, and effectually prevented the Enemy from sending any Detachments to his Left.

On the 3d at Day-break, the Enemy evacuated their strongly fortified Posts at Oudt Carspel and the Lange Dyke, retiring upon Saint Pancras and Alkmaar: the above Posts were very soon after occupied by Lieutenant-General Sir James Pulteney.

The Enemy still continued in the Woods and Town of Bergen, and appeared with Cannon and in some Force on that Side of it next to the Koe Dyke. They had, however, withdrawn the greater Part of their Force during the Night, and before Midday the Village was taken Possession of by the 85th Regiment. About One, General Sir Ralph Abercromby entered Egmont-op-Zee, and in the Evening the Russians under Major-General D'Essen advanced from the Ground where (as I have already stated) they had halted the preceding Day, to Egmont-op-te-Hooss. Major-General

Burrard, who when the Enemy retired from Bergen had advanced to Koe Dyke, was ordered in the Evening to occupy with a Detachment from his Brigade the Town of Alkmaar, which had been abandoned by the Enemy, and had been entered nearly at the same Time by Patroles from his and Lieutenant-General Sir James Pulteney's Corps.

The exhausted State of the Troops, from the almost unparalleled Difficulties and Fatigues which they had to encounter, prevented me from taking that Advantage of the Enemy's Retreat to Beverwyck and Wyck-op-Zee which, in any other Country and under any other Circumstances, would have been the Consequences of the Operations of the Army upon the 2d.

Of the Loss sustained by the Enemy, the Reports are so various that I cannot venture to say any Thing decisive; but from all Circumstances I have Reason to think it must have exceeded Four Thousand Men. Seven Pieces of Cannon and a great Proportion of Tumbrils were taken. The Prisoners having been immediately sent to the Helder, I cannot at present give any Statement of their Number, but I do not believe it exceeds a few Hundred Men.

Under Divine Providence this signal Victory obtained over the Enemy is to be attributed to the animating and persevering Exertions which have at all Times been the Characteristics of the British Soldier, and which on no Occasion were ever more eminently displayed; nor has it often fallen to the Lot of any General to have such just Cause of Acknowledgment for the distinguished Support he that Day experienced from the Officers under his Command.

I cannot in sufficient Terms express the Obligations I owe to General Sir Ralph Abercromby and Lieutenant-General Dundas, for the able Manner in which they conducted their respective Columns, whose Success is in no small Degree to be attributed to their personal Exertions and Example. The former had Two Horses shot under him.

I must also state my warm Acknowledgments to Lieutenant-General Hulse, Major-Generals Lord Chatham, Coote, D'Oyley, Burrard, and Moore, for their spirited Efforts upon this Occasion, and the Abilities which they shewed in the Conduct of their respective Brigades.

The latter, by his Ability and personal Exertion, very materially contributed to the Success of this Column; and, although severely wounded through the Thigh, continued in Action for near Two Hours, until a Second Wound in the Face obliged him to quit the Field. Much Praise is due to Major-General Hutchinson for the Manner in which he led the 5th or Lord Cavan's Brigade; and I hope it will not be considered as an improper Intrusion, if I take this Occasion to express my sincere Regret that an unfortunate Blow from a Horse in going into Action, by fracturing his Leg, should have deprived me of his Lordship's Services. Colonel McDonald distinguished himself by his usual Spirit and Ability in the Command of the Reserve, as did Lord Paget, who commanded the Cavalry upon the Beach, and whose Exertions are deserving of every Praise. Nor must I omit expressing my thanks to Lieutenant-Colonels Whitworth and Smyth, who commanded the Artillery of Reserve, and to Major Judson of the Horse Artillery. – The Detachment of Seamen under the

Command of Captains Goddard and Jurcoing were upon this, as upon a former Occasion, of the most essential Service in the Direction of the Gun Boats. – The Conduct of Major-General Knox, who was attached to the Column of Russian Troops, was such as to afford me the greatest Satisfaction.

I enclose the Returns of the Loss of the British and Russian Troops, and must repeat my sincere Regret that the Advantages we have obtained (however brilliant) have been so dearly bought.

In closing this Dispatch, I cannot deny myself the Pleasure of expressing my Approbation of the Staff of my Army, and in particular of the Exertions and Abilities shewn by Lieutenant-Colonel Anstruther, Deputy-Quarter Master-General.

I am, &c.
FREDERICK.

38

Battle Of Castricum

Head Quarters, Alkmaar, October 7, 1799.

SIR,

THE Enemy, after the Action of the 2d, having taken up the Position between Beverwyck and Wyck-op-Zee, I determined to endeavour to force him thence before he had an Opportunity of strengthening by Works the short and very defensible Line which he occupied, and to oblige him still further to retire before he could be joined by the Reinforcements which I had Information were upon their March.

Preparatory, therefore, to a general forward Movement, I ordered the Advanced Posts which the Army took up on the 3d Instant in Front of this Place, of Egmont-op-te-Hooff and Egmont-op-Zee, to be pushed forward, which Operation took place, yesterday Morning. At first little Opposition was shewn, and we succeeded in taking Possession of the Villages of Schermerhoorn, Acher Sloot Limmen, Baccum, and of a Position on the Sand Hills near Wyck-op-Zee: the Column of Russian Troops under the Command of Major-General D'Essen, in endeavouring to gain a Height in Front of their intended Advanced Post at Baccum, (which was material to the Security of that Point,) was vigorously opposed and afterwards attacked by a strong Body of the Enemy, which, obliged General Sir Ralph Abercromby to move up in Support with the Reserve of his Corps.

The Enemy on their Part advanced their whole Force; the Action became general along the whole Line from Limmen to the Sea, and was maintained with great Obstinacy on both Sides until Night, when the Enemy retired, leaving us Masters of the Field of Battle. The Conflict however has, I am concerned to state, been as severe, and has been attended with as serious a Loss (in Proportion to the Numbers engaged), as any of those which have been fought by the brave Troops composing this Army since their Arrival in Holland. The Gallantry they displayed, and the Perseverance with which they supported the Fatigues of this Day, rival their former Exertions.

The Corps engaged were:
Major-General D'Oyley's Brigade of Guards
Major-General Burrard's Ditto
Major-General Earl of Chatham's Brigade.
Major-General Coote's Ditto,

Major-General the Earl of Cavan's Brigades, commanded by Major-General Hutchinson,

The Reserve under the Command of Colonel McDonald,

Part of the 7th and 11th Light Dragoons,

And Seven Battalions of Russians.

To General Sir Ralph Abercromby, and the other General Officers in Command of the Brigades before-mentioned, as also to Colonel McDonald, my warmest Acknowledgments are due, for their spirited and judicious Exertions during this Affair; nor ought I to omit the Praise due to Colonel Clephane, commanding Four Companies of the 3d and One of the Coldstream Regiments of Guards, who, by a spirited Charge, drove Two Battalions of the Enemy from the Post of Acher Sloot making Two Hundred Prisoners. I have sincerely to regret that in the Course of the Action Major-General Hutchinson received a Musket-shot Wound in the Thigh, which, however is not serious. I have not yet received any Reports of the Killed and Wounded, but I am apprehensive that the Number of British is not less than Five Hundred, and that the Loss of the Russian Troops, as far as I can understand amounts to Twelve Hundred Men. I shall, as early as Circumstances possibly admit, transmit particular Returns.

The Loss of the Enemy upon this Occasion has been very great; and, in Addition to their Killed and Wounded, Five Hundred Prisoners fell into our Hands.

I am, &c.
FREDERICK.

Head-Quarters Schagen Brug, October 9, 1799.

SIR,

I Have already acquainted you with the Result of the Action of the 6th Instant, which terminated successfully to the Allied Arms, and at the same Time pointed out the Necessity of the Movement which produced this Affair.

From the Prisoners taken upon the 6th Instant, I learnt the Certainty of the Enemy having been reinforced since the Action of the 2d by Two Demi-Brigades, amounting to about Six Thousand Infantry, and of their having strengthened the Position of Beverwyck, and fortified strongly in the Rear of it Points which it would still be necessary to carry before Haerlem could be attacked.

It ought also to be stated, that the Enemy had retired a large Force upon Purmirind in an almost inaccessible Position, covered by an inundated Country, and the Debouches from which were strongly fortified and in the Hands of the Enemy; and further, that as our Army advanced this Corps was placed in our Rear.

But such Obstacles would have been overcome, had not the State of the Weather, the ruined Condition of the Roads, and total Want of the necessary Supplies arising from the above Causes, presented Difficulties which required the most serious Consideration.

Having maturely weighed the Circumstances in which the Army was thus placed, and having felt it my Duty on a Point of so much Importance to consult with General Sir Ralph Abercromby and the Lieutenant-Generals of this Army, I could not but consider (and their Opinion Was unanimous on the Subject) that it would be for the Benefit of the general Cause to withdraw the Troops from their advanced position, in order to wait His Majesty's further Instructions.

I must request you will again represent to His Majesty the distinguished Conduct of His Army; which, whilst acting under the Pressure of uncommon Difficulties, never for a Moment ceased to be actuated by the noblest Feelings for the Success of the public Cause, and the Honor of the British Arms.

As there are many Points resulting from our present Situation upon which you may require particular Information, and such Details as cannot be brought within the Compass of a Letter, I have thought it necessary to charge my Secretary Colonel Brownrigg with this Dispatch, who will be able to explain fully all Matters relating to this Army.

I transmit a Return of Killed, Wounded, and Missing of His Majesty's and the Russian Troops in the Action of the 6th Instant; I most heartily lament that it has again been so serious, and that, so many brave and valuable Men have fallen.

I am, yours,
FREDERICK.

39

Battle Of Brión (Ferrol)

Downing-Street, September 6, 1800.

A DISPATCH, of which the following is a Copy, has been this Day received at the Office of the Right Honourable Henry Dundas, one of His Majesty's Principal Secretaries of State, from Lieutenant-General Sir James Pulteney, Bart, dated on board His Majesty's Ship Renown, at Sea, 27th August 1800.

SIR,

I Have the Honor to inform you, that the Meet, on board of which the Troops under my Command were embarked, arrived before the Harbour of Ferrol, on the 25th Instant.

I determined immediately to make a landing, with a View, if practicable to attempt the Town of Ferrol, being certain, if I found either the Strength of the Place or the Force of the Enemy too great to justify an Attack, that in the landing there was no considerable Risk.

The Disembarkation was effected, without Opposition, in a small Bay near Cape Prior; the Reserve followed by the other Troops as they landed immediately ascended a Ridge of Hills adjoining to the Bay; just as they had gained the Summit the Rifle Corps fell in with a Party of the Enemy which they drove Back. I have to regret that Lieutenant-Colonel Stewart, who commanded this Corps, was wounded on the Occasion. At Day break the following Morning a considerable Body of the Enemy was driven back by Major-General the Earl of Cavan's Brigade, supported by some other Troops, to that we remained in complete Possession of the Heights which overlook the Town and Harbour of Ferrol; but from the Nature of the Ground, which is steep and rocky, unfortunately this Service could not be performed without Loss; the 1st Battalion of the 52d Regiment had the principal Share in this Action. The Enemy lost about One Hundred Men killed and wounded, and Thirty or Forty Prisoners.

I had now an Opportunity of observing minutely the Situation of the Place, and of forming, from the Reports of Prisoners, an Idea of the Strength of the Enemy when, comparing the Difficulties which presented themselves, and the Risk attendant on Failure on one Hand, with the Prospect of Success and the Advantages to be derived from it on the other, I came to the Determination of reimbarking the Troops, in order to proceed without Delay on my further Destination. The Embarkation was effected the same Evening in perfect Order, and without Loss of any Kind.

The Spirit and Alacrity shewn by the Troops merit every Commendation; and if Circumstances had admitted of their being led against the Enemy I should have had every Reason to expect Success.

I am under the greatest Obligations to the Admiral Sir John Borlase Warren and the Officers of the Navy, for the judicious Arrangements made for the Landing and Reimbarkation of the Troops, and the Activity with which they were put in Execution.

The immediate Direction of this Service was intrusted to Sir Edward Pellew, who performed it in a Manner highly creditable to himself, and advantageous to the Service.

I have the Honor to be, &c.
JAMES PULTENEY.

Copy of a Letter from Rear-Admiral Sir John Borlase Warren, K.B. to Admiral the Earl of Saint Vincent, K.B. dated Renown, Bay of Play a de Dominos, August 27, 1800.

MY LORD,

I Beg Leave to inform you that the Squadron and Convoy under my Command arrived off this Bay on the 25th Instant, without having fell in with any Thing excepting the St. Vincent Schooner, who had parted from Captain Curzon.

General Sir James Pulteney having desired that the Troops might be disembarked, I directed Sir Edward Pellew to superintend that Service, assisted by Captains Hood, Dalrymple, Fyffe, and Stackpool, with Captains Guion, Searle, and Young, which was most ably performed on the same Night in the Bay above-mentioned, after a Fort of Eight Twenty-four-Pounders had been silenced by the Fire of the Impetueux, Brilliant, Cynthia and St. Vincent Gun-Boat; the whole Army were on Shore without the Loss of a Man, together with Sixteen Field-Pieces, attended by Seamen from the Men of War to carry Scaling Ladders, and to get the Guns up the Heights above Ferrol.

On the Morning of the 26th the General informed me, by Letter, that from the Strength of the country and Works, no further Operations could be carried on, and that it was his Intention to re-embark the Troops, which I ordered to take place, and the Captains of the Squadron to attend; and I have the Satisfaction to add that, by their indefatigable Exertion, the whole Army, Artillery, and Horses, were again taken on board the Transports and Men of War before Day-break on the 27th.

I shall immediately proceed with the Squadron and Convoy, in pursuance of the latter Part of your Lordship's Orders.

I have the Honor to be, &c. &c. &c,
J.B. WARREN.

40

Battle Of Alexandria

Downing-Street, October 21, 1801.

A DISPATCH, of which the following is a Copy, was this Day received (in Duplicate) at the Office of the Right Honourable Lord Hobart, One of His Majesty's Principal Secretaries of State.

Head-Quarters, Camp before Alexandria, September 5, 1801.

MY LORD,

I Have now the satisfaction to inform your Lordship, that the Forts and Town of Alexandria have surrendered to His Majesty's Troops, who, on the 2d Instant, took Possession of the entrenched Camp, the Heights above Pompey's Pillar, the Redoubt de Bain, and the Fort Triangular. By the Capitulation the Garrison are to be embarked for France in the Course of Ten Days, provided the Shipping is in a State of Preparation to receive them.

The Operations against the Enemy's Works commenced on the 17th of August.

Major-General Coote embarked with a strong Corps on the Inundation in the Night between the 16th and 17th of August. He effected his landing to the Westward of Alexandria with little or no Opposition, and immediately invested the strong Castle of Marabout, situated at the Entrance of the Western Harbour of Alexandria.

On the East Side of the Town two Attacks were made to get possession of some Heights in Front of the entrenched Position of the Enemy. I instructed the Conduct of the Attack against their Right, to Major-General Cradock; and that against their Left to Major-General Moore. Those Two Officers perfectly executed my Intentions, and performed the Service committed to their Care with much Precision and Ability. – The Action was neither obstinate or severe, and our loss is but small; but it afforded One more Opportunity to display the Promptness of British Officers, and the Heroism of British Soldiers. A Part of General Doyle's Brigade, the 30th Regiment, (but under the immediate Command of Colonel Spencer,) had taken Possession of a Hill in Front of the Enemy's Right. General Menou, who was in Person in that Part of the French Intrenched Camp, directly opposite to our Post, ordered about Six Hundred Men to make a Sortie, to drive us from our Position. – The Enemy advanced in Column with fixed Bayonets and without firing a Shot, till they got very close to the 30th Regiment, to whom Colonel Spencer gave an immediate Order to charge, though they did not consist of more than Two Hundred Men; he was obeyed with a Spirit and a Determination worthy the highest Panegyric. The Enemy were driven back to their Intrenchments in the greatest Confusion – they had many killed and wounded, and several taken Prisoners.

On the Night between the 18th and 19th, Major-General Coote opened Batteries against the Castle of Marabout; an Attack was also made from the Sea by several Turkish Corvettes, and the Launches and Boats of the Fleet, under the Guidance of the Honourable Captain Cochrane; great Perseverance and Exertions were required to get up heavy Guns through a difficult and almost impracticable Country; but the Troops executed this painful and arduous Service with such Zeal and continued Firmness, that the Fort capitulated in the Night of the 21st; the Garrison consisted of about One Hundred and Eighty Men, and were commanded by a Chef de Brigade.

On the Morning of the 22d, Major-General Coote marched from Marabout to attack a strong Corps posted in his Front, in order to cover the Approach to Alexandria; the Managements of that excellent Officer appear to have been able and judicious, and were attended with the most complete Success; he drove the Enemy every where, though Strongly posted, and in a Country which opposed uncommon Obstacles to the Progress of Troops. The French suffered extremely in the Action, and retreated in much Confusion, leaving their Wounded and Seven Pieces of Cannon behind them.

On the 24th, Batteries were opened against the Redoubt de Bain; and on the 25th, at Night, Major-General Coote surprised the Enemy's Advanced Posts, when Seven Officers and Fifty Men were taken Prisoners; this Service was gallantly performed by Lieutenant-Colonel Smith, with the 1st Battalion of the 20th Regiment, and a small Detachment of Dragoons under the orders of Lieutenant Kelly, of the 26th. The Enemy endeavoured to regain Possession of the Ground from which they had been driven, but were repulsed with Loss.

On the Morning of the 26th we opened Four Batteries on each Side of the Town against the intrenched Camp of the French, which soon silenced their Fire, and induced them to withdraw many of their Guns.

On the 27th, in the Evening, General Menou sent an Aid-de-Camp to request an Armistice for Three Days, in order to give Time to prepare a Capitulation, which, after some Difficulties and Delays, was signed on the 2d of September.

I have the Honor to enclose you a Copy of the Capitulation, and also a List of the Number of Persons for whom the Enemy have required Shipping; by this it appears, that the Total of the Garrison of Alexandria consisted of upwards of Eight Thousand Soldiers, and One Thousand Three Hundred Sailors.

This arduous and important Service has at length been brought to a Conclusion. The Exertions of Individuals have been splendid and meritorious. I regret that the Bounds of a Dispatch will not allow me to specify the Whole, or to mention the Name of every Person who has distinguished himself in the public Service. I have received the greatest Support and Assistance from the General Officers of the Army. The Conduct of the Troops of every Description has been exemplary in the highest Degree; there has been much to applaud and nothing to reprehend; their Order and Regularity in the Camp have been as conspicuous as their Courage in the Field. To the Quarter-Master General Lieutenant-Colonel Anstruther I owe much for his unwearied Industry and Zeal in the public Service, and for the Aid, Advice, and Cooperation, which he has at all Times afforded me. Brigadier-General Lawson, who commanded the Artillery, and Captain Bryce, the Chief Engineer, have both great Merit in their different Departments. The local Situation of Egypt presents Obstacles of a most serious Kind to military Operations on an extended Scale. The Skill and Perseverance of those Two Officers have overcome Difficulties which at first appeared almost insurmountable.

Lieutenant-Colonel Lindenthal, who has always acted with the Turks, deserves my utmost Acknowledgments; his Activity and Diligence have been unremitted, and he has introduced amongst them an Order and Regularity which does him the highest Honor.

During the Course of the long Service on which we have been engaged, Lord Keith has, at all Times, given me the most able Assistance and Counsel. The Labour and Fatigue of the Navy have been continued and excessive; – it have not been of One Day or of One Week, but for Months together. In the Bay of Aboukir, on the New Inundation, and on the Nile, for One Hundred and Sixty Miles, they have been employed without Intermission, and have submitted to many Privations with a Chearfulness and Patience highly creditable to them, and advantageous to the public Service.

Sir Sidney Smith had originally the Command of the Seamen who landed from the Fleet; he continued on Shore till after the Capture of Rosetta, and returned on board the Tigre a short Time before the Appearance of Admiral Gantheaume's Squadron on the Coast. He was present in the Three Actions of the 8th, 13th, and 21st of March, when he displayed that Ardour of Mind for the Service of his Country, and that noble Intrepidity for which he has been ever so conspicuous. Captain Stevenson, of the Europa, succeeded him, and I have every Reason to be satisfied with his Zeal and Conduct. The Crews of the Gun-Boats displayed great Gallantry, under his Guidance, in the New Inundation; and much Approbation is also due to the Naval Officers who acted under his Orders.

Captain Pressland of the Regulus has had the Direction for many Months past of all Greek Ships in our Employment, and of those belonging to the Commissariot. He has been active, zealous, and indefatigable, and merits my warmest Approbation. I must therefore beg Leave particularly to recommend this old and meritorious Officer to your Lordship's Protection.

Allow me to express an humble Hope, that the Army in Egypt have gratified the warmest Wishes and Expectations of their Country. To them every Thing is due, and to me nothing. It was my Fate to succeed a Man who created such a Spirit and established such a Discipline amongst them, that little has been left for me to perform except to follow his Maxims, and to endeavour to imitate his Conduct.

This Dispatch will be delivered to your Lordship by Colonel Abercromby, an Officer of considerable Ability, and worthy of the great Name which he bears. He will one day, I trust, emulate the Virtue and Talents of his never sufficiently to be lamented Father.

I have the Honor to be, &c. &c. &c.
J. HELY HUTCHINSON, Lieutenant-General.

41

Battle Of Copenhagen

Admiralty-Office, April 15, 1801.

CAPTAIN OTWAY, of His Majesty's Ship the London, arrived in Town this Morning with Dispatches from Admiral Sir Hyde Parker, Commander in Chief of a Squadron of His Majesty's Ships employed on a particular Service, to Evan Nepean Esq; dated on board the London, in Copenhagen-Roads, the 6th Instant, of which the following are Copies:

SIR,

YOU will be pleased to acquaint the Lords Commissioners of the Admiralty, that since my Letter of the 23d of March, no Opportunity of Wind offered for going up the Sound until the 25th, when the Wind shifted in a most violent Squall from the S.W. to the N.W. and North, and blew with such Violence, and with so great a Sea, as to render it impossible for any Ship to have weighed her Anchor. The Wind and Sea were even so violent as to oblige many Ships to let go a second Anchor to prevent them from driving, notwithstanding they were riding with Two Cables an End; and, by the Morning, the Wind Veered again to the Southward of the West.

On the 30th of last Month, the Wind having come to the Northward, we passed into the Sound with the Fleet, but not before I had assured myself of the hostile Intentions of the Danes to oppose our Passage, as the Papers marked No. 1, 2, 3, and 4, will prove; after this Intercourse, there could be no Doubt remaining of their Determination to resist.

After anchoring about Five or Six Miles from the Island of Huin, I reconnoitered, with Vice Admiral Lord Nelson, and Rear-Admiral Graves, the formidable Line of Ships, Radeaus, Pontoons, Galleys, Fire-Ships, and Gun-Boats, flanked and supported by extensive Batteries on the Two Islands called the Crowns; the largest of which was mounted with from Fifty to Seventy Pieces of Cannon; these were again commanded by Two Ships of Seventy Guns, and a large Frigate in the Inner Road of Copenhagen; and Two Sixty-four Gun Ships, (without Masts) were moored on the Flat, on the Starboard Side of the Entrance into the Arsenal.

The Day after, the Wind being Southerly, we again examined their Position, and came to the Resolution of attacking them from the Southward.

Vice-Admiral Lord Nelson, having offered his Services for conducting the Attack, had, some Days before we entered the Sound, shifted his Flag to the Elephant; and after having examined and buoyed the Outer Channel of the Middle Ground, his Lordship proceeded with the Twelve Ships of the Line named in the Margin*, all the Frigates, Bombs, Fire-Ships, and all the small Vessels, and that Evening anchored off Draco Point to make his Disposition for the Attack, and wait for the Wind to the Southward.

It was agreed between us, that the remaining Ships with me should weigh at the same Moment his Lordship did, and menace the Crown Batteries, and the Four Ships of the Line that lay at the Entrance of the Arsenal; as also to cover our disabled Ships as they came out of Action.

I have now the Honor to enclose a Copy of Vice Admiral Lord Nelson's Report to me of the Action on the 2d Instant. His Lordship has stated so fully the Whole of his Proceedings on that Day, as only to leave me the Opportunity to testify my entire Acquiescence and Testimony of the Bravery and Intrepidity with which the Action was supported throughout the Line.

Was It possible for me to add any Thing to the well-earned Renown of Lord Nelson, it would be by asserting, that his Exertions, great as they have heretofore been, never were carried to a higher Pitch of Zeal for his Country's Service.

I have only to lament that the Sort of Attack, confined within an intricate and narrow Passage, excluded the Ships particularly under my Command from the Opportunity of exhibiting their Valour; but I can, with great Truth assert, that the same Spirit and Zeal animated the Whole of the Fleet; and I trust that the Contest in which we are engaged, will, on some future Day, afford them an Occasion of shewing that the Whole were inspired with the same Spirit, had the Field been sufficiently extensive to have brought it into Action.

It is with the deepest Concern I mention the Loss of Captains Mosse and Riou, Two very brave and gallant Officers, and whose Loss, as I am well informed, will be sensibly felt by the Families they have left behind them; the former, a Wife and Children, the latter, an aged Mother.

From the known Gallantry of Sir Thomas Thompson on former Occasions, the Naval Service will have to regret the Loss of the future Exertions of that brave Officer, whose Leg was shot off.

For all other Particulars I beg Leave to refer their Lordships to Captain Otway, who was with Lord Nelson in the latter Part of the Action, and able to answer any Questions that may be thought necessary to put to him.

I have the Honor to be, &c.
H. PARKER.

* Elephant, Defiance, Monarch, Bellona, Edgar, Russel, Ganges, Glatton, Isis, Agamemnon, Polyphemus, Ardent.

Elephant, off Copenhagen, 3 April, 1801.

SIR,

IN Obedience to your Directions to report the Proceedings of the Squadron named in the Margin*, which you did me the Honor to place under my Command; I beg Leave to inform you that having, by the Assistance of that able Officer, Captain Riou, and the unremitting Exertions of Captain Brisbane, and the Masters of the Amazon and Cruizer, in particular, buoyed the Channel of the Outer Deep, and the Position of the Middle Ground, the Squadron passed in Safety, and anchored off Draco the Evening of the First; and that Yesterday Morning I made the Signal for the Squadron to weigh, and to engage the Danish Line, consisting of Six Sail of the Line, Eleven Floating Batteries, mounting from Twenty-six Twenty-four Pounders, to Eighteen Eighteen Pounders, and one Bomb-Ship, besides Schooner Gun-Vessels.

These were supported by the Crown Islands mounting Eighty-eight Cannon, and Four Sail of the Line moored in the Harbour's Mouth, and some Batteries on the Island of Amak.

The Bomb-Ship and Schooner Gun-Vessels made their Escape, the other Seventeen Sail are sunk, burnt, or taken, being the Whole of the Danish Line to the Southward of the Crown Islands, after a Battle of Four Hours.

From the very intricate Navigation, the Bellona and Russel unfortunately grounded, but although not in the Situation aligned them, yet to placed as to be of great Service. The Agamemnon could not weather the Shoal of the Middle, and was obliged to anchor; but not the smallest Blame can be attached to Captain Fancourt; it was an Event to which all the Ships were liable. These Accidents prevented the Extension of our Line by the Three Ships before mentioned, who would, I am confident, have silenced the Crown Islands, the Two outer Ships in the Harbour's Mouth, and prevented the heavy Loss in the Defiance and Monarch, and which unhappily threw the gallant and good Captain Riou, to whom I had given the Command of the Frigates and Sloops named in the Margin**, to assist in the Attack of the Ships at the Harbour's Mouth under very heavy Fire; the Consequence has been the Death of Captain Riou, and many brave Officers and Men in the Frigates and Sloops.

The Bombs were directed and took their Stations abreast of the Elephant, and threw some Shells into the Arsenal.

Capt. Rose, who volunteered his Services to direct the Gun Brigs, did every Thing that was possible to get them forward, but the Current was too strong for them to be of Service during the Action; but not the less Merit is due to Captain Rose, and, I believe, all the Officers and Crews of the Gun-Brigs for their Exertions.

The Boats of those Ships of the Fleet, who were not ordered on the Attack, afforded us every Assistance; and the Officers and Men who were in them, merit my warmest Approbation.

The Desiree took her Station in raking the Southermost Danish Ship of the Line, and performed the greatest Service.

The Action began at Five Minutes past Ten. The Van, led by Captain George

Murray of the Edgar, who set a noble Example of Intrepidity, which was as well followed up by every Captain, Officer, and Man in the Squadron.

It is my Duty to state to you the high and distinguished Merit and Gallantry of Rear Admiral Graves.

To Captain Foley, who permitted me the Honor of hoisting my Flag in the Elephant, I feel under the greatest Obligations; his Advice was necessary on many and important Occasions during the Battle.

I beg Leave to express how much I feel indebted to every Captain, Officer, and Man, for their Zeal and distinguished Bravery on this Occasion. The Honourable Colonel Stewart did me the Favor to be on board the Elephant, and himself, with every Officer and Soldier under his Orders, shared with Pleasure the Toils and Dangers of the Day.

The Loss in such a Battle has naturally been very heavy. Amongst many other brave Officers and Men who were killed, I have with Sorrow to place the Name of Captain Mosse, of the Monarch, who has left a Wife and Six Children to lament his Loss; and, among the Wounded, that of Captain Sir Thomas B. Thompson of the Bellona.

I have the Honor to be, &c. &c. &c.
NELSON and BRONTE.

Elephant, Defiance, Monarch, Bellona, Edgar, Russel, Ganges, Glatton, Isis, Agamemnon Polyphemus, Ardent, Amazon, Desiree, Blanche, Alcmene; Sloops Dart, Arrow, Cruizer, and Harpy; Fire-Ships Zephyr and Otter; Bombs Discovery, Sulphur, Hecla, Explosion, Zebra, Terror, and Volcano.

**Blanche, Alcmene, Dart, Arrow, Zephyr, and Otter.*

42

Battle Of Algeciras Bay

Admiralty-Office, August 1, 1801.

Copy of a Letter from Rear-Admiral Sir James Saumarez, to Evan Nepean, Esq; dated on board His Majesty's Ship Caesar, at Gibraltar, the 6th July 1801.

SIR,

I HAVE to request you will be pleased to Inform my Lords Commissioners of the Admiralty, that, conformably to my Letter of Yesterday's Date, I stood through the Streights, with His Majesty's Squadron under my Orders, with the Intention of attacking Three French Line of Battle Ships and a Frigate, that I had received Information of being at Anchor off Algeziras; on opening Cabareta Point, I found the Ships lay at a considerable Distance from the Enemy's Batteries, and having a leading Wind up to them, afforded every reasonable Hope of Success in the Attack.

    I had previously directed Captain Hood, in the Venerable, from his Experience and Knowledge of the Anchorage, to lead the Squadron, which he executed with his accustomed Gallantry, and although it was not intended he should anchor, he found himself under the Necessity so to do, from the Wind's failing, (a Circumstance so much to be apprehended in this Country) and to which Circumstance I have to regret the Want of Success in this well-intended Enterprise; Captain Stirling anchored opposite to the inner Ship of the Enemy, and brought the Pompée to Action in the most spirited and gallant Manner, which was also followed by the Commanders of every Ship in the Squadron.

    Captains Darby and Ferris, owing to light Winds, were prevented for a considerable Time from coming into Action; at length the Hannibal getting a Breeze, Captain Ferris had the most favorable Prospect of being alongside one of the Enemy's Ships, when the Hannibal unfortunately took the Ground, and I am extremely concerned to acquaint their Lordships, that after having made every possible Effort with this Ship and the Audacious, to cover her from the Enemy, I was under the Necessity to make Sail, being at the Time only Three Cables Length from one of the Enemy's Batteries.

    My Thanks are particularly due to all the Captains, Officers, and Men under my Orders; and although their Endeavours have not been crowned with Success, I trust the Thousands of Spectators from His Majesty's Garrison, and also the surrounding

Coast, will do Justice to their Valour and Intrepidity, which was not to be checked by the Fire from the numerous Batteries, however formidable, that surround Algeziras.

I feel it incumbent upon me to state to their Lordships the great Merits of Captain Brenton, of the Cæsar, whose cool Judgment and intrepid Conduct, I will venture to pronounce, were never surpassed.

I also beg Leave to recommend to their Lordships' Notice my Flag-Lieutenant, Mr. Philip Dumaresq, who has served with me from the Commencement of this War, and is a most deserving Officer. Mr. Lamborne and the other Lieutenants are also entitled to great Praise, as well as Captain Maxwell of the Marines, and the Officers of his Corps serving on board the Cæsar.

The Enemy's Ships consisted of Two of Eighty-four Guns, and One of Seventy-four, with a large Frigate; Two of the former are aground, and the Whole are rendered totally unserviceable.

I cannot close this Letter without rendering the most ample Justice to the great Bravery of Captain Ferris: the Loss in his Ship must have been very considerable both in Officers and Men; but I have the Satisfaction to be informed, that His Majesty has not lost so valuable an Officer.

I have the Honor to be, &c. &c.
JAMES SAUMAREZ.

The Honourable Captain Dundas, of His Majesty's Polacre the Calpe, made his Vessel as useful as possible, and kept up a spirited Fire on one of the Enemy's Batteries. I have also to express my Approbation of Lieutenant Janverin, Commander of the Gun Boats, who having joined me with Intelligence served as Volunteer on board the Cæsar.

Admiralty-Office, August 1, 1801.

Copy of a Letter from Rear-Admiral Sir James Saumarez, dated, on board His Majesty's Ship Caesar, Gibraltar Mole, 10th July 1801, to Evan Nepean, Esq.

SIR,

I Herewith enclose the Copy of a Letter from Captain Ferris, of His Majesty's late Ship Hannibal, which I request you will please to lay before their Lordships; and I have only to express my deep Regret that his well-meant Endeavours to bring his Ship to close Action should have occasioned so severe a Loss.

J. SAUMAREZ.

SIR,

Algeziras, July 7, 1801.

I Have little more to tell you of the Fate of His Majesty's Ship Hannibal than yourself must have observed, only, that from the Number of Batteries and Ships, Gun-Boats, &c. we had to encounter, our Guns soon got knocked up; and I found it was impossible to do any Thing either for the Preservation of the Ship or for the Good of the Service, our Boats, Sails, Rigging, and Springs being all shot away; and having so many Killed and Wounded, which will appear by the annexed List, I thought it prudent to strike, and thereby preserve the Lives of the brave Men that remained.

Had I been successful in the View before me, previous to the Ship's taking the Ground, my Praises of the Conduct of my Officers and Ship's Company could not have exceeded their Merits; but I have, notwithstanding, the Satisfaction to say, that every Order was observed and carried into Execution with that promptitude and Alacrity becoming British Officers and Seamen.

I am, &c. (Signed) S. FERRIS.

Rear Admiral Sir James Saumarez &c. &c. &c
Caesar, off Cape Trafalgar, July 13, 1801

SIR,

IT has pleased the Almighty to crown the Exertions of this Squadron with the most decisive Success over the Enemies of their Country.

The Three French Line of Battle Ships disabled in the Action of the 6th Instant, off Algeziras, were, on the 8th, reinforced by a Squadron of Five Spanish Line of Battle Ships under the Command of Don Juan Joaquin de Moreno, and a French Ship of Seventy-four Guns, wearing a Broad Pendant, besides Three Frigates, and an incredible Number of Gun-boats and other Vessels, and got under Sail Yesterday Morning, together with His Majesty's late Ship Hannibal, which they had succeeded in getting off the Shoal on which she struck.

I almost despaired of having a sufficient Force in Readiness to oppose to such Numbers, but, through the great Exertions of Captain Brenton, the Officers and Men belonging to the Cæsar, the Ship was in Readiness to warp out of the Mole Yesterday Morning, and got under Weigh immediately after with all the Squadron, except the Pompée, which Ship had not had Time to get in her Masts.

Confiding in the Zeal and Intrepidity of the Officers and Men I had the Happiness to serve with, I determined, if possible, to obstruct the Passage of this very powerful Force to Cadiz. Late in the Evening I observed the Enemy's Ships to have cleared Cabareta Point, and at Eight I bore up I with the Squadron to stand after them. His Majesty's Ship Superb being stationed a-head of the Cæsar, I directed Captain Keats to make Sail and attack the Sternmost Ships in the Enemy's Rear, using his Endeavours to keep in shore of them.

At Eleven the Superb opened her Fire close to the Enemy's Ships, and on the Caesar's coming up and preparing to engage a Three Decker that had hauled her Wind, she was perceived to have taken Fire, and the Flames having communicated to a Ship to Leeward of her, both were seen in a Blaze, and presented a most awful Sight. No Possibility existing of offering the least Assistance in so distressing a Situation, the Cæsar passed to close with the Ship engaged by the Superb, but by the cool and determined Fire kept upon her, which must ever reflect the highest Credit on that Ship, the Enemy's Ship was completely silenced, and soon after hauled down her Colours.

The Venerable and Spencer having at this Time come up, I bore up after the Enemy, who were carrying a Press of Sail standing out of the Straits, and lost Sight of them during the Night. It blew excessively hard till Day-light, and in the Morning the only Ships in Company were the Venerable and Thames ahead of the Cæsar, and one of the French Ships at some Distance from them, standing towards the Shoals of Conil, besides the Spencer astern coming up.

All the Ships immediately made Sail with a fresh Breeze, but, as we approached, the Wind suddenly failing, the Venerable was alone able to bring her to Action, which Captain Hood did in the most gallant Manner, and had nearly silenced the French Ship, when his Main Mast (which Had been before Wounded) was unfortunately shot away, and it coming nearly calm, the Enemy's Ship was enabled to get off without any Possibility of following her.

The highest Praise is due to Captain Hood, the Officers and Men of the Venerable, to their Spirit and Gallantry in the Action, which entitled them to better Success. The French Ship was an Eighty-four, with additional Guns on the Gunwale.

This Action was so near the Shore, that the Venerable struck on one of the Shoals, but was soon after got off and taken in Tow by the Thames, but with the Loss of all her Masts.

The Enemy's Ships are now in Sight to the Westward, standing in for Cadiz. The Superb and Audacious, with the captured Ship, are also in Sight, with the Carlotta Portuguese Frigate commanded by Captain Crawfurd Duncan, who very handsomely came out with the Squadron, and has been of the greatest Assistance to Captain Keats, in staying by the Enemy's Ship captured by the Superb.

I am proceeding with the Squadron for Rosier Bay, and shall proceed the Moment the Ships are refitted to resume my Station.

No Praises that I can bestow are adequate to the Merits of the Officers and Ships' Companies of all the Squadron, particularly for their unremitted Exertions in refitting the Ships at Gibraltar, to which, in a great Degree, is to be ascribed the Success of the Squadron against the Enemy.

Although the Spencer and Audacious had not the good Fortune to partake of this Action, I have no Doubt of their Exertion, had they come up in Time to close With the Enemy's Ships.

My Thanks are also due to Captain Holies of the Thames, and to the Honourable

Captain Dundas of the Calpe, whose Assistance was particularly useful to Captain Keats in securing the Enemy's Ship, and enabling the Superb to stand after the Squadron, in case of having been enabled to renew the Action.

I have the Honor to be, &c. &c. &c.
(Signed) J. SAUMAREZ

43

Raid On Boulogne

Admiralty-Office, August 18, 1801.

Copy of a Letter from Lord Viscount Nelson, K.B. Vice-Admiral of the Red, dated on board the Medusa, off Boulogne, August 16, 1801.

SIR,

HAVING judged it proper to attempt bringing off the Enemy's Flotilla, moored in the Front of Boulogne, I directed the Attack to be made by four Divisions of Boats for boarding, under the Command of Captains Somerville, Cotgrave, Jones and Parker, and a Division of Howitzer Boats under Captain Conn. The Boats put off from the Medusa at Half past Eleven o'Clock last Night in the best possible Order, and before One o'Clock this Morning the firing began, and I had, from the Judgment of the Officers, and the Zeal and Gallantry of every Man, the most perfect Confidence of complete Success, but the Darkness of the Night, with the Tide and Half Tide, separated the Divisions, and from all not arriving at the same happy Moment with Captain Parker, is to be attributed the Failure of Success; but I beg to be perfectly understood that not the smallest Blame attaches itself to any Person; for although the Divisions did not arrive together, yet each (except the Fourth Division, which could not be got up before Day) made a successful Attack on that Part of the Enemy they fell in with, and actually took possession of many Brigs and Flats, and cut their Cables, but many of them being aground, and the Moment of the Battle's ceasing on board them, the Vessels were filled with Vollies upon Vollies of Musketry, the Enemy being perfectly regardless of their own Men, who must have suffered equally with us, it was therefore impossible to remain on board even to burn them; but allow me to say, who have seen much Service this War, that more determined persevering Courage I never witnessed, and that nothing but the Impossibility of being successful, from the Causes I have mentioned, could have prevented me from having to congratulate their Lordships; but although in Value the loss of such gallant and good Men is incalculable, yet, in Point of Numbers, it has fallen short of my Expectations. I must also beg leave to state, that greater Zeal and ardent Desire to distinguish themselves by an Attack on the Enemy was never shewn than by all the Captains, Officers, and Crews of all the different Descriptions of Vessels under my Command.

The Commanders of the Hunter and Greyhound Revenue Cutters went in their

Boats in the most handsome and gallant Manner to the Attack. Amongst the many brave Men wounded, I have with the deepest Regret to place the Name of my gallant good Friend and able Assistant Captain Edward T. Parker; also my Flag Lieutenant Frederick Langford, who has served With me many Years; they were both wounded in attempting to board the French Commodore. To Captain Gore of the Medusa I feel the highest Obligations; and when their Lordships look at the Loss of the Medusa on this Occasion, they will agree with me, that the Honor of my Flag, and the Cause of their King and Country, could never have been placed in more gallant Hands.

Captain Bedford of the Leyden, with Captain Gore, very handsomely volunteered their Services to serve under a Master and Con... 'er; but I did not think it fair to the latter, and I only mention it to mark the Z... ose Officers. From the Nature of the Attack only a few prisoners were made; a Lieutenant, Eight Seamen, and Eight Soldiers, are all they brought off. Herewith I send the Reports of the several Commanders of Divisions.

I have the Honor to be, &c.
NELSON and BRONTE.

P.S. Captain Somerville was the senior Master and Commander employed.

Eugenie off Boulogne, August 16, 1801.

MY LORD,

IN Obedience to your Lordship's Direction to state the Proceedings of the First Division of Boats which you did me the Honor to place under my Command, for the Purpose of attacking the Enemy's Flotilla in the Bay of Boulogne, I beg Leave to acquaint you, that after leaving the Medusa last Night, I found myself, on getting on Shore, carried considerably, by the Rapidity of the Tide, to the Eastward of the above-mentioned Place; and finding that I was not likely to reach it in the Order prescribed, I gave Directions for the Boats to cast each other off. By so doing, I was enabled to get to the Enemy's Flotilla a little before the Dawn of Day, and in the best Order possible attacked, close to the Pier Head, a Brig, which, after a sharp Contest, I carried. Previous to so doing, her Cables were cut; but I was prevented from towing her out by her being secured with a Chain, and in consequence of a very heavy Fire of Musquetry and Grape Shot that was directed at us from the Shore, Three Luggers, and another Brig within Half Pistol Shot; and not seeing the least Prospect of being able to get her off, I was obligated to abandon her, and push out of the Bay, as it was then completely Day-light.

The undaunted and resolute Behaviour of the Officers, Seamen, and Marines was unparalleled; and I have to lament the Loss of several of those brave Men, a List of whom I enclose you herewith.

I have the Honor to be, &c.

P. SOMERVILLE.

Medusa, off Boulogne, August 16, 1801.

MY LORD,

AFTER the complete Arrangement which was made, the perfect good Understanding and Regularity with which the Boats you did me the Honor to put under my Command left the Medusa, I have an anxious Feeling to explain to your Lordship the Failure of our Enterprise, that, on its outset, promised every Success.

Agreeable to your Lordship's Instructions, I proceeded with the Second Division of the Boats under my Direction, (the Half of which were under the Direction of Lieutenant Williams, Senior of the Medusa,) to attack the Part of the Enemy's Flotilla, appointed for me, and at Half-past Twelve had the good Fortune to find myself close to them, when I ordered Lieutenant Williams, with his Subdivision, to push on to attack the Vessels to the Northward of me, while I, with the others, ran alongside a large Brig off the Mole Head, wearing the Commodore's Pendant. It is at this Moment I feel myself at a Loss for Words to do Justice to the Officers and Crew of the Medusa who were in the Boat with me, and to Lieutenant Langford, the Officers and Crew of the same Ship, who nobly seconded us in the Barge, until all her Crew were killed or wounded; and to the Honourable Mr. Cathcart who commanded the Medusa's Cutter, and sustained the Attack with the greatest Intrepidity, until the desperate Situation I was left in obliged me to call him to the Assistance of the Sufferers in my Boat.

The Boats were no sooner alongside than we attempted to board; but a very strong Netting, traced up to her Lower Yards, baffled all our Endeavours, and an instantaneous Discharge of her Guns and small Arms, from about Two Hundred Soldiers on her Gunwale, knocked myself, Mr. Kirby, the Master of the Medusa, and Mr. Gore, a Midshipman, with Two-Thirds of the Crew, upon our Backs into the Boat, all either killed or wounded desperately, the Barge and Cutter being on the Outside, sheered off with the Tide, but the Flat Boat in which I was hung alongside, and as there was not an Officer or Man left to govern her, must have fallen into the Hands of the Enemy, had not Mr. Cathcart taken her in Tow, and carried her off.

Mr. Williams led his Subdivision up to the Enemy with the most intrepid Gallantry, took One Lugger, and attacked a Brig, while his Crews, I am concerned to say, suffered equally with ourselves, nearly the Whole of his Boat's Crew were killed or wounded; Lieutenant Pelley, who commanded the Medusa's Launch, and the Honourable Mr. Maitland, Midshipman, were severely wounded; and Mr. William Bristow, Master's Mate, in the Medusa's Cutter, under Lieutenant Stewart, was killed.

I now feel it my Duty to assure your Lordship, that nothing could surpass the Zeal, Courage, and Readiness of every Description of Officer and Man under my Command; and I am sorry that my Words fall short of their Merits, though we could not accomplish the Object we were ordered to.

I have the Honor to be, &c.

(Signed) EDWARD T. PARKER.

Ganet, August 16, 1801.

MY LORD

ON the Night of the 15th Instant, the Third Division of Boats which I had the Honor to command, assembled on board His Majesty's Ship York, agreeable to your Lordship's Directions, and at Eleven P. M. by Signal from the Medusa, proceeded, without Loss of Time, to attack the Enemy's Flotilla, off Boulogne, as directed by your Lordship; and as I thought it most adviseable to endeavour to reduce the largest Vessel first, I lost no Time in making the Attack; but in consequence of my leading the Division, and the Enemy opening a heavy Fire from several Batteries, thought it adviseable to give the Enemy as little Time as possible, cut the Tow-Rope, and did not wait for the other Boat, so that it was some little Time before the heavy Boats could get up; received so many Shots through the Boat's Bottom, that I soon found her in a sinking State, and as it was not possible to stop so many Shot Holes, was obliged with the Men, to take to another Boat, and have the Pleasure to acquaint your Lordship, that I received particular Support from the Boats of His Majesty's Ship York, which soon came up with the rest of the Division I had the Honor to command; but finding no Prospect of Success and the Number of Men killed and wounded in the different Boats, and the constant Fire from the Shore of Grape and small Arms, thought it for the Good of His Majesty's Service to withdraw the Boats between Two and Three in the Morning, as we could not board her, although every Effort was made.

I have the Honor to be, &c.
(Signed) ISAAC COTGRAVE.

His Majsty's Ship Isis, Sunday, Aug. 16 1801.

MY LORD

IN consequence of Directions received from your Lordsthip, I last Night, on the Signal being made on board the Medusa, left this Ship with the Boats of the Fourth Division, formed with two close Lines, and immediately joined the other Divisions under the Stern of the Medusa, and from thence proceeded to put your Lordship's Order into Execution, attacking the Westernmost Part of the Enemy's Flotilla: but notwithstanding every Exertion made, owing to the Rapidity of the Tide we could not, until near Day-light, get to the Westward of any Part of the Enemy's Line; on approaching the Eastern part of which, in order to assist the First Division then engaged, we met them returning.

Under these Circumstances, and the Day breaking apace, I judged it prudent to direct the Officers commanding the different Boats to return to their respective Ships.

> I have the Honor to be, &c.
> ROB. JONES

P.S. None killed or wounded on board any of the Fourth Division.

> *Discovery off Boulogne, 16 August, 1801.*

MY LORD,

I Beg Leave to make my Report to your Lordship of the Four Howitzer Boats that I had the Honor to command, in the Attack of the Enemy last Night.

Having led in to support Captain Parker's Division, keeping between his Lines until the Enemy opened their Fire on him, we keeping on towards the Pier until I was aground in the headmost Boat, then opened our Fire, and threw about Eight Shells into it; but, from the Strength of the Tide coming out of the Harbour, was not able to keep our Station off the Pier Head, but continued our Fire on the Camp, until the Enemy's Fire had totally slackened, and Captain Parker's Division had passed without me. I beg Leave to mention to your Lordship, that I was ably supported by the other Boats. Captain Broome and Lieutenant Beam, of the Royal Artillery, did every Thing in their Power to annoy the Enemy. The other Officers of Artillery were detached in the other Four Howitzer Boats.

> I have the Honor to be, &c.
> JOHN CONN.

44

Battle Of St Lucia

Downing-Street, July 30, 1803.

A DISPATCH, of which the following is a Copy, has been this Day received from Lieutenant-General Grinfield, Commander in Chief of His Majesty's Troops in the Windward and Leeward Charibbee Islands, by the Right Honourable Lord Hobart, His Majesty's Principal Secretary of State for the War Department:

St Lucia, June 22, 1803.

SIR,

IT is with Satisfaction I have the Honor to acquaint your Lordship, that this Day the Fortress of Morne Fortunee was carried by Assault, and the Island of St. Lucia is in consequence unconditionally restored to the British Government.

I have to state to your Lordship, that in consequence of His Majesty's Order, signified to me in your Letter, dated the 16th of May, and received on the 14th Instant, which I immediately communicated to Commodore Hood, he arrived at Barbadoes on the 17th; the Troops, Stores, &c. were on board, or embarked on the 19th; sailed on the 20th. On the 21st, at Day-break, they were off the North End of St. Lucia, in the Course of the Day the greatest Part of the Troops were disembarked in Choque Bay; about Half-past Five, the Out-Posts of the Enemy were driven in, the Town of Castries taken, and a Summons was sent to the Commander of the Troops of the French Republic.

In consequence of the Refusal of Brigade General Nogues to accede to any Terms, and the Expectation of approaching Rains, it became necessary to get Possession of the Morne with as little Delay as possible. It was therefore determined, this Morning, to attack the Fortress by Assault, which was done accordingly at Four o'Clock, and it was carried in about Half an Hour, and with less Loss, considering the Resistance, than could have been expected; but the Loss has been chiefly among the higher Ranks of Officers, and those the most truly valuable: but it is yet to be hoped most of them will recover, for the real Benefit of His Majesty's Service.

I cannot omit a Circumstance which reflects so much Credit, as well on the British

Nation, as on the Conduct of the Soldiers actually employed, that, notwithstanding the severe and spirited Resistance of the French Troops, yet, no sooner were the Works carried by Assault, and the Opposition no longer existed, than every Idea of Animosity appeared to cease, and not a French Soldier was either killed or wounded.

These Dispatches will be delivered to your Lordship by my Aid de Camp Captain Weir, to whom I beg to refer your Lordship for any Information you may require.

(Signed) W. TATUM , Captain, Assistant Adjutant-General.

Copy of a letter from Commodore Hood, Commander in Cheif of His Majesty's Ships and Vessels at the Leeward Islands, to Sir Evan Nepean Bart. dated on board the Centaur, in Choc Bay, St. Lucia, 22nd June 1803.

SIR,

I HAVE the Honor to acquaint you, for the Information of the Lords Commissioners of the Admiralty that, on my Arrival at Barbadoes on the 17th, late in the Evening, having consulted Lieutenant-General Grinfield with respect to the intended Co-operations of the Army and Navy, I instantly took Measures to prevent further Supplies being thrown into St. Lucia, (the Ships on this Service, under the Orders of Captain O'Bryen, of the Emerald, made some Captures of Trading Vessels,) and every Disposition was settled for embarking the Troops and Light Artillery on board the Ships of War, and the necessary Stores, &c. in small Vessels for the Expedition; by great Exertions the Whole was effected on the 20th, and the Arrangements completed: The Lieutenant-General having embarked with the Troops I put to Sea with the Ships named in the Margin*; was joined the next Morning by the Emerald and Osprey, having Brigadier-General Prevost on board, and were all anchored by Eleven o'Clock in this Bay.

There being a strong Breeze, the Boats of the Squadron had a heavy Pull with the First Division of the Army, composed of the 2d Battalion of the Royals, and Two Field-Pieces, under the Command of Brigadier-General Brereton; but, by the great Energy and excellent Disposition made by Captain Hallowell, were landed in good Order about Two P. M. and by the Perseverance of every Officer and Man employed in landing the Remainder of the Troops, the Lieutenant-General was enabled to make an early Arrangement for an Attack on that very important and strong Post, Morne Fortunée, where the Force of the Enemy was assembled, which, on the Commandant refusing to give up when summoned, was ordered to be attacked with that Decision and Promptitude which has always been the characteristic Mark of Lieutenant-General Grinfield, and carried by Storm at half-past Four this Morning, with the superior Bravery which has ever distinguished the British Soldier: this placed the Colony completely in our Possession.

To Captain Hallowell's Merit it is impossible for me to give additional Encomium, as it is so generally known; but I must beg Leave to say, on this Expedition, his Activity could not be exceeded; and by his friendly Advice I have obtained the most effectual Aid to this Service, for which he has been a Volunteer, and, after the final Disembarkation, proceeded on with the Seamen to co-operate with the Army. The Marines of the Squadron, by Desire of the Lieutenant-General, were landed and ordered to take Post near Gros Ilet, to prevent Supplies being thrown into Pigeon Island, which, on the Fall of Morne Fortunée, was delivered up.

We are already occupied in re-embarking Troops and other necessary Service for future Operations.

Captain Littlehales (of this Ship) is charged with the Dispatch, whose Assiduity and Attention. I with much Satisfaction acknowledge, will be able to give their Lordships any further Information.

I have the Honor to be, &c.
SAM HOOD

Centaur, Courageux, Argo, Chichester, Hornet, and *Cyane.*

45

Battle Of Ally Ghur

Fort William, Thursday, Sept. 8, 1803.
To His Excellency the Most Noble Marquis Wellesley, Governor-General, &c. &c.

MY LORD,

I HAVE the Honor to inform your Lordship, that I attacked M. Peròn's Force this Morning, which was strongly posted with their Right extending to the Fort of Ally Ghur, and their entire Front protected by a deep Morass, which obliged me to change my original Plan of Attack, and detour considerably to the Right to turn their Left Flank, which I completely effected, dislodging a Body of Troops which were posted in a Village in the Enemy's Front.

On moving forward with the Cavalry in Two Lines, supported by the Line of Infantry and Guns, the Enemy immediately retired after a very few Shots from the Cavalry Guns, which did some Execution.

Several Attempts were made to charge some considerable Bodies of Cavalry, who made an Appearance of standing, but the Rapidity of their Retreat prevented the Possibility of effecting it so completely as I could have wished, but I have Reason to believe that, in consequence of the Operations of this Day, many of his Confederates have left him.

My Loss in Men and Horses is very inconsiderable, and no Officer.

I have the Pleasure to assure your Lordship, that the Zeal, Activity, and Steadiness displayed by both Officers and Men, afforded me entire Satisfaction, and deserve my warmest Praise.

My Staff afforded me every Assistance, and I feel myself under great Obligations to them.

From every Information l can obtain, immediately upon our advancing, M. Peron, with his Body Guard, retired towards Agra, and has left Colonel Pedron in Charge of the Fort.

I am at present encamped to the Southward of the Fort, and the Town of Coel is occupied by one of my Battalions.

I have the Honor to be,
My Lord,
Your Lordship's most faithful and humble Servant,
(Signed) G. LAKE.

46

Battle Of Assaye

Whitehall, March 31, 1804.

THE following Dispatches have been received at the East India House from the Governor in Council at Bombay:

Jonathon Duncan, Esq. &c. &c. &c.

SIR,

I ATTACKED the united Armies of Doulut Rao Sindia and the Rajah of Berar with my Division on the 23d, and the Result of the Action which ensued was that they were completely defeated with the Loss of Ninety Pieces of Cannon which I have taken. I have suffered a great Loss of Officers and Men.

I enclose a Copy of my Letter to the Governor General, in which I have given him a detailed Account of the Events which led to, and occurred in, the Action.

I have the Honor to be, &c. &c. &c.
ARTHUR WELLESLEY

Camp, Sept 25, 1803.

To His Excellency the Governor General, &c. &c. &c.

MY LORD,

I WAS joined by Major Hill with the last of the Convoys expected from the River Kistna, on the 18th, and on the 20th was enabled to move forward towards the Enemy, who had been joined in the Course of the last Seven or Eight Days by the Infantry under Colonel Pohlman, by that belonging to Begum Sumreo, and by another Brigade, the Name of whose Commander I have not ascertained. The Enemy's Army was collected about Bakerdun, and between that Place and Jasserabad.

I was near Colonel Stevenson's Corps on the 21st, and had a Conference with that Officer, in which we concerted a Plan to attack the Enemy's Army, with the Divisions under our Command, on the 24th in the Morning; and we marched on the 22d, Colonel Stevenson by the Western Route and I by the Eastern Route, round the Hills between Beed Naporah and Jalnah.

On the 23d I arrived at Naulaiah, and there received a Report that Sindia and the Rajah of Berar had moved off in the Morning with their Cavalry, and that the Infantry were about to follow, but were still in Camp, at the Distance of about six Miles from the Ground on which I intended to encamp. It was obvious that the Attack was no longer to be delayed, and having provided for the Security of my Baggage and Stores at Naulaiah, I marched on to attack the Enemy.

I found the whole combined Army of Sindia and the Rajah of Berar encamped on the Bank of the Kistna River, nearly on the Ground which I had been informed that they occupied. Their Right, which consisted entirely of Cavalry, was about Bakterdun, and extended to their Corps of Infantry, which were encamped in the Neighbourhood of Assye. Although I came first in Front of their Right, I determined to attack their Left, as the Defeat of their Corps of Infantry was most likely to be effectual; accordingly, I marched round to their left Flank, covering the March of the Column of Infantry by the British Cavalry in the Rear, and by the Mahratta and Mysore Cavalry on the Right Flank.

We passed the River Kistna at a Ford beyond the Enemy's left Flank, and I formed the Infantry immediately in two Lines, with the British Cavalry as a Reserve, in a Third, in an open Space between that River and a Nullah running parallel to it. The Mahratta and Mysore Cavalry occupied the Ground beyond the Kistna on our left Flank, and kept in check a large Body of the Enemy's Cavalry, which had followed our March from the Right of their own Position.

The Enemy had altered the Position of their Infantry previous to our Attack. It was no longer as at first, along the Kistna, but extended from that River across to the Village of Assye, upon the Nullah which was upon our Right. We attacked them immediately, and the Troops advanced under a very hot Fire from Cannon, the Execution of which was terrible.

The Picquets of the Infantry and the 74th Regiment, which were on the Right of the first and second Lines, suffered particularly from the Fire of the Guns on the Left of the Enemy's Position, near Assye. The Enemy's Cavalry also made an Attempt to charge the 74th Regiment, at the Moment when they were most exposed to this Fire; but they were cut up by the British Cavalry, which moved on at that Moment.

At Length the Enemy's Line gave Way in all Directions; and the British Cavalry cut in among their broken infantry, but some of their Corps went off in good Order; and a Fire was kept up on our Troops from many of the Guns from which the Enemy had been first driven, by Individuals who had been passed by the Line, under the Supposition that they were dead.

Lieutenant-Colonel Maxwell, with the British Cavalry, charged a large Body of Infantry, which had retired, and was formed again, in which Operation he was killed; and some Time elapsed before he could put an End to the straggling Fire which was kept up by Individuals from the Guns from which the Enemy were driven. The Enemy's Cavalry also, which had been hovering round us throughout the Action, was still near us. At length, when the last formed Body of Infantry gave way, the Whole went off, and left in our Hands Ninety Pieces of Cannon. This Victory, which was certainly complete, has, however, cost us dear, your Excellency will perceive by the enclosed Return, that our Loss in Officers and Men has been very great, and in that of Lieutenant-Colonel Maxwell and other Officers, whose Names are therein included, greatly to be regretted.

I cannot write in too strong Terms of the Conduct of the Troops. They advanced in the best Order, and with the greatest Steadiness, under a most destructive Fire, against a Body of Infantry far superior in Numbers who appeared determined to contend with them to the last, and who were driven from their Guns only by the Bayonet, and, notwithstanding the Numbers of the Enemy's Cavalry, and the repeated Demonstrations they made of an Intention to charge, they were kept at a Distance by the Infantry.

I am particularly indebted to Lieutenant-Colonel Harness and Lieutenant-Colonel Wallace, for the Manner in which they conducted their Brigades, and to all the Officers of the Staff for the Assistance I received from them.

The Officers commanding Brigades, nearly all those of the Staff, and the mounted Officers of the Infantry, had their Horses shot under them.

I have also to draw your Excellency's Notice to the Conduct of the Cavalry Commanded by Lieutenant-Colonel Maxwell, particularly that of the 19th Dragoons.

The Enemy are gone off towards the Adjuntee Chant, and I propose to follow them as soon as I can place my captured Guns, and the Wounded, in Security.

I have the Honor to be, &c.
A. WELLESLEY, M.G.

47

Battle Of Pulo Aura

Admiralty-Office, August 11, 1804.

THE Court of Directors of the East India Company have transmitted to this Office an Account of an Action which took place in the China Seas, on the 15th of February last, between a Division of the Company's Ships and a French Squadron, of which the following is a Copy.

SIR,

FOR the Information of the Honourable Court, I beg Leave to acquaint you, that the Earl Camden was dispatched from Canton by the Select Committee the 31st of January last, and the Ships noted in the Margin* were put under my Orders as Senior Commander, also the Rolla Botany Bay Ship, and the Country Ships, as per Margin†, were put under my Charge to convoy as far as our Courses lay in the same Direction. I was also ordered to take under my Protection a Portuguese Europe Ship that was lying in Macao Roads, whose Supra Cargo had solicited it from the Select Committee.

    Our Passage down the River was tedious, and the Fleet much dispersed, the Ships being under the Directions of their several Chinese Pilots, I could not keep them collected as I wished.

    The Ganges, a fast-failing Brig, was put under my Orders by the Select Committee to employ in any Manner that might tend to the Safety or Convenience of the Fleet, till we had passed the Streights of Malacca; I was then to dispatch her to Bengal.

    We passed Macao Roads on the Night of the 5th of February and I conceive the Rolla had anchored so near Macao as not to see the Fleet get under Weigh, and pass through, although, at the Time, I had no Idea that could be possible, especially as I saw the Ocean in shore of us getting under Weigh, burning Blue Lights, and firing a Gun; the Portuguese Ship, I suppose, must have been in the same Situation as the Rolla.

    During the Night of the 5th of February, I carried an easy Sail, and on the following Day hove-to for above Two Hours, hoping to see those Ships, but there was no Appearance of them, nor did they ever join the Fleet.

    On the 14th February, at Daybreak, we saw Pulo Auro, bearing W. S. W. and at Eight A. M. the Royal George made the Signal for seeing Four strange Sail in the S. W. I made the Signal for the Four Ships noted in the Margin‡, to go down and

Battle Of Pulo Aura

examine them, and Lieutenant Fowler, of the Royal Navy, late Commander of the Porpoise, and Passenger with me, having handsomely offered to go in the Ganges Brig, and inspect them nearly, I afterwards sent her down likewise; and from their Signals I perceived it was an Enemy's Squadron, consisting of a Line of Battle Ship, Three Frigates, and a Brig.

At One P. M. I recalled the look-out Ships by Signal, and formed the Line of Battle in close Order.

As soon as the Enemy could fetch in our Wake they put about, we kept on our Course under an easy Sail; at near Sunset they were close in our Rear, and I was in momentary Expectation of an Attack there, and preparing to support them but at the Close of the Day we perceived them haul to Windward. I sent Lieutenant Fowler, in the Ganges Brig, to station the Country Ships on our Lee-Bow, by which Means we were between them and the Enemy; and having done so, he returned with some Volunteers from the Country Ships.

We lay-to in Line of Battle all Night, our Men at their Quarters; at Day-break of the 15th, we saw the Enemy about Three Miles to Windward, laying-to. We hoisted our Colours, offering him Battle if he chose to come down. The Enemy's Four Ships hoisted French Colours, the Line of Battle Ship carrying a Rear-Admiral's Flag; the Brig was under Batavian Colours.

At Nine A. M. finding they would not come down, we formed the Order of Sailing, and steered our Course under an easy Sail; the Enemy then filled their Sails, and edged towards us.

At One P. M. finding they propose to attack and endeavour to cut off our Rear, I made the Signal to tack and bear down on him, and engage in Succession – the Royal George being the leading Ship, the Ganges next, and then the Earl Camden. This Manoeuvre was correctly performed, and we stood towards him under a Press of Sail. The Enemy then formed in a very close Line, and opened their Fire on the headmost Ships, which was not returned by us till we approached him nearer. The Royal George bore the Brunt of the Action, and got as near the Enemy as he would permit him. The Ganges and Earl Camden opened their Fire as soon as their Guns could have Effect; but before any other Ship could get into Action, the Enemy hauled their Wind, and stood away to the Eastward under all the Sail they could set. At Two P.M. I made the Signal for a general Chase, and we pursued them till Four P.M. when fearing a longer Pursuit would carry us too far from the Mouth of the Straits, and considering the immense Property at Stake, I made the Signal to tack; and at Eight P. M. we anchored in a Situation to proceed for the Entrance of the Straits in the Morning. As long as we could distinguish the Enemy, we perceived him steering to the Eastward under a Press of Sail.

The Royal George had One Man killed and another wounded, many Shot in her Hull, and more in her Sails; but few Shot touched either the Camden or Ganges, and the Fire of the Enemy seemed to be ill directed, his Shot either falling short or passing over us.

Captain Timins carried the Royal George into Action in the most gallant Manner. In justice to my Brother Commanders I must state, that every Ship was clear and prepared for Action; and as I had Communication with almost all of them during the Two Days we were in Presence of the Enemy, I found them unanimous in the determined Resolution to defend the valuable Property entrusted to their Charge to the last Extremity, with a full Conviction of the successful Event of their Exertions; and this Spirit was fully seconded by the gallant Ardour of all our Officers and Ships' Companies.

I received great Assistance from the Advice and Exertions of Lieutenant Fowler, whose meritorious Conduct in this Instance I hope the Honourable Court will communicate to the Lords of the Admiralty.

From Malacca I dispatched Lieutenant Fowler in the Ganges Brig to Pulo Perang, with a Packet from the Select Committee to the Captain of any of His Majesty's Ships, soliciting their Convoy to this very valuable Fleet.

On Arrival at Malacca we were informed that the Squadron we had engaged was that of Admiral Linois, consisting of the Marengo, of Eighty-four Guns, the Belle Poule and Smillante heavy Frigates, a Corvette of Twenty-eight, and the Batavian Brig William, of Eighteen Guns.

The 28th February, in the Straits of Malacca, Lat. 4 Deg. 3 Min. N. we fell in with His Majesty's Ships Albion and Sceptre; I was then in a very poor State of Health, and Mr. Lance went on Board the Albion, and by his very able Representation to Captain Ferrier, of the great national Consequence of the Honourable Company's Ships, he was induced to take Charge of the Fleet.

On the 3d of March I dispatched the Ganges Brig with a Letter to the Right Honourable the Governor General, giving an Account of our Action, to be conveyed to the Honourable Court.

We arrived at St. Helena the 9th of June, under Convoy of His Majesty's Ships Albion and Sceptres, and sailed the 18th, under Convoy of His Majesty's Ship Plantagenet, with the Addition of the Carmarthen, Captain Dobree, and Five Whalers.

Accompanying this, I send a Chart of the Entrance of the Streights of Malacca, with the Situation of the Fleet on the 14th and 15th February, which will, I trust, convey a more distinct Idea of the Action, than any written Description.

I have the Honor to be, &c.
NATH. DANCE.

---

* *Warley, Alfred, Royal George, Coults, Wexford, Ganges, Exeter, Earl of Abergavenny, Henry Addington, Bombay Castle, Cumberland, Hope, Dorsetshire, Warren Hastings, and Ocean.*

† *Lord Castlereagh, Carron, David Scott, Minerva, Ardasein, Charlotte, Friendship, Shan Kissaroo, Jahaungeer, Gilwell, and Neptune.*

‡ *Alfred, Royal George, Bombay Castle, and Hope.*

48

Battle Of Cape Finistere

Admiralty-Office, July 31, 1805.

A Copy of a Letter from the Honourable Admiral Cornwallis, Commander in Chief of His Majesty's Ships and Vessels in the Channel, &c. to William Marsden, Esq; dated Ville de Paris, off Ushant, 28th July 1805. Eight P.M.

SIR,

I HAVE the Pleasure to enclose, for the Information of the Lords Commissioners of the Admiralty, a Letter from Vice-Admiral Sir Robert Calder, giving an Account of his Success against the Combined Squadron of France and Spain.

I have the Honor to be, &c.
W. CORNWALLIS

Prince of Wales, July 23, 1805.

SIR,

YESTERDAY at Noon, Lat. 43 Deg. 30 Min. N., Long. 11 Deg. 17 Min. W., I was favoured with a View of the Combined Squadrons of France and Spain, consisting of Twenty Sail of the Line, also Three large Ships, armed en flute, of about Fifty Guns each, with Five Frigates and Three Brigs; the Force under my Directions at this Time consisting of Fifteen Sail of the Line, Two Frigates, a Cutter, and Lugger, I immediately stood towards the Enemy with the Squadron, making the needful Signals for Battle in the closest Order; and, on closing with them, I made the Signal for attacking their Centre. When I had reached their Rear, I tacked the Squadron in Succession; this brought us close up under their Lee, and when our Headmost Ships reached their Centre the Enemy were tacking in Succession; this obliged me to make again the same Manoeuvre, by which I brought on an Action which lasted upwards of Four Hours, when I found it necessary to bring-to the Squadron to cover the Two captured Ships, whose Names, are in the Margin*. I have to observe, the Enemy had every Advantage of Wind and Weather during the Whole Day. The Weather had been foggy, at Times, a great Part of the Morning; and very soon after we had brought them to Action, the Fog was so very thick at Intervals, that we could, with great Difficulty, see the Ship ahead or a-stern of us; this rendered it impossible to take the Advantages of the Enemy by Signals I could have wished to have done; had the Weather been more favourable, I am led to believe the Victory would have been more complete.

I have very great Pleasure in saying, every Ship was conducted in the most masterly Style; and I beg Leave here publicly to return every Captain, Officer, and Man whom I had the Honor to command on that Day, my most grateful Thanks, for their conspicuously gallant and very judicious good Conduct. The Honourable Captain Gardner, of the Hero led the Van Squadron in a most masterly and officer-like Manner, to whom I feel myself particularly indebted; as also to Captain Cuming for his Assistance during the Action.

If I may judge from the great Slaughter on board the captured Ships, the Enemy must have suffered greatly. They are now in Sight to Windward, and when I have secured the captured Ships, and put the Squadron to rights, I shall endeavour to avail myself of any Opportunity that may offer to give you some further Account of these Combined Squadrons.

I have the Honor to be, &c.
R. CALDER.

* *St. Rafael, 84 Guns; Firm, 74 Guns.*

49

Battle Of Trafalgar

Admiralty-Office, November 6, 1805.

DISPATCHES, of which the following are Copies, were received at the Admiralty this Day, at One o'Clock A. M. from Vice-Admiral Collingwood, Commander in Chief of His Majesty's Ships and Vessels off Cadiz:

Euryalus, off Cape Trafalgar, October 22, 1805.

SIR,

THE ever to be lamented Death of Vice-Admiral Lord Viscount Nelson, who, in the late Conflict with the Enemy, fell in the Hour of Victory, leaves to me the Duty of informing my Lords Commissioners of the Admiralty, that on the 19th Instant, it was communicated to the Commander in Chief from the Ships watching the Motions of the Enemy in Cadiz, that the Combined Fleet had put to Sea; as they sailed with light Winds westerly, his Lordship concluded their Destination was the Mediterranean, and immediately made all Sail for the Streights' Entrance, with the British Squadron, consisting of Twenty-seven Ships, Three of them Sixty fours, where his Lordship was informed by Captain Blackwood, (whose Vigilance in watching, and giving Notice of the Enemy's Movements, has been highly meritorious,) that they had not yet passed the Streights.

On Monday the 21st Instant, at Daylight, when Cape Trafalgar bore E. by S. about Seven Leagues, the Enemy was discovered Six or Seven Miles to the Eastward, the Wind about West, and very light, the Commander in Chief immediately made the Signal for the Fleet to bear up in Two Columns, as they are formed in order of sailing; a Mode of Attack his Lordship had previously directed, to avoid the Inconvenience and Delay in forming a Line of Battle in the usual Manner. The Enemy's Line consisted of Thirty-three Ships (of which Eighteen were French and Fifteen Spanish), commanded in Chief by Admiral Villeneuve; the Spaniards, under the Direction of Gravina, wore, with their Heads to the Northward, and formed their Line of Battle with great Closeness and Correctness; but as the Mode of Attack was unusual, so the Structure of their Line was new; - it formed a Crescent convexing to Leeward – so that, in leading down to their Centre, I had both their Van, and Rear, abast the Beam; before the Fire opened, every alternate Ship was about a Cable's Length to Windward of her Second a-head and a-stern, forming a Kind of double Line, and appeared, when on their Beam, to leave a very little Interval between them; and this without crowding their Ships. Admiral Villeneuve was in the Bucentaure in the Centre, and the Prince of Asturias bore Gravina's Flag in the Rear; but the French and Spanish Ships were mixed without any apparent Regard to Order of national Squadron. As the Mode of our Attack had been previously determined on, and communicated to the Flag-Officers, and Captains, few Signals were necessary, and none were made, except to direct close Order as the Lines bore down.

The Commander in Chief in the Victory led the Weather Column, and the Royal Sovereign, which bore my Flag, the Lee.

The Action began at Twelve o'Clock, by the leading Ships of the Columns breaking through the Enemy's Line, the Commander in Chief about the Tenth Ship from the Van, the Second in Command about the Twelfth from the Rear, leaving the Van of the Enemy unoccupied; the succeeding Ships breaking through, in all Parts, astern of their Leaders, and engaging the Enemy at the Muzzles of their Guns; the Conflict was severe; the Enemy's Ships were fought with a Gallantry highly honourable to their Officers; but the Attack on them was irresistible, and it pleased the Almighty Disposer of all Events to grant His Majesty's Arms a complete and glorious Victory; about Three P.M. many of the Enemy's Ships having struck their Colours, their Line gave way; Admiral Gravina, With Ten Ships joining their Frigates to Leeward, stood, towards Cadiz. The Five headmost Ships in their Van tacked, and standing to the Southward, to Windward of the British Line, were engaged, and the Sternmost of them taken; the others went off, leaving to His Majesty's Squadron Nineteen Ships of the Line, (of which Two are First Rates, the Santisima Trinidad and the Santa Anna,) with Three Flag Officers, viz. Admiral Villeneuve, the Commander in Chief, Don Ignatio Maria D'Aliva, Vice-Admiral, and the Spanish Rear-Admiral Don Baltazar Hidalgo Cisneros.

After such a Victory it may appear unnecessary to enter into Encomiums on the particular Parts taken by the several Commanders; the Conclusion says more on the Subject than I have Language to express; the Spirit which animated all was the same; when all exert themselves zealously in their Country's Service, all deserve that their high Merits should stand recorded; and never was high Merit more conspicuous than in the Battle I have described.

The Achille (a French 74), after having surrendered, by some Mismanagement of the Frenchmen took Fire and blew up; Two hundred of her Men were saved by the Tenders. A Circumstance occurred during the Action, which so strongly marks the invincible Spirit of British Seamen, when engaging the Enemies of their Country, that I cannot resist the Pleasure I have in making it known to their Lordships; the Temeraire was boarded by Accident, or Design, by a French Ship on one Side, and a Spaniard on the other; the Contest was vigorous, but in the End, the combined Ensigns were torn from the poop, and the British hoisted in their Places.

Such a Battle could not be fought without sustaining a great Loss of Men. I have not only to lament, in common with the British Navy, and the British Nation, in the Fall of the Commander in Chief, the Loss of a Hero, whose Name will be immortal, and his Memory ever dear to his Country; but my Heart is rent with the most poignant Grief for the Death of a Friend, to whom, by many Years' Intimacy, and a perfect Knowledge of the Virtues of his Mind, which inspired Ideas superior to the common Race of Men, I was bound by the strongest Ties of Affection; a Grief to which even the glorious Occasion in which he fell, does not bring the Consolation which perhaps it ought; his Lordship received a Musket Ball in his Left Breast, about the Middle of the Action, and sent an Officer to me immediately with his last Farewell; and soon after expired.

I have also, to lament the Loss of those excellent Officers Captains Duff of the Mars, and Cooke of the Bellerophon; I have yet heard of none others.

I fear the Numbers that have fallen will be found very great when the Returns come to me; but it having blown a Gale of Wind ever since the Action, I have not yet had it in my Power to collect any Reports from the Ships.

The Royal Sovereign having lost her Masts, except the tottering Foremast, I called the Euryalus to me, while the Action continued which Ship lying within Hail, made my Signals, a Service Captain Blackwood, performed with great Attention. After the Action, I shifted my Flag to her, that I might more easily communicate my Orders to, and collect the Ships, and towed the Royal Sovereign out to Seaward. The whole Fleet were now in a very perilous Situation, many dismasted; all shattered in Thirteen Fathom Water, off the Shoals of Trafalgar; and when I made the Signal to prepare to anchor, few of the Ships had an Anchor to let go, their Cables being shot; but the same good Providence which aided us through such a Day preserved us in the Night, by the Wind shifting a few Points, and drifting the Ships off the Land, except Four of the captured dismasted Ships, which are now at Anchor off Trafalgar, and I hope will ride safe, until those Gales are over.

Having thus detailed the Proceedings of the Fleet on this Occasion, I beg to congratulate their Lordships on a Victory which, I hope, will add a Ray to the Glory of His Majesty's Crown, and be attended with public Benefit to our Country.

I am, &c.
(Signed) C. COLLINGWOOD.

The Order in which the Ships of the British Squadron attacked the Combined Fleets, on the 21st of October, 1805.

VAN.	REAR.
Victory.	Royal Sovereign.
Temeraire.	Mars.
Neptune.	Belleisle.
Conqueror.	Tonnant.
Leviathan.	Bellerophon.
Ajax.	Colossus.
Orion.	Achille.
Agamemnon.	Polyphemus.
Minotaur.	Revenge.
Spartiate.	Swiftsure.
Britannia.	Defence.
Africa.	Thunderer.
Euryalus.	Defiance.
Sirius.	Prince.
Phoebe.	Dreadnought.
Naiad.	
Pickle Schooner.	
Entreprenante Cutter.	

(Signed) C. COLLINGWOOD.

50
Battle Of Cape Ortegal

Admiralty Office, November 11, 1805.

THE Letter, (and its Enclosures,) of which the following are Copies, were received at this Office last Night, from Captain (now Rear-Admiral) Sir Richard John Strachan, Bart. Commander of His Majesty's Ship the Cæsar, addressed to William Marsden, Esq.

Caesar, West of Rochfort 264 Miles,
Nov. 4, 1805, Wind S. E.

SIR,

BEING off Ferrol, working to the Westward, with the Wind Westerly, on the Evening of the 2d, we observed a Frigate in the N. W. making Signals; made all Sail to join her before Night, and followed by the Ships named in the Margin*, we came up with her at Eleven at Night; and at the Moment she joined us, we saw Six large Ships near us. Captain Baker informed me he had been chased by the Rochfort Squadron, then close to Leeward of us.

We were delighted. I desired him to tell the Captains of the Ships of the Line astern to follow me, as I meant to engage them directly; and immediately bore away in the Cæsar for the Purpose, making all the Signals I could to indicate our Movements to our Ships; the Moon enabled us to see the Enemy bear away in a Line abreast, closely formed; but we lost Sight of them when it set, and I was obliged to reduce our Sails; the Hero, Courageux, and Æolus being the only Ships we could see. We continued steering to the E. N. E. all Night, and in the Morning observed the Santa Margarita near us; at Nine we discovered the Enemy of Four Sail of the Line in the N. E. under all Sail. We had also every Thing set and came up with them fast; in the Evening, we observed Three Sail astern; and the Phoenix spoke me at Night. I found that active Officer, Captain Baker, had delivered my Orders, and I sent him on to assist the Santa Margarita in leading us up to the Enemy. At Daylight we were near them, and the Santa Margarita had begun in a very gallant Manner to fire upon their Rear and was soon joined by the Phoenix.

A little before Noon, the French finding an Action unavoidable began to take in their small Sails, and form in a Line, bearing on the Starboard Tack; we did the same, and I communicated my Intentions by hailing to the Captains, that I should attack the Centre and Rear and at Noon began the Battle; in a short Time the Van Ship of the Enemy tacked, which almost directly made the Action close and general; the Namur joined soon after we tacked, which we did as soon as we could get the Ships round, and I directed her by Signal, to engage the Van; at half-past Three the Action ceased the Enemy having fought to admiration, and not surrendering till their Ships were unmanageable. I have returned Thanks to the Captains of the Ships of the Line and the Frigates, and they speak in high Terms of Approbation of their respective Officers and ships' Companies. If any Thing could add to the good Opinion I had already formed of the Officers and Crew of the Cæsar, it is their gallant Conduct in this Day's Battle. The Enemy have suffered much, but our Ships not more than is to be expected on these Occasions. You may judge of my Surprise, Sir, when I found the Ships we had, taken, were not the Rochfort Squadron, but from Cadiz.

I have the Honor to be, &c.
R.J. STRACHAN.

* *Cæsar, Hero, Courageux, and Namur.*
  Bellona, Æolus, Santa-Margarita far to Leeward in the South East.

FIRST LINE
STARBOARD TACK.
British Line.
Cæsar, of 80 Guns.
Hero, of 74 Guns.
Courageux, of 74 Guns.
French Line.
Duguay Trouin, of 74 Guns, Captain Tousset.
Formidable, of 80 Guns, Rear-Admiral Dumanoir.
Mont Blanc, of 74 Guns, Captain Villegrey.
Scipion, of 74 Guns, Captain Barouger.

SECOND LINE
(When the Namur joined).
LARBOARD TACK.
British Line.
Hero, of 74 Guns, Honourable Captain Gardner.
Namur, of 74 Guns, Captain Halsted.
Ceasar, of 80 Guns, Sir Richard J. Strachan.
Courageux, of 74 Guns, Captain Lee.
French Line.
Duguay Trouin
Formidable
Mont Blanc

Scipion

N.B. The Duguay Trouin and Scipion totally dismasted; the Formidable and Mont Blanc have their Foremasts standing.

Our Frigates — Santa Margarita, Æolus, Phoenix and Revolutionaire.

The Revolutionaire joined at the Time the Namur did, but, with the rest of our Frigates, in consequence of the French tacking, were to Leeward of the Enemy.

I do not know what is become of the Bellona, or the other Two Sail we saw on the Night of the 2d Instant.

The Reports of Damage, Killed, and Wounded, have not been all received. The Enemy have suffered much.

51

Battle Of Blaauwberg (Cape Of Good Hope)

Downing-Street, February 28, 1806.

DISPATCHES, of which the following are a Copy and Extract, addressed to Lord Viscount Castlereagh, were received Yesterday Evening, at the Office of the Right Honourable William Windham, one of His Majesty's Principal Secretaries of State, from Major-General Sir David Baird:

Cape-Town, January 12, 1806.

My LORD,

I HAVE the Honor to announce to your Lord-ship the Capitulation of the Town and Garrison of the Cape of Good Hope to His Majesty's Arms.

In my Dispatches of the 24th November last, from St. Salvador, I had the Honor to apprize your Lordship of the Measures adopted to refresh the Force under my command; and having, with much difficulty, procured about sixty or seventy Horses for the Cavalry, and the Sick being recruited, the Expedition sailed on the 26th of that Month; and we had the good Fortune to reach Table Bay on the 14th instant.

It had been intended to disembark the Army immediately, and with a View of covering our Design, before entering the Bay, the 24th Regiment, commanded by the Honourable Lieutenant-Colonel McDonald, was detached, under Charge of the Leda Frigate, to make a Demonstration of landing in Campo Bay, but the wind having failed, the Fleet did not arrive at its Anchorage until the Day was too far advanced to attempt a Landing.

On the Morning of the 5th the First Brigade, under the Orders of Brigadier General Beresford, was embarked in Boats, and proceeded towards the only accessible part of the Shore, in a small Bay, sixteen Miles to the Northward of Cape-Town, where it appeared practicable to effect a Disembarkation, but the Surf had increased so considerably that, combined with the local Difficulties of the Spot, it was found necessary to abandon the Attempt.

The Rest of the Day was devoted to a careful Examination of the whole Shore, from Lospards Bay to within Gunshot of the Batteries at Cape-Town, but which produced only the distressing Conclusion that the Chance of effecting a Landing depended upon Contingencies, very unlikely to be realized but in a perfect Calm.

In consequence of this Inference, in order to obviate the Disadvantages of Delay in the Adoption of a Resolution which I apprehended would at last be necessarily imposed on me, I directed Brigadier-General Beresford to proceed with the 38th Regiment, and the 20th Light Dragoons, escorted by His Majesty's Ship Diomede, to Saldanha Bay, where the Disembarkation could be accomplished with Facility, and a Prospect was afforded us of procuring Horses and Cattle; and I purposed following with the main Body of the Army in the Event of the Beach being impracticable the ensuing Morning.

The Surf along the Shore of Lospards Bay having considerably abated the ensuing Morning, I determined, with the Concurrence of Commodore Sir Home Popham, to make an Effort to get the Troops on Shore, and accordingly the Highland Brigade, composed of the 71, 72, and 93d Regiments effected that Object, under the Command of Brigadier General Ferguson.

The Shore had been previously very closely inspected by the Brigadier, and by his spirited Exertions and Example, our Efforts were crowned with Success; although a confined and Intricate Channel to the Shore, which had been accurately pointed out by Beacons laid down by the Diligence and Activity of the Boats of His Majesty's Ship Diadem, and a tremendous Surf, opposed the Passage of the Troops.

The Enemy had scattered a Party of Sharp Shooters over the contiguous Heights, and commanded the Landing, but the Casualties of this Service arose principally from natural Difficulties, and it is with the deepest Concern I have the Honor to inform your Lordship that we lost Thirty-five Rank and File of the 93d Regiment by the oversetting of One of the Boats, notwithstanding every possible Effort to rescue those unfortunate Men.

The Remainder of the Troops could only be brought on Shore on the succeeding Day, when the extraordinary Obstacles to all Intercourse with the Fleet, which nothing but the Courage and Perseverance of British Seamen could surmount, barely enabled us to obtain the indispensable Supplies of Water and Provisions for immediate Subsistence.

On the Morning of the 8th the Army, consisting of the 24th, 59th, 71st, 72d, 83d, and 93d Regiments, about Four Thousand strong, was formed into Two Brigades, with Two Howitzers and Six light Field Pieces, and moved off towards the Road which leads to Cape-Town; and, having ascended the Summit of the Blaw-Berg, or Blue Mountains, and dislodged the Enemy's Light Troops, I discovered their main Body, drawn up in Two Lines, prepared to receive us, and even in Motion to anticipate our Approach.

The Enemy's Force apparently consisted of about Five Thousand Men, the greater Proportion of which was Cavalry, and Twenty-three Pieces of Cannon, yoked to Horses, the Disposition of which, and the Nature of the Ground occupied by the Enemy's Troops, made it evident that they intended to refuse their Right Wing, and with their Left attempt to turn our Right Flank; but, to frustrate their Design, I formed the Army into Two Columns, the Second Brigade under Brigadier-General Ferguson keeping the Road, whilst the First struck to the Right, and took the Defile of the Mountains. Having accomplished my Purpose, our Line was formed with equal Celerity and Order; and the Left Wing, composed of the Highland Brigade, was thrown forward, and advanced with the steadiest Step under a very heavy Fire of Round Shot, Grape and Musquetry. Nothing could surpass or resist the determined Bravery of the Troops, headed by their gallant Leader, Brigadier-General Ferguson, and the Number of the Enemy, who swarmed the Plain, served only to augment their Ardour and confirm their Discipline. The Enemy received our Fire, and maintained his Position obstinately, but in the Moment of charging, the Valour of British Troops bore down all Opposition, and forced him to a precipitate Retreat.

The first Brigade, composed of the 24th, 59th, and 83d Regiments, and commanded in the Absence of Brigadier-General Beresford, by Lieutenant-Colonel Baird, was unavoidably precluded, by their Situation, from any considerable Participation in the Triumph of the British Arms, though the Flank Companies of the 24th had however an Opportunity of distinguishing themselves in dislodging a Number of Horse and Riflemen from the Heights on our Right Flank. This brilliant Achievement however was clouded by the Loss of Captain Foster, of the Grenadiers, whose Gallantry is best recorded in the Bosoms of his Brother Soldiers, and the universal Regret of the Army.

It is utterly impossible to convey to your Lordship an adequate Idea of the Obstacles which opposed the Advance, and retarded the Success of our Army, but it is my Duty to inform your Lordship, that the Nature of the Country – a deep, heavy, and arid Land, covered with Shrubs, scarcely pervious to light Bodies of Infantry; and above all, the total Privation of Water under the Effects of a burning Sun, had nearly exhausted our gallant Fellows in the Moment of Victory, and with the utmost Difficulty were we able to reach the Reit Valley, where we took our Position for the Night. A considerable Portion of the Provisions and Necessaries with which we started, had been lost during the Action, and we occupied our Ground under an Apprehension that even the great Exertions of Sir Home Popham and the Navy could not relieve us from Starvation.

My Lord, on every Occasion where it has been found necessary to call for the Co-operation of British Seamen in Land Enterprizes, their Valour has been so conspicuous, and their Spirit of Labour and Perseverance so unconquerable, that no Tribute of my Applause can add a Lustre to their Character; but I discharge a most agreeable Portion of my Duty in assuring your Lordship, that on the recent Employment of their Services, they have maintained their Reputation: And in this Place it behoves me to inform your Lordship, that the uniform good Conduct of those gallant Fellows, and the Zeal of Captain George Byng who commanded them, together with that of every subordinate Officer, have merited my fullest Approbation.

The Loss of the Enemy in this Engagement is reputed to exceed seven hundred Men in killed and Wounded; and it is with the most sensible Gratification that I contrast it with the inclosed Return of our Casualties. Your Lordship will perceive the Name of Lieutenant Colonel Grant among the wounded, but the heroic Spirit of this Officer was not subdued by his Misfortune, and he continued to lead his Men to Glory, as long as an Enemy was opposed to his Majesty's 72d Regiment. I have the cordial Satisfaction to add, that his Wound, though very severe, is not pronounced dangerous; and I indulge the Hope and Expectation of his early Recovery and Resumption of Command.

On the Morning of the 9th, recruited by such Supplies as the unwearied Diligence and Efforts of the Navy could throw on more the 59th Regiment however, being almost completely destitute of Food, we prosecuted our March towards Cape-Town, and took up a Position South of Salt River, which we trusted might preserve a free communication with the Squadron; for our Battering Train, as well as every other Necessary, except Water, was to pass to us from His Majesty's Ships. In this Situation, a Flag of Truce was sent to me by the Commandant of the Garrison of Cape-Town, (the Governor General Janserif, having retired after the Action of the 8th into the Country, moving by Hottentots Holland Kloof,) requesting a suspension of Hostilities for Forty-eight Hours, in order to negotiate a Capitulation. In Answer to this Overture, I dispatched Brigadier-General Ferguson, accompanied by Lieutenant Colonel Brownrigg, to stipulate, as the Condition of my Acquiescence, the Surrender of the Outworks of the Town within Six Hours, allowing Thirty six Hours for arranging the Articles of Capitulation.

My Proposition being assented to, the 59th Regiment marched into Fort Knokke; and the next Day, in Conjunction with Sir Home Popham, the Terms were agreed upon, and His Majesty's Forces were put in Possession of the several Defences of the Town.

The cordial, able, and zealous Co-operation of Commodore Sir Home Popham, emulated by all the Officers under his Command, merits my warmest Acknowledgments and Commendation; and I have the Satisfaction to add, that no united Service was ever performed with more true Harmony than has uniformly been manifested by both Branches of His Majesty's Forces. Such of His Majesty's Ships as could be spared from the Service of Lospards Bay, constantly coasted the Enemy's Shore, throwing Shot among his Troops and People, and contributing to keep him ignorant of the actual Place of our Disembarkation; and a very spirited Effort was made by the Marines of the Fleet, and a Party of Seamen from the Diadem, under the Commodore's immediate Command, to occupy a Position in Reit Valley, and co-operate with the Army.

The Marines and the Honourable Company's Recruits, as well as their Cadets, headed by Lieutenant-Colonel Willett, of the Bengal Establishment, have been usefully employed in different Branches of the Service; but I have to regret the Deprivation of the Services of the 20th Dragoons, and 38th Regiment, under a Conviction that they could not have failed to discharge their Duty in the same exemplary manner as the rest of His Majesty's Troops engaged in the Action.

Public as well as Honourable Considerations induce me to lament the Absence of Brigadier-General Beresford, from whose Talents and Experience I should have derived the most essential Assistance in our disputed and difficult Progress from Lospards Bay.

The Duties of the Quarter-Master General's Department were very ably and judiciously discharged by Lieutenant-Colonel Brownrigg; and although the Army had the greatest Cause to lament the Absence, from severe Illness, of Major Tucker, Deputy Adjutant-General, yet the Zeal and Activity manifested by Major Trotter of the 83d Regiment, and the Assistant-Adjutant General Captain Munro, happily precluded all Deficiency in that Department.

The Absence of Captain Smyth, of the Royal Engineers, with the Saldanha Detachment, was also a Matter of great Regret to me, for his Knowledge of the Country would have relieved me from much Embarrassment.

To the several Officers commanding Corps, I am under considerable Obligations for their gallant, spirited, zealous, and judicious Conduct and Example, in leading their Men up to the Enemy. British Troops, headed by such Men, must ever under Providence, command Success; and every Man in this Army has, I trust it will be considered, preserved the Character of the British soldier, and faithfully discharged his Duty to His King and Country.

This Dispatch will be delivered to your Lordship by Lieutenant-Colonel Baird, and to whom I beg Leave to refer for any additional Information your Lordship may wish to obtain, respecting our Proceedings; and I beg Leave to recommend this zealous and meritorious Officer to your Lordship's Protection.

I take the Liberty of mentioning to your Lordship, that not saving been joined by the Narcissus Frigate prior to our Disembarkation, and subsequent Operations in the Field, I was unfortunately deprived of the Services of Captain Sorell, Assistant-Adjutant-General, who was charged with my Dispatches from Madeira to Governor Patton, and with the Execution of my Wishes to procure Intelligence relative to the Strength and Condition of this Colony; and from whose extensive local Knowledge and professional Talents, I expected to derive great Assistance.

> I have the Honor to be, &c.
> D. BAIRD, Major-General,
> Commanding in Chief.

> His Majesty's Ship the Diadem, in Table-Bay, the
> 13th January 1806.

SIR,

WHEN I address you, for the Information of the Lords Commissioners of the Admiralty, on an Occasion of such public Interest and Importance as the Capture of the Cape of Good Hope which is now in Possession of His Majesty's Troops under that renowned General Sir David Baird, I consider it unnecessary to trouble their Lordships with a detailed Account of the Proceedings of the Fleet from St. Salvador, which, however will be conveyed in another Dispatch.

On the 3d Instant, we made Table Land, and on the 4th, in the Evening, we reached our preconcerted Anchorage to the Westward of Robben Island, though too late to do any Thing but take a superficial View of Blue Berg Bay, where it was proposed that the main Body of the Army, making however a Demonstration off Green Point, with the Leda Frigate, and the Transports containing the 24th Regiment; which was certainly well executed by Captain Honyman.

On the 5th, at Three o'Clock in the Morning, the Troops were put in the Boats and assembled alongside of the Espoir, but the Surf ran so high, that a Landing was deemed totally impracticable, and consequently the Troops returned to their Ships; and I immediately accompanied the General aboard the Espoir for the Purpose of making a close Examination of the whole Coast from Craig's Tower to Lospard's Bay; on no Part of which did it appear possible to land a single Boat without extreme Danger.

To the evil Consequences of Delay in commencing Operations on an Enemy's Coast, was to be added the very alarming Possibility that some Reinforcement might arrive by one of the various Squadrons in Motion when we left Europe; and therefore the General and myself were induced to consider that however difficult the Task might be of advancing from Saldanha Bay, yet it was an Object of very great Moment to accomplish a safe and speedy Landing for the Troops; and the instant the Decision was made, the Diomede, with the Transports of the 38th Regiment, the Cavalry Ships, and a Proportion of Artillery, under the Orders of Brigadier General Beresford sailed for Saldanha, preceded by Captain King in the Espoir, having on board Captain Smyth of the Engineers (an Officer well acquainted with the Country) with a View of seizing the Post Mailer, and as many Cattle as possible, antecedent to the Arrival of the advanced Division of the Fleet.

Soon after the Diomede weighed, the Westerly Wind began to abate; and on the 6th in the Morning, the Officers examining the Beach reported that the Surf had considerably subsided during the Night; which indeed was so evident from the Diadem when she stood in Shore, that I requested Sir David Baird to permit General Ferguson, and Colonel Brownrigg, the Quarter-Master-General, to attend the Officer on his second Examination, that their Feelings might in some Measure be balanced against those of professional Men, and to satisfy the Army that no Measure in which its Safety was so intimately connected, should be determined on without due and proper Deliberation.

In the mean Time the Diadem, Leda, and Encounter were placed in a Situation to render the most effectual Assistance; and the 71st and 72d Regiments with Two Field Pieces and a Howitzer ready if mounted, in the Boats of the Raisonable and Belliqueux, rendezvoused alongside the Two former Ships, I manifesting the most ardent Desire for the Signal from General Ferguson; at this Moment the Protector joined the Squadron, and Captain Rowley who was well acquainted with the Anchorage, volunteered his Services to place her to the Northward, so as to cross the Fire of the Encounter and more effectually cover the landing of the Troops.

Captain Downman at the same Time went in Shore with a light Transport Brig drawing only six Feet, to run her on the Beach as a Break Water, if it would in any Degree facilitate the Debarkation of the Troops.

At Half past Twelve the Encounter conveyed by Signal General Ferguson's Opinion, that a Landing might be effected, and the joy that was manifest in the Countenance of every Officer, heightened the characteristic Ardour of the Troops, and under an anxiety probably to be first on shore, induced them to urge the Boats to extend their Line of Beach further than was prudent, and occasioned the Loss of One Boat, with a Party of the 93d Regiment.

I report this Event to their Lordships with the most unfeigned Regret and It is doubly painful to me, because from all the Efforts of an Enemy posted on an advantageous Height, the Army had only Two Men wounded in landing. This Circumstance must fully prove how well the Covering Vessels were placed, and how ably their Guns were served; and I trust my Country will acquit me of having applied every Expedient that could be devised to prevent the Occurrence of an Accident which I so sincerely deplore.

The Surf increased, considerably towards the Close of the Evening, and about Eight o'Clock the Landing of any more Troops was stopped, but recommenced in the Morning, when all the Men, and Prisoners which the General judged necessary to take, were disembarked without a Moment's Loss of Time.

Conceiving that a Detachment of the Squadron might be of Service at the Head of the Bay, I proceeded there with the Leda, Encounter, and Protector, and a Division of Transports, and I understand, from firing occasionally that Evening over the Bank towards the Salt Pan, that the Enemy was obliged to move from an eligible Situation which he had before occupied.

On the following Morning we discovered the British Army advancing, with an unparalleled Rapidity, over a heavy Country, defended by a numerous Train of well-served Artillery; and as I conceived a few fresh Troops might be applied to Advantage, I desired Captain Downman to land with the Marines of the Squadron, and Two Field Pieces, to await the Arrival of Sir David Baird at Reit Valley, whom I very soon after had the Pleasure of personally congratulating on the Victory he had obtained over a General of such high Military Fame as General Jansens.

When the Army was in Motion to take up its Position at Craig's Tower, and while I was proceeding up the Bay to anchor in the most convenient Place for landing the Battering Train, a Flag of Truce was discovered coming towards the Diadem, by which I received the Letter No. 1. From the Commandant of the Town and Castle; and the next Day, in Conjunction with Sir David Baird, the Capitulation No. 2 was accepted, and at Six a Royal Salute was fired from the Squadron, on His Majesty's Colours being once more hoisted on the Castle. Although their Lordships will perceive by the detailed Account of our Transactions here, and the accompanying Plan of the different Dispositions which were made, that no brilliant Service fell to the Lot of the Squadron I have the honor to command, yet it is what I owe every Officer and Seaman to state, that under the most laborious Duty I ever experienced, Their Zeal never abated. To Captain Rowley I feel personally indebted for his Readiness on every Occasion; and I have no Doubt but the highest Satisfaction will be expressed of the Conduct of Captain Byng, who commanded the Marine Battalion, by an Authority far exceeding mine: And I inclose, for their Lordships Information, a Copy of the Report he made me on the Conduct of the Officers serving in that Battalion; to which exclusive of those belonging to the Squadron, are added Captain Hardinge, of the Salsette, and several other Officers, now on their Passage to India to join their Ships.

Captain Butterfield and Lieutenant Cochrane of the Transports, were on all Occasions ready to forward the Service, and we are particularly indebted to Captains Cameron, Christopher, and Moring, of the Honourable Company's Ships Dutchess of Gordon, Sir William Pultney, and Comet, who particularly exerted themselves in assisting the Troops through the Surf.

It is impossible for me to transmit any Returns of the Stores taken, by this Opportunity, or of the State of the Bato of Sixty-eight Guns, in Seamen's Bay; but it is, however, so strongly reported that the Enemy has not completely succeeded in his Attempt to burn her, that I have sent Captain Percy to take Possession of her, and, if possible, to move her into Safety, as the Enemy has totally abandoned her.

Captain Downman, of the Diadem, will have the Honor of delivering this Dispatch to their Lordships, and from the intelligent Manner in which I am satisfied he will explain every Movement; and the Causes by which I have been actuated, I trust he will require no further Recommendation to their Lordships' Protection.

I cannot, however, conclude this Letter without assuring their Lordships that I know no Instance where a stronger Degree of Confidence and Unanimity has been exemplified between the two Professions than on the present Occasion, and I humbly hope this Circumstance, coupled with the meritorious and successful issue of Sir David Baird's Military Dispositions will recommend this Armament to His Majesty's most gracious Favour and Protection.

I have the Honor to be, Sir,
Your most obedient humble Servant,
HOME POPHAM.

52

Battle Of San Domingo

Admiralty-Office, March 24, 1806.

DISPATCHES, of which the following are Copies, from Vice-Admiral Sir John Thomas Duckworth, K.B. commanding a Squadron of His Majesty's Ships, addressed to William Marsden, Esq; and brought to England by Captain Nathaniel Day Cochrane, were Yesterday received at the Admiralty:

Superb, to Leeward of the Town of St. Domingue, about 12 Leagues, Feb. 7, 1806

SIR,

AS I feel it highly momentous for His Majesty's Service, that the Lords Commissioners of the Admiralty should have the earliest Information of the Movements of the Squadron under my Command, and as I have no other Vessel than the Kingfisher that I feel justified in dispatching, I hope neither their Lordships or Vice-Admiral Lord Collingwood will deem me defective in my Duty towards his Lordship by addressing you on the happy Event of Yesterday; and as you will receive my Letter of the 3d Instant herewith, I shall only say, I lost not a Moment in getting through the Mona Passage, and on the 5th in the Afternoon was joined by the Magicienne, with a further Corroboration from various Vessels spoken, of an Enemy's Force of Ten Sail of the Line, with as many Frigates and Corvettes, being in these Seas; I therefore continued under easy Sail for the Night, in my Approach off the Town of St. Domingue, having given Orders to Captain Dunn of the Acasta, whose Zeal and Activity I have experienced for a Series of Years, to make Sail with the Magicienne, Captain McKenzie, Two Hours before Day-light, to reconnoitre; when at Six o'Clock the Acasta, to our great Joy, made the Signal for Two of the Enemy's Frigates; and before Seven, for Nine Sail at an Anchor at Half past, that they were getting under Weigh; the Squadron under my Command then in close Order with all Sail set, and the Superb, bearing my Flag, leading, and approaching fast, so as to Discover before Eight o'Clock that the Enemy were in a compact Line under all Sail, going before the Wind for Cape Nisao, to Windward of Ocoa Bay; and as they consisted of only Five Sail of the Line, Two Frigates, and a Corvette, (which hereafter will be named,) I concluded, from the Information I was in Possession of, that they were endeavouring to form a Junction with their remaining Force, and in consequence shaped my Course to render abortive such Intention, which was completely effected by a little after Nine, so as to make an Action certain. I therefore telegraphed the Squadron, that the principal Object of Attack would be the Admiral and his Seconds, and at Three Quarters past Nine, for the Ships to take Stations for their mutual Support, and engage the Enemy as they got up, and a few Minutes after, to engage as close as possible, when, at a short Period after Ten, the Superb closed upon the Bow of the Alexander, the leading Ship and commenced the Action; but after three Broadsides, she sheered off: the Signal was now made for closer Action, and we were enabled to attack the Admiral in the Imperial, (formerly Le Vengeur,) the Fire of which had been heavy on the Northumberland, bearing the Hon. Rear-Admiral Cochranes's Flag. By this Time, the Movement of the Alexander had thrown her among the Lee Division, which Rear-Admiral Louis happily availed himself of, and the Action became general, and continued with great Severity till half past Eleven; when the French Admiral, much shattered, and completely beat, hauled direct for the Land, and not being a Mile off, at Twenty Minutes before Noon ran on Shore; his Foremast then only standing, which fell directly on her striking; at which Time the Superb being only in Seventeen Fathom Water, was forced to haul off to avoid the same Evil; but not long after, the Diomede of Eighty-four Guns pushed on Shore near his Admiral, when all his Masts went; and I think it a Duty I owe to Character and my Country to add, from the Information of Sir Edward Berry, after she had struck, and the Agamemnon desisted from firing into her, from the Captain taking off his Hat, and making every Token of Surrender; and Captain Dunn assures me both Ensign and pendant were down; to comment on which, I leave to the World. About Fifty Minutes after Eleven the Firing ceased, and upon the Smoke clearing away I found Le Brave, bearing a Commodore's Pendant, the Alexander, and Le Jupitre in our Possession.

When I contemplate on the Result of this Action, when five Sail of the Line had surrendered, or were apparently destroyed in less than two Hours, I cannot, though bound to pay every Tribute to the noble and gallant Efforts of the Honourable Rear-Admiral Cochrane, Rear-Admiral Louis, the Captains, Officers, Seamen, and Royal Marines, under my Command, be vain enough to suppose that, without the aiding Hand of Providence, such Result could have been effected, and with a Loss so comparatively small; and though I shall ever sympathize with the Connections of those that fell, the Reflection on the Cause will, I hope, afford much Consolation.

To speak individually to the Conduct of any one would be injurious to all; for all were equally animated with the same zealous Ardour in support of their King and Country. Yet, possessed of these Feelings, I cannot be silent without Injustice to the firm and manly Support for which I was indebted to Captain Keats, and the Effect that the System of Discipline and good Order in which I found the Superb must ever produce; and the Pre-eminence of the British Seaman could never be more highly conspicuous than in this Contest.

After the Action, the Water being too deep to anchor in the Bay off St. Domingue, it was-requisite to bring to with the Prizes to repair Damages, put the Ships in a manageable State, and shift the Prisoners, which took me till this Afternoon; when Idetached the Honourable Captain Stopford in the Spencer, with the Donegal and Atlas, which latter had lost her Bowsprit, with the Prizes to Jamaica; and being anxious, with Rear-Admiral Cochrane, that he should return to his Command, where his Services must be wanted, a Jury Mainmast is fitting to the Northumberland, under this Island, to enable her to get to Windward, when I shall order the Agamemnon, which is staying by her, to accompany the Rear-Admiral to his Station; and I am now proceeding with the Canopus, Rear-Admiral Louis, Acasta, and Magicienne, off St. Domingue, to make certain of the Imperial and Diomede being completely wrecked, after which, I shall repair to Jamaica.

Having recited the Transactions of this glorious Combat, which will fairly add another Sprig of Laurel to our Naval History, and assist in promoting our Country's good,

I am, Sir, &c.
J.T. DUCKWORTH.

53

Battle Of Maida

Downing-Street, September 4, 1806.

A DISPATCH has been this Day received by the Right Honourable William Windham, one of His Majesty's Principal Secretaries of State, from Major-General Sir John Stuart, commanding His Majesty's Troops acting in Calabria, of which the following is a Copy:

Camp on the Plain of Maida, July 6, 1806.

SIR,

It is with the most heartfelt Satisfaction that I have the Honor of reporting to you, for the Information of His Majesty, the Particulars of an Action, in which the French Army quartered in this Province have sustained a signal Defeat by the Troops under my Command.

General Regnier, having been apprised of our Disembarkation at St. Eufemia, appears to have made a rapid March from Reggio, uniting, as he advanced, his detached Corps, for the Purpose of attacking, and with his characteristic Confidence, of defeating us.

On the Afternoon of the 3d Instant, I received Intelligence that he had that Day encamped near Maida, about Ten Miles distant from our Position, that his Force consisted at the Moment of about Four Thousand Infantry and Three Hundred Cavalry, together with Four Pieces of Artillery, and that he was in Expectation of being joined within a Day or Two by Three Thousand more Troops who were marching after him in a Second Division.

I determined therefore to advance towards his Position, and, having left Four Companies of Watteville's Regiment under Major Fisher to protect the Stores, and occupy a Work which had been thrown up at our Landing Place, the Body of the Army marched the next Morning according to the following Detail.

Advanced Corps - Lieutenant-Colonel Kempt, with Two Four-Pounders.
Light Infantry Battalion.
Detachment Royal Corsican Rangers.

Detachment Royal Sicilian Volunteers.

1st Brigade - Brigadier-General Cole, with Three Four-Pounders.
Grenadier Battalion.
27th Regiment.

2d Brigade - Brigadier-General Ackland, with Three Four-Pounders.
78th Regiment.
81st Regiment.

3d Brigade - Colonel Oswald, with Two Four-Pounders.
58th Regiment.
Watteville's Regiment, Five Companies.
20th Regiment, Lieutenant-Colonel Ross, landed during the Action.

Reserve of Artillery - Major Lemoine.
4 Six-Pounders and 2 Howitzers.
Total. - Rank and File, including the Royal Artillery, 4795.

General Regnier was encamped on the Side of a woody Hill, below the Village of Maida, sloping into the Plain of St. Eufemia; his Flanks were strengthened by a thick impervious Underwood. The Amato, a River perfectly fordable, but of which the Sides are extremely marshy, ran along his Front; my Approach to him from the Sea Side (along the Borders of which, I directed my March, until I had nearly turned his Left) was across a spacious Plain; which gave him every Opportunity of minutely observing my Movements.

After some loose firing of the Flankers to cover the Deploiements of the Two Armies, by Nine o'Clock in the Morning the opposing Fronts were warmly engaged, when the Prowess of the Rival Nations seemed now fairly to be at Trial before the World, and the Superiority was greatly and gloriously decided to be our own.

The Corps which formed the Right of the advanced Line, was the Battalion of Light Infantry commanded by Lieutenant Colonel Kempt, consisting of the Light Companies of the 20th, 27th, 35th, 58th, 61st, 81st, and Watteville's, together with One Hundred and Fifty chosen Battalion Men of the 35th Regiment, under Major Robinson. Directly opposed to them, was the favourite French Regiment the 1st Légére. The Two Corps at the distance of about One Hundred Yards fired reciprocally a few Rounds, when, as if by mutual Agreement, the Firing was suspended, and in close compact Order and awful Silence, they advanced towards each other, until their Bayonets began to cross. At this momentous Crisis the Enemy became appalled. They broke, and endeavoured to fly, but it was too late; they were overtaken with the most dreadful Slaughter.

Brigadier-General Ackland, whose Brigade was immediately on the Left of the Light Infantry, with great Spirit availed himself of this favorable Moment to press instantly forward upon the Corps in his Front; the brave 78th Regiment, commanded by Lieutenant-Colonel Macleod, and the 81st Regiment, under Major Plenderleath, both distinguished themselves on this Occasion. The Enemy fled with Dismay and Disorder before them, leaving the Plain covered with their dead and wounded.

The Enemy being thus completely discomfited on their Left, began to make a new Effort, with their Right, in the Hopes of recovering the Day. They were resisted most gallantly by the Brigade under Brigadier-General Cole. Nothing could shake the undaunted Firmness of the Grenadiers under Lieutenant-Colonel O'Callaghan, and of the 27th Regiment under Lieutenant-Colonel Smith. The Cavalry, successively repelled from before their Front, made an Effort to turn their Left, when Lieutenant-Colonel Ross, who had that Morning landed from Messina with the 20th Regiment, and was coming up to the Army during the Action, having observed the Movement, threw his Regiment opportunely into a small Cover upon their Flank, and by a heavy and well directed Fire, entirely disconcerted this Attempt.

This was the last feeble Struggle of the Enemy, who now, astonished and dismayed by the Intrepidity with which they were assailed, began precipitately to retire, leaving the Field covered with Carnage. Above Seven Hundred Bodies of their Dead have been buried upon the Ground. - The Wounded and Prisoners already in our Hands (among which are General Compère, and an Aid-de Camp, the Lieutenant Colonel of the Swiss Regiment, and a long List of Officers of different Ranks) amount to above One Thousand. There are also above One Thousand Men left in Monteleone and the different Posts between this and Reggio, who have mostly notified their Readiness to surrender, whenever a British Force shall be sent to receive their Submission, and to protect them from the Fury of the People. - The Peasantry are hourly bringing in Fugitives, who dispersed in the Woods and Mountains after the Battle. In short, never has the Pride of our presumptuous Enemy been more severely humbled, nor the Superiority of the British Troops more gloriously proved, than in the Events of this memorable Day.

His Majesty may, perhaps, still deign to appreciate more highly the Achievements of this little Army, when it is known that the Second Division which the Enemy were said to be expecting had all joined them the Night before the Action; no Statement that I have heard of their Numbers places them at a less Calculation than Seven Thousand Men.

Our victorious Infantry continued the Pursuit of the routed Enemy so long as they were able; but as the latter dispersed in every Direction, and we were under the Necessity of preserving our Order, the Trial of Speed became unequal.

The total Loss occasioned to the Enemy by this Conflict cannot be less than Four Thousand Men. When I oppose to the above our own small comparative Loss, as underneath detailed, His Majesty will, I hope, discern in the Fact, the happy Effects of that established Discipline to which we owe the Triumphs by which our Army has been latterly so highly distinguished.

I am now beginning my March Southward preparatory to my return to Sicily, for which Station I shall re-embark with the Army, as soon as His Sicilian Majesty shall have arranged a Disposition of his own Forces to secure those Advantages which have been gained by the present Expedition.

There seldom has happened an Action in which the Zeal and Personal Exertions of Individuals were so imperiously called for as in the present; seldom an Occasion where a General had a fairer Opportunity of observing them.

The General Officers, and those who commanded Regiments, will feel a stronger Test of their Merits in the Circumstances that have been detailed of their Conduct, than in any Eulogium I could presume to pass upon them.

The 58th and Watteville's Regiment, commanded by Lieutenant-Colonels Johnston and Watteville, which formed the Reserve, under Colonel Oswald, were ably directed in their Application to that essential Duty.

The Judgment and Effect with which our Artillery was directed by Major Lemoine, was, in our Dearth of Cavalry, of most essential Use; and I have a Pleasure in reporting the effective Services of that valuable and distinguished Corps.

To the several Departments of the Army, every Acknowledgement is due; but to no Officer, am I bound to express them so fully, on my Part, as to Lieutenant-Colonel Bunbury, the Deputy Quarter-Master-General, to whose Zeal and Activity, and able Arrangements in the important Branch of Service which he directs, the Army as well as myself are under every marked Obligation.

From Captain Tomlin the acting Head of the Adjutant-General's Department, and from the Officers of my own Family, I have received much active Assistance. Among the latter I am to mention Lieutenant-Colonel Moore of the 23d Light Dragoons, who being in Sicily for his Health at the Time of our Departure, solicited Permission to accompany me on this Expedition; he was wounded in the Execution of my Orders.

From the Medical Department under the Direction of Mr. Grieves, the Deputy Inspector, I am to acknowledge much professional Attention, the more so as their Labours have been greatly accumulated by the Number of wounded Prisoners who have become equally with our own, the Subject of their Care.

The Scene of Action was too far from the Sea to enable us to derive any direct Co-operation from the Navy: but Admiral Sir Sidney Smith, who had arrived in the Bay the Evening before the Action, had directed such a Disposition of Ships and Gun boats as would have greatly favoured us, had Events obliged us to retire. The Solicitude however of every Part of the Navy to be of use to us, the Promptitude with which the Seamen hastened on Shore with our Supplies, their Anxiety to assist our wounded, and the Tenderness with which they treated them, would have been an affecting Circumstance to Observers even the most indifferent. To me it was particularly so.

Captain Fellowes, of His Majesty's Ship Apollo, has been specially attached to this Expedition by the Rear-Admiral; and, in every Circumstance of professional Service, I beg Leave to mention our grateful Obligations to this Officer, as well as to Captains Cocket and Watson, Agents of Transports, who acted under his Orders.

Captain Bulkeley, my Aide-de-Camp, who will have the Honor of presenting this Letter to you, has attended me throughout the Whole of the Services in the Mediterranean, and will therefore be able to give you every additional Information on the Subject of my present Communication.

I have the Honor to be, &c.
J. STUART, Maj. Gen.

NAPOLEONIC WARS INDEX
INDEX OF PERSONS

Abercromby, Lieutenant General Sir Ralph, 8, 9, 10, 12-3, 14, 24, 27, 59-60, 72, 81-7, 92-3, 94-5, 98-9, 126-8, 129, 131-2, 133, 135, 137, 139-44, 146-8

Apodaca, Rear-Admiral Don Sebastian Ruiz de, 94

Balcarres, Alexander Lindsay, Earl of, 111, 115

Barrow, Lieutenant Colonel Thomas, 11, 111-5

Baird, General Sir David, 18, 123-4, 188-92, 193-5

Beresford, General William Carr, 188-93

Bonaparte, Joseph, King of Naples and Sicily, 18

Bonaparte, Napoleon, 3, 10, 11, 17

Brune, Marshal of France, Guillaume-Marie-Anne, 13-4, 138

Brueys d'Aigalliers, Vice-Admiral François-Paul, 11

Brunswick, Charles William Ferdinand, Duke of, 1, 3

Burrard, Lieutenant General Sir Harry, 127, 131, 136, 139-46

Calder, Admiral Sir Robert, 17, 89-90, 179-80

Carteaux, General Jean François, 3

Castagnier, Commodore Jean-Joseph, 10

Cavan, General Richard Ford William Lambart, Earl of, 139, 143-4, 147, 149

Cawdor, John Campbell Ist Baron, 96-7

Chapuy, General René-Bernard, 5, 55, 57, 125

Chatham, General John Pitt, 140-6

Christian, Rear-Admiral Sir Hugh Cloberry, 83, 85

Clairfayt, General Count François Sebastien Charles Joseph de Croix, 58-9, 70

Cochrane, Admiral Sir Alexander Inglis, 152, 197-8

Collingwood, Vice-Admiral Cuthbert, 181-4, 196

Collot, General Victor, 4, 53-4

Congreve, Lieutenant Colonel Sir William, 56

Conn, Captain John, 168

Coote, General Sir Eyre, 44, 46, 53, 104, 106-8, 127, 134, 140-2, 146, 151-2

Cordóba, Admiral Don José de, 9

Cornwallis, Admiral Sir William, 179

Cornwallis, General Charles, Governor-General of Ireland, 12, 118-9, 124-5

Cradock, General John Francis, 119-20, 151

Craufurd, Major General Robert, 23-5, 119-20

Dance, Commodore Sir Nathaniel, 17, 176-8
De Winter, Admiral, 102-3
D'Oyley (Oyley), Major General, 127, 134, 136, 139, 143-6
Duckworth, Admiral Sir John Thomas, 18, 196-8
Duke of Cambridge, Prince Adolphus, 29
Duke of York (Prince Frederick), 2, 5, 6, 7, 13-4, 23-5, 26-8, 55-7, 58-61, 62-3, 70-1, 72-3, 133-36, 137-45
Duncan, Admiral Adam, 10, 102-3, 128
Duncan, Major Alexander, 37, 49, 69
Dundas, Henry, Secretary of State for the Home Department and Secretary of State for War, 1, 26, 27, 28, 30, 39, 43, 48, 51, 52, 55, 56, 58, 62, 67, 70, 72, 81, 84, 92, 98, 107, 126, 131, 133, 137, 138, 149
Dundas, General Sir David, 4, 31, 38, 39-41, 46, 52, 53-4, 133-6, 137, 140-4
Dundas, Rear-Admiral the Honourable George Heneage Laurence, 160, 163

Elphinstone, Admiral George Keith, 30-1, 37
Erskine, Lieutenant General William, 29
Erskine, Lieutenant General Sir James, 69

Ferguson, General Sir Ronald Craufurd, 189-94
Ferraris, General Joseph, 23-4
Fox, General Henry Edward, 59-60, 62-3
Freytag, Field Marshal Heinrich Wilhelm von, 2, 27, 28

Garlies, Admiral George Stewart, 46, 51

Goodall, Admiral Samuel Granston, 48-9
Gordon, Major General Sir Charles George, 51, 54
Graves, Admiral Thomas, 65, 155, 158
Gravina y Nápoli, Admiral Frederico Carlos, 36, 38, 181-2
Grey, General Sir Charles, 4, 5, 11, 43-5, 51-2

Harris, General George, 12, 123-5
Harvey, Admiral Sir Henry, 9, 99
Hobart, Robert Earl of Buckinghamshire, Secretary of State for War, 151, 169
Hood, Admiral Alexander, 1st Viscount Bridport, 7, 77-8
Hood, Admiral Samuel, 3-4, 16, 30-1, 37, 39-41, 48-50, 67
Hood, Vice-Admiral Sir Samuel, 42, 101, 109, 150, 162, 169-70
Hotham, Admiral William, 8, 30, 74-6, 79-80
Houchard, General Jean Nicholas, 2, 29
Howe, Admiral Richard, 6, 64-6
Humbert, General Jean Joseph Amable, 12
Hunter, Major General, 85
Hely-Hutchinson, General John, 144, 147, 154

Imbert, Baron d', 3

Jervis, Admiral John, 1st Earl of St. Vincent, 4, 9, 46-7, 89-91
Jourdan, Marshal of France Jean-Baptiste, 6

Keats, Admiral Sir Richard Goodwin, 163, 197
Kingsmill, Admiral Sir Robert Brice, 121

Lake, General Gerard, 12, 16, 118-20, 172

Lamarch, General François Drouet, 2
Linzee, Commodore Robert Gordon Hood, 40-2
Louis XVI, King of France, 1,
Louis XVII, 3,
Louis, Rear-Admiral Sir Thomas, 197-8

Macbride, Admiral John, 28
Mack, Lieutenant-Marshal Karl von Leiberich, 5-6
Manners, Lieutenant General Robert, 133-6, 140
Martin, Admiral Pierre, 8
Menou de Boussay, General Jacques-François de, 14, 151-2
Mitchell, Vice Admiral Sir Andrew, 128-30
Moira, Francis Rawdon-Hastings, Earl of, 6
Montagu, Admiral Sir George, 64
Moore, Lieutenant General Sir John, 39-41, 68-9, 82, 84, 118, 127, 132-3, 138-44, 151, 202
Morshead, Major General, 85
Moss, Captain, 111-17
Murray, Sir James, later General Pulteney, 13, 14, 23, 25, 26, 27, 28, 29, 56, 127, 134-6, 140, 143-4, 149-50

Nepean, Sir Ivan, Under Secretary of State for War, Secretary to the Board of Admiralty, 79, 89, 100, 102, 104, 109, 115, 155, 159, 160, 170
Nelson, Vice-Admiral Horatio, 4, 8, 9, 11, 15, 17, 49, 67-9, 75, 79, 100-1, 109-10, 155-56, 157-8, 164-5, 181
Nicolls, Major General, 84, 86-8

O'Hara, General Charles, 38
Otto, Lieutenant General, 56-60

Paget, Field Marshal Henry William, 139, 143-4

Parker, Admiral Sir Hyde, 15, 115, 155-6
Parker, Admiral Sir William, 9
Parker, Captain Edward T, 46-7, 164-8
Pichegru, General Jean-Charles, 5, 7
Portland, William Cavendish-Bentinck Duke of, Secretary of State for the Home Department, 96, 111, 118
Prescott, General Robert, 44, 54
Prince Edward, Major General, 43-4, 46, 52-3

Regnier (Reynier), General François-Augustin, 200-2
Reynier, General Jean Louis Ebénézer, 18
Rochambeau, Marshal of France, Jean Baptiste Donatien de Vimeure, 44-5, 53, 54

Saumarez, Vice-Admiral James, 15, 159-60, 161-3
Saxe-Coburg-Saalfeld, Prince Frederick Josias, 2, 5-6, 70
Schwarzenberg, Field Marshal Karl Philipp Fürst zu, 57
Smith, Admiral Sir William Sidney, 3, 18, 30-1, 31-4, 153, 202
Souham, Joseph General, 2, 5
Strachan, Admiral Sir Richard John, 18, 185-6
Stuart, Lieutenant General Sir Charles, 4, 67-9
Stuart, Lieutenant General Sir John, 18, 199-202

Tippu (Tipu, Tippoo), Sultan, 12, 124-5
Tone, Theobald Wolfe, 12
Trogoff de Kerlessy, Admiral Jean-Honoré, 31
Troubridge, Rear-Admiral Sir Thomas, 9, 101

Vandamme, General Dominique-Joseph René, 138

Villaret de Joyeuse, Admiral Louis Thomas, 6, 7
Villeneuve, Vice-Admiral Pierre-Charles-Jean-Baptiste-Silvestre de, 17, 181-2

Wallmoden, General Ludwig Georg Thedel Graf von, 7, 28, 29, 62, 70,
Ward, Lieutenant Colonel, 107-8
Warren, Admiral Sir John Borlase, 7, 12, 121-2, 150

Wellesley, Richard, Ist Earl of Mornington, Governor-General of India, 7, 16, 172
Wellesley, Sir Arthur, Duke of Wellington, 7, 16, 173-5
William V, Prince of Orange, 1, 5, 29, 38, 129, 134-40

Young, Admiral Sir William, 42, 48, 49, 150

INDEX OF MILITARY AND NAVAL UNITS

Austrian Army, 1, 2, 5, 6, 7, 10, 17, 23-4, 27, 58-9, 62
    Arch-Duke Ferdinand Hussars, 57
    Cuirassier Regiment of Zetchwitz, 56
    Jordis Regiment, 27
    Starray, 27

British Army,
    Royal Artillery, 7, 36-7, 44, 46, 49, 58, 60, 68-9, 82-3, 84-5, 86, 88, 98-9, 113, 139-40, 143-4, 153, 168, 193-4, 199-200, 202
    Guards, Brigade of, 2, 24, 59-60, 105, 131-2, 134, 146
        1st Regiment, 107, 135
        Coldstream Regiment, 26, 60, 108, 147
        3rd Regiment, 108, 135, 147
    Royal Horse Guards (Blues), 56
    1st Dragoons (Royals), 56
    1st Dragoon Guards, 56
    3rd Dragoon Guards, 55, 56
    5th Dragoon Guards, 56

7th Light Dragoons, 57, 59, 133, 147
11th Light Dragoons, 24-5, 49, 57, 133-4, 147
15th Light Dragoons, 59
16th Light Dragoons, 60
18th Light Dragoons, 133, 140
20th Light Dragoons, 189, 191
23rd Light Dragoons, 119, 202
1st Regiment (Royals), 33, 68, 127, 170
Queen's Regiment, 94
5th Regiment, 135
8th Regiment, 93
11th Regiment, 108
12th Regiment, 123
14th Regiment, 24, 27, 94
18th Regiment, 35
20th Regiment, 132, 152, 200-1
23rd Regiment, 108, 133, 140, 127
24th regiment, 189-90
25th Regiment, 49
27th Regiment, 82, 142, 200-1
29th Regiment, 127, 142

30th Regiment, 68, 151-2
31st Regiment, 81-2
33rd Regiment, 123
35th Regiment, 200
38th Regiment, 87, 189, 191, 193
40th Regiment, 135
43rd Regiment, 51, 53
45th Regiment, 92-4
49th Regiment, 108
50th Regiment, 68
51st Regiment, 68
52nd Regiment, 149
53rd Regiment, 24, 82
55th Regiment, 83, 127, 133, 140
57th Regiment, 82, 87
58th Regiment, 200, 202
59th Regiment, 189-91
61st Regiment, 200
64th Regiment, 119
71st Regiment, 189, 193
72nd Regiment, 189-91, 193
73rd Regiment, 123
74th Regiment, 123, 174
78th Regiment, 200
81st Regiment, 200
83rd regiment, 189-92
85th Regiment, 127, 141-3
92nd Regiment, 127
93rd Regiment, 189, 194
Royal Engineers, 36, 44, 49, 85, 86, 120, 192-3
Cardigan Militia, 96

French Naval Vessels,
    Arethusa, 31
    Bucentaure, 182
    Ca-ira, 75-6
    Censeur, 75
    Commerce de Marseilles, 31
    Duguay Trouin, 186
    Formidable, 186
    Hoche, 122
    La Juste, 66
    L'Achille, 66
    L'Alcide, 80
    L'America, 66
    L'Impetueux, 66
    L'Orient, 110
    Mont Blanc, 186
    Northumberland, 66, 197-8
    Pearl, 31
    Pompée, 31
    Puissant, 31
    Revolutionaire, 66,
    Sans Pareille, 66
    Scipion, 186-7
    Topaze, 31
    Vengeur (later Imperial), 66, 197

Hanoverian Army,
    Garde de Corps, 24
Hesse Darmstadt Troops, 72-3
Hessian Troops, 27, 28, 58-60

British Naval Vessels,
    Acasta, 196-98
    Achille, 184
    Acute, 107
    Aeolus, 185-7
    Africa, 184
    Agamemnon, 49, 67, 75, 80, 156, 157-8, 184, 197-8, 208
    Ajax, 184
    Alcide, 41
    Alcmene, 158
    Alert, 33
    Amazon, 157-8
    Anson, 121
    Apollo, 202
    Ardent, 39, 103, 156, 158
    Arethusa, 31, 85, 93-5, 98
    Argo, 171
    Ariadne, 80, 104, 106
    Arrow, 158
    Asp, 105
    Astraea, 77
    Atlas, 198
    Audacious, 62, 159, 162
    Barfleur, 90

Belleisle, 184
Bellerophon, 183-4
Bellona, 95, 156, 157-8, 186-7
Berwick, 74, 76
Biter, 105
Blanche, 46, 51, 158
Blenheim, 90
Boxer, 107
Boyne, 46-7, 51-3
Britannia, 30, 32, 74, 76, 79, 90, 184
Caesar, 159-62, 185-6
Canada, 121-2
Canopus, 198
Captain, 90
Centaur, 170-1
Ceres, 51
Champion, 107
Chichester, 171
Circe, 104-7
Colossus, 77, 90, 184
Conqueror, 184
Courageux, 49, 75, 171, 185-6
Crash, 107
Cruizer, 157-8
Culloden, 9, 90, 101
Cyane, 171
Cyclops, 79
Dart, 105, 107, 158
Defence, 184
Defiance, 156-8, 184
Desiree, 157-8
Diadem, 40, 90, 189, 191, 192-5
Diomede, 189, 193, 197-8
Discovery, 158, 168
Donegal, 198
Doris, 121
Dreadnought, 184
Druid, 107
Edgar, 156, 158
Egmont, 90, 102
Elephant, 156-8
Emerald, 100-1, 170
Ethalion, 121-2

Eugenie, 165
Euryalus, 181-4
Excellent, 90
Expedition, 104-7
Explosion, 158
Favourite, 93-5
Fortitude, 40-2, 49
Foudroyant, 122
Fox, 101
Furnace, 107
Ganges, 156, 176-8
Glatton, 156, 158
Goliath, 90
Gorgon, 40
Harpy, 104-6, 158
Hebe, 86, 107
Hecla, 105-6, 158
Hero, 180, 185-6
Hornet, 171
Irresistible, 46, 77, 90
Isis, 128-9, 156, 158, 167
Juno, 40-2
Kangaroo, 121
Kent, 128
La Bonne Citoyenne, 89
La Fleche, 79
Leviathan, 184
Lion, 107
London, 155
Magnanime, 122
Majestic, 109
Mars, 184
Medusa, 164-7
Melampus, 121
Meleager, 80
Merlin, 111-16
Minerva, 105-7, 178
Minotaur, 184
Monarch, 156-8
Moselle (Mozelle), 74, 80
Mutine, 109
Naiad, 184
Namur, 90, 186-7
Neptune, 184

Niger, 89
Nymphe, 77
Orion, 77, 90, 184
Otter, 158
Phoebe, 184
Phoenix, 18, 185-7
Polyphemus, 156, 158, 184
Prince, 184
Prince of Wales, 95, 98, 179
Prince Orange, 90
Princess Royal, 40
Quebec, 51-3
Queen Charlotte, 64-5, 77, 178
Rattlesnake, 46
Renown, 149-50
Revolutionaire, 187
Revenge, 184
Robust, 31, 78, 121-2
Rose, 51, 102
Royal George, 77-8, 176-8
Royal Sovereign, 182-4
Russel, 77, 156-8
Sans Pareil, 77
Santa Margaritta, 46, 186
Sarah Christiana, 123
Savage, 106
Scipio, 95, 186-7
Sea Flower, 52
Seahorse, 100, 101
Sirius, 184
Spartiate, 184
Spencer, 198
Standard, 78
Sulphur, 158
Superb, 162-3, 196-7
Swallow, 31-2, 34
Swiftsure, 184
Sylph, 121
Tarleton, 74
Tartarus, 105
Temerair, 182-4
Terpsichore, 101
Terrible, 33
Terrier, 107

Terror, 95, 158
Theseus, 101
Thorn, 94
Thunderer, 78, 184
Tonnant, 184
Vanguard, 109
Venerable, 102-3, 159, 162
Vengeance, 46, 95
Venus, 64
Vestal, 107
Vesuve, 107
Veteran, 46, 51
Victory, 30-1, 35, 39-40, 48, 78, 80, 89-90, 182, 184
Ville de Paris, 100-1, 179
Volcano, 158
Vulcan, 30
Winchelsea, 46, 51
Windsor Castle, 30, 34
Wolverene, 105
Woolwich, 46
Zealous, 101, 109
Zebra, 43, 94, 158
Zyphyr, 95, 158

Spanish Naval Vessels
  Atlante, 91
  Bahama, 91
    Concepcion, 91
  Conde de Regla, 91
  Conquestador, 91
  Fiane, 91
  Glorioso, 91
  Mexicana, 91
  Neptuna, 91
  Oriente, 91
  Pelayo, 91
  Principe De Asturias, 91
  Salvador Del Mundo, 90-1
  San Antonio, 91
  San Firmin, 91
  San Francisco de Paula, 91
  San Genaro, 91
  San Ildephonso, 91

San Isidro, 91
San Josef, 90-1
San Juan Nepomuceno, 91
San Nicolas, 90-1
San Pablo, 90-1
Santissima Trinidad, 91
Soberano, 91